Fragile Victory

Fragile Victory

A Nicaraguan Community at War

Alison Rooper

Weidenfeld and Nicolson
London

Copyright © by Alison Rooper 1987

First published in Great Britain by
George Weidenfeld & Nicolson Limited
91 Clapham High Street
London SW4 7TA

Set in Old Style Roman by
Butler & Tanner Ltd.
Printed and bound in Great Britain by
Butler & Tanner Ltd, Frome and London

ISBN 0 297 79224 5 cased
     0 297 79248 2 paperback

For Donatila, who shared scant resources
and opened a door on Nicaragua.

Contents

20. A heart of hard sticks 216

Illustrations

Photographs are by Alison Rooper unless otherwise credited

Cover/jacket picture: woman at the San Jerónimo co-operative

Mass funeral in Condega

Urban youth in the front line of the insurrection (Susan
   Meiselas/John Hillelson Agency)

Daniel Ortega (Patrick Chauvel/John Hillelson Agency)

The body of Juan Guillén (photo courtesy of Alfredo Pintero)

Managua, 19 July 1979

General Augusto César Sandino

Don Leandro Córdoba

Anastasio Somoza Debayle (Benoit Gysembergh/Camera Press)

Donatila and Antonio Centeno

School pupils celebrate the anniversary of the Literacy Campaign

Luisa Centeno

Volunteer picking coffee

At the health centre in Condega

Bertilda Villareyna with Nicola, her cousin's widow

The village school at San Jerónimo, before its destruction by the
   Contras

Roberto Pineda Rivas, of El Jocote, with his mother

Father Enrique Oggier

Moisés Córdoba with his wife

Bishop Pablo Vega

Condegans celebrate the Stations of the Cross

Ampara Irías

Julia Meza

Miriam Centeno

AMNLAE day, Condega, 1983 (photo courtesy of Henry Vargas)

The gallery of heroes and martyrs in Jalapa

Workers from Condega marching to Ducualí in protest against the
   attack on the depot

One of the lorries destroyed in the attack on the depot at Ducualí

Members of the Juanita Viscaya co-operative at work

Daniel Flores

Militias guard the San Jerónimo co-operative

Children from the San Jerónimo co-operative

Acknowledgements

Countless people in and around Condega gave me access to their lives and made time for my questions. They are the inspiration for this book and I must thank them above all.

I would like to thank all those individuals and organizations, in England and in Nicaragua, who helped me with the research.

For their encouragement in the early stages of writing I thank in particular Jerry Kuehl, Paul Pickering, Jenny Rathbone and John Uden, and Juliet Gardiner at Weidenfeld.

I am grateful to Hermione Harris for her support and permission to quote from her interview with Luisa and Amanda Centeno; to Irene Vance and Carlos Madriz for the many consultations on matters of fact and translation; and to all those who gave me support, advice or suggestions for the manuscript, in particular Ros Hayes, Nick Lewis, Fiona Mackintosh, Yvonne Richards, Hazel Smith and Humphrey Trevelyan.

Finally my thanks to Stephanie Henry for her creative attention to the prints, to Rachel Calder, and to Linden Lawson at Weidenfeld for her work on the manuscript.

Preface

This book is the story of a continuing war in a place called Condega, a mountainous district in the north of Nicaragua, centred around a small town.

The war began in the late 1920s when local peasants joined a guerilla army to fight US marines for an independent Nicaragua. It continues today as a war against shortages and economic isolation, against ignorance, illiteracy and disease. It is a war for the survival of a revolution fought against a US puppet army, the Contras.

The story of Condega was told to me during a visit I made there to look at the impact that the 1979 Revolution had on ordinary Nicaraguans; it was the people themselves who encouraged me to write it down. These are people who for at least ten years have been caught up in tumultuous events and who have neither time nor energy left to record what is happening.

Part of my purpose in writing this book was to describe those people and their lives, as I saw them, at a particular time – the mid-1980s. The other was to place those people in the context of their own past, a past that is too often ignored by the media when reporting Nicaragua. It is a past that is also underestimated by Ronald Reagan, the CIA and the Contras' commanders who believe that brute force will destroy the Nicaraguan Revolution. In Condega people remember the bloody repression of Somoza and the National Guard as if it were yesterday. It is my belief that no one can fully comprehend the spirit of Nicaragua today – the speeches of President Ortega, the defiance of a seventeen-year-old soldier, the determination and pride of a woman who works the field with a rifle at the ready – without understanding this history.

Condega is a Sandinista community. I make no claim that it is typical of Nicaragua, whose population of three million is scattered over a wide area, much of it isolated from towns and cities. Neither can I claim the status of unassailable objective truth for my own observations and impressions. I have included them in order to illuminate the story and to bring the reader, probably an outsider like myself, closer to the people of Nicaragua and what is happening to them.

Alison Rooper
May 1987

Glossary

Spanish terms

barrio	urban district, neighbourhood
brigadista	literacy teacher, health or coffee-picking volunteer
campesino	peasant-farmer or member of his family
compañero	comrade, companion
compa	abbreviation of *compañero*, applied to soldiers in the Sandinista army
córdoba	national currency of Nicaragua
expendio popular	local CDS shop
Frente	abbreviation of Frente Sandinista de Liberación Nacional – the FSLN
Frente Sur	southern battle front
gringo	derogatory term for citizen of the USA: Yankee
Guardia	member of Somoza's National Guard, used also to denote the Contras
internacionalista	foreigner sympathetic with and working for the revolution
juez de mesta	local magistrate or sheriff in Somoza's time
junta	board, town administration
mestizo	of mixed descent. (Most Nicaraguans are *mestizos*, descended from indigenous indians and Spanish settlers.)
muchachos	boys, used of young combatants of the FSLN
oreja	a Somocista informer – 'ear'
piricuaco	insulting term coined by the National Guard to denote a Sandinista – 'running dog'
Somocista	adherent of Somoza
tortilla	flat maize pancake, staple food in Nicaragua

Organizations

AMNLAE	Asociación de Mujeres Nicaraguenses 'Luisa Amanda Espinoza' (Association of Nicaraguan Women 'Luisa Amanda Espinoza')
AMPRONAC	Asociación de Mujeres Ante la Problemática Nacional (Association of Women Confronting the National Problem)
ATC	Asociación de Trabajadores del Campo (Rural Workers' Association)

Barricada	daily newspaper of the FSLN
BLI	Batallónes de Lucha Irregular (Irregular Warfare Battalions)
CAS	Cooperativa Agrícola Sandinista (Sandinista Agricultural Co-operative)
CCS	Cooperativa de Crédito y Servicios (Credit and Service Co-operative)
CDC	Comité de Defensa Civil (Civil Defence Committee)
CDS	Comité de Defensa Sandinista (Sandinista Defence Committee)
CST	Central Sandinista de Trabajadores (Sandinista Workers' Federation)
EEBI	Escuela de Entrenamiento Básico de Infantería (Basic Infantry Training School [National Guard])
EPS	Ejército Popular Sandinista (Sandinista People's Army)
FAO	Frente Amplio Opositor (Broad Opposition Front)
FDN	Fuerza Democrática Nicaraguense (Nicaraguan Democratic Force [the main Contra grouping])
FER	Frente Estudiantil Revolucionario (Revolutionary Students' Front)
FETSALUD	Federación de Trabajadores de la Salud (Health Workers' Federation)
FPN	Frente Patriótico Nacional (National Patriotic Front)
FSLN	Frente Sandinista de Liberación Nacional (Sandinista National Liberation Front)
GPP	Guerra Popular Prolongada (Prolonged Popular War – FSLN Tendency)
MPS	Milicias Populares Sandinistas (Sandinista People's Militias)
MPU	Movimiento Pueblo Unido (United People's Movement)
OAS	Organization of American States
SMP	Servicio Militar Patriótico (Patriotic Military Service)
UNAG	Unión Nacional de Agricultores y Ganaderos (National Union of Farmers and Livestock Producers)

Central America and the Caribbean region

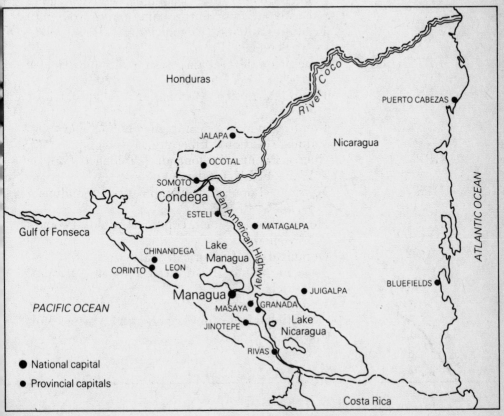

Nicaragua

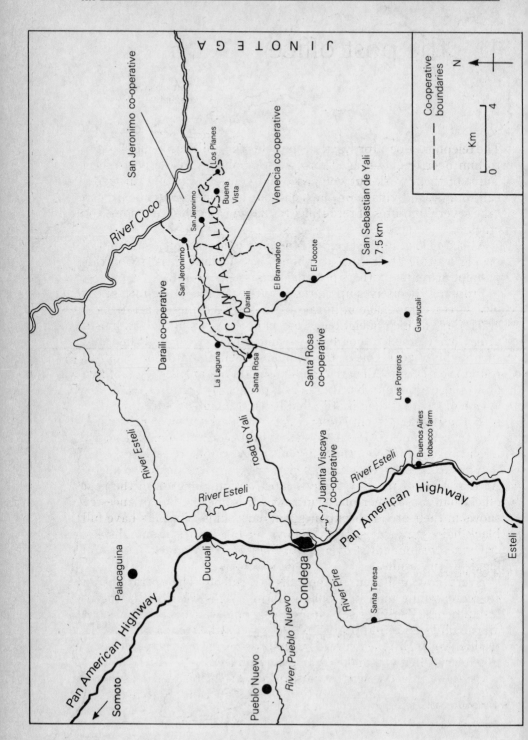

1.   The post office

The telephone operator sweats as he fields the numbers being shouted to him over the counter. There are four phones in the post office. Three of them work but you can't dial yourself. Putting through a call to a nearby village on the small old-fashioned switchboard can take several minutes of rerouting, re-dialling and shouting down the crackle.

At six o'clock in the evening, the post office in Condega is full of people waiting their turn to phone; boys calling girls, schoolkids phoning parents, mothers phoning sons.

Propping themselves up on the counter are five young men in the olive-green camouflage uniforms of the special combat battalions; a crack force formed of eighteen-year-old conscripts in the Sandinista army. They smell of combat – a mixture of sweat and dust and several days' wear. One or two still have their ammunition strapped round their chests. All carry Russian-made AK47 rifles – something almost as common in Nicaragua as a packet of cigarettes.

One of the battalion is still on duty and reading a coded message over the phone: 'Twenty-four, thirty-six, seventy-two. Fifty-nine, sixteen, zero nine . . .' It is a lesson in the dire state of communications in Nicaragua that even the army has to use public telephones.

A group of teenagers sit on a ledge smoking. They are in no hurry. At that time of the day there is more action going on in the post office than most other places in town. In some the indian ancestry shows in their broad cheekbones and dark skins. The girls have full black hair, some cut short; the boys jet-black curls. Some display crucifixes prominently over their t-shirts. They crack jokes and giggle at the adults.

Every now and then all the calls are cut off. The operator – an energetic young man in a blue uniform – sighs wearily, playing to his audience. Tension rises among the people waiting as he pulls out all the plugs and disappears next door to fix the generator – a well-trodden route, by the expression on his face. There is no point being in a hurry when you make a call from Condega.

On the wall a typewritten notice calls attention to 'violations of our territory, massacres, torture and abductions systematically being carried out against our civilian population'. An emergency drill follows:

(1) If an emergency arises requiring the population to be placed on alert, a warning will be given by continuous rings on the church bells.

(2) Brigades must report immediately to their respective command posts.

(3) To protect our children, elderly, and pregnant women we will retire to the shelters maintaining communication between our houses.

(4) In case there is no electricity, keep candle, gas and matches ready.

(5) Try to get provisions down in the established time.

(6) Promote revolutionary vigilance.[1]

No one appears to be interested in the notice. Perhaps they know it off by heart. Outside, barefoot children play in the dust.

2. Condega

Condega lies in a valley just south of the River Coco, the river which twists its way through the inhospitable mountains of the north of Nicaragua to the Atlantic ocean. It was in these mountains and near this river that Nicaragua's first guerilla army under one General Sandino fought US marines occupying the country in the late 1920s. Fifty years later it was in these mountains that a group of student guerillas calling themselves the Sandinista National Liberation Front, the FSLN, hid and trained in preparation for the revolution to overthrow the Somoza dictatorship.

For many miles the River Coco forms the border between Nicaragua and Honduras. Its banks mark the northern boundaries of the district of Condega: an arid, rocky and mountainous terrain, broken up by the occasional cluster of poor peasant dwellings sheltering in valleys or by the roadside.

The town itself – it is more of a village really – is built where two rivers meet and below a low range of hills which provide little relief from the burning sun.

The layout is symmetrical and centres round a rather uninspiring square with trees and benches, dominated by a modern Catholic church. Its one thousand single-storey dwellings face one another down wide straight streets. The older ones are made of what used to be called wattle and daub, better known now as adobe. On some where the old mud has come away, you can see a criss-cross lattice which provides a structure for the walls. Near the square, the houses are more substantial and of brick – no doubt built by the wealthier families and landowners of the district. At the bottom near the river there are little one-room shacks made of rotting planks of wood.

Few people have glass in their windows – just wooden shutters. The back yards have hens and pigs and concrete sinks, and they are the focal point of domestic life. In the front the doors open straight onto the dust and stones of the streets. In the daytime women and children fight a constant battle to sweep out the dust which passing vehicles and horses send swirling into their homes. Children play in the doorways and shout hello to passers-by. At night the doors and windows remain wide open for fresh air. There is no traffic then, just crickets, crackly radios and voices. Walking past, the only sound you hear is that of your own footsteps crunching in the stones. A shaft of light, usually from a single bulb, frames adults – men and women of all ages – studying hard on makeshift tables. It seems that every house has become a college and that Condegans are in a race to catch up with the schooling they were denied in the past.

There is not much industry. Outside on the main road is the slaughterhouse, part of an important meat-exporting business once owned by friends of Anastasio Somoza. It is now a state enterprise run by a consensus of trade unions and management. Further down the road are state-owned tobacco farms. Together with the tannery in Condega these are the only significant sources of employment, apart from farming, in the district. Traditionally, the vast majority of Condega's six thousand inhabitants were land workers, deriving a meagre existence cultivating maize and beans on nearby plots of land or doing seasonal work on local coffee estates.

Condega's main lifeline is the Pan American Highway – part of the artery that connects Alaska to Tierra del Fuego. From the Honduran border, twenty-five miles north-east of Condega, the road cuts through the mountains, past the town of Estelí, down to the capital Managua, on past the lakes and volcanoes of southern Nicaragua and into Costa Rica. Around Condega it is not a busy road these days. In a full hour you might see a jeep taking government employees to a town in the region, or agricultural technicians to a local farm; one or two lorries transporting rice or beans to or from Managua; a farmer's truck loaded with skinny cattle on the way to market, and others carrying people – peasant-farmers, women and children holding themselves onto the wooden boards round the sides, hair flying in the wind.

Occasionally a bus labours by, its bodywork nearly scraping the road, its tyres barely visible under the weight of its occupants. Built to hold fifty, it regularly carries three times as many. A tangled mass of human faces, bodies and limbs is crammed inside, bundles, cases, boxes, baskets piled on top. And every now and then a juggernaut thunders through, destined for Costa Rica or Panama in the south, or north towards Honduras, Guatemala or El Salvador. Maybe even Mexico. Heard from a house in Condega, the rumble of lorries breaks the silence of the night, drawing Central America into a unity, and making Condega feel like a small dot on the map.

Ambushed

All evening families had been gathering in the building opposite the post office. It belongs to the local branch of the Sandinista Defence Committee, known as the CDS. Some half a million Nicaraguans all over the country are drawn into the revolution via their local CDS. In towns each neighbourhood or block has its own committee. Before 1979 the CDS office in Condega was the home of one of the few wealthy families in the village. It is a large town house with flagstones and plastered walls. Since the revolution it has lost any previous claim to elegance; slogans daub the flaking plaster on walls which have not seen a coat of paint in years.

When CDS meetings are well-attended, Condegans cram into the courtyard of the building; men in their wide stetson hats and women in brightly-coloured nylon dresses, babies clinging to their sides. Their concerns are mainly domestic and local. They complain about the lack of sugar in their local shop, the overcrowded buses, increased bus fares, an empty house in their neighbourhood which could surely be used to house a family; what to do about their seventeen-year-old son who has been called for military service. . . .

Much of the day-to-day organizing of the CDS is done by full-time workers. There are three employed in Condega. They are a new breed of Nicaraguan: young Sandinista activists who had been drawn into the struggle against Somoza and who are now responsible for keeping up the momentum of the revolution. CDS workers explain why there are shortages of certain foods, of agricultural equipment, why military conscription had to be introduced. Yes, they will go and sort out the local shop which is overcharging. Yes, they will find out from the Ministry of Commerce when the next delivery of cement or car tyres can be expected.

At CDS meetings everyone is a *compañero* – a word meaning companion or comrade. CDS activists urge the compañeros to help explain to others the problems facing Nicaragua now that it has won its freedom. Some men and women nod their approval. Others are not consoled. The meetings break up late and people disperse through the darkened streets – the generator in Condega is in need of overhaul and power cuts are common.

But it was not a meeting that had brought people to the CDS on this occasion. The whole day rumours had been spreading about the death of several young soldiers who were ambushed while patrolling a road in the nearby mountains.

These days the mountains around Condega are the hiding place

for a new set of guerillas – the Contras (short for 'counter-revolutionaries'). The Contras wear blue uniforms manufactured in the
USA and carry rifles supplied and paid for by the US Government.
Since 1983 they have made their presence felt in the district. They
raid small communities and farms, burn the homes of peasant-
farmers, assassinate teachers, health-workers and activists and
foreign workers, and ambush passing vehicles. Their objective is to
overthrow the Sandinista Government and destroy the revolution.

News of the ambush had travelled fast. People in Condega have
close family ties with the nineteen thousand inhabitants of nearby
mountain communities. The bank, the market, the church, the
health centre, a secondary school, the farmers' union and, perhaps
most important of all, the offices of the Sandinista National Liberation Front (known as the Frente) – all these make Condega a
focal point for the zone.

Outside the CDS building the news was confirmed. The bodies of
seven soldiers would be brought there shortly. Most of the dead were
part of the volunteer militia of a nearby hamlet, La Laguna. An
eighth victim was a girl volunteer who had been accompanying
the patrol. Her name was Angela. She had disappeared, assumed
kidnapped. People shook their heads sadly. No one spelt it out, but
everyone knew she would have been raped and probably killed.

Inside were the families of the dead, many in shock. A single light
bulb glared in the middle of the room. Women, crying softly, leant
against the flaking wall, surrounded by huddles of relatives comforting each other. There was a low murmur of sound. The families
had been told but still did not quite believe it could be true. Maybe
they had the wrong boy? The room became more and more crowded
as more onlookers and relatives poured in. People blocked the
entrance, peering over the tops of heads to catch a glimpse of the
scene. Curiosity might have brought some of them but also an
overwhelming desire to share the grief of this disaster.

Beyond a doorway onto the courtyard, another family stood over
a woman who had fainted onto a mattress. They would rather keep
their tragedy private.

The coffins arrived on two army trucks which roared up in a cloud
of dust. It was decided to open the large church hall in the central
square to accommodate the crowd. People rushed and pushed their
way in. Benches were hastily put together to form a platform for
the coffins.

As the coffins arrived, relatives rushed forward to open the lids
and identify the corpses. They were heavily bandaged, their faces,

where you could see them, an eerie waxen yellow. The youngest of
the victims was only fifteen years old; the oldest twenty-one. Women
started to scream, to faint and throw themselves on the lids. Many
people stood around speechless and helpless. Soon the hall was full –
the whole village was arriving, it seemed. Mothers collapsed into the
little wooden school chairs, comforted by their children. It is not
easy to forget their wailing and screaming.

Someone brought in two flags – red and black for the Sandinistas
and blue and white for Nicaragua. They seemed incongruous in such
a personal scene.

Condega's Sandinista officials and activists were there too. Eunice,
a quiet, slim, gentle woman in her twenties, moved briefly amongst
the families, paying her respects, and comforting. As the Frente
secretary she is one of the most important local figures. From a
distance she stood observing the tragedy that had struck the village,
shaking her head in disbelief. She was joined by Luisa, a CDS worker
and Luisa's older sister, Miriam, in charge of education in the town.
Their parents, the Centenos, were to be my hosts in Condega.

Several conscripts were present from the platoon which had been
attacked. They tried hard to keep calm. Bottles of rum were passed
round. Their young lieutenant was eager to tell me about the
ambush. They were a company of forty on a reconnaissance patrol.
At mid-day a large group of Contras – maybe as many as 500 –
attacked them on a bend in the road. They fought for several hours.
Most of the company were sons of local *campesino* families and
longstanding volunteers in the local defence militias. Some had just
begun a period of full-time military service. He had recovered the
bodies himself. Amongst them he found his twenty-year-old brother.
The lieutenant was agitated but disciplined, and tried hard to conceal
his grief.

The stench of the bodies, dead for some eighteen hours, was
beginning to waft out of the coffins into the evening heat. A distraught father suddenly started hitting the coffin lid and thrashing
out wildly. In a matter of seconds the hall had emptied in a mad
stampede to get to the door. It seemed they expected the man to
begin a shoot-out, crazed by grief. Firm hands were laid on him by
the young soldiers and he was calmed. The hall filled again. But the
communal haste to get out of his way betrayed a history of violent
clashes at public gatherings – the legacy of Somoza's police, the
National Guard.

A mass funeral

The next morning I visited one of the bereaved families who had stayed overnight in Condega. The family were holding a vigil around the coffin. Outside the two-roomed house a group of mourners were gathered in the dusty street. The father had been drinking. He was distraught, but angry and eager to talk.

They were a peasant family. Their community had known many deaths through the Contras. This was the second in the family. A cousin had died six months before in combat.... The father was almost shouting as he spoke:

> We are from a small community with just 400 families. It is a revolutionary community. We have been fighting the Contras for four years. We haven't done anything to the Contras and yet they come to attack us. But they can't affect our morale. The only way they can hit us is with the ambushes. We have suffered but we are going to get stronger. My son was twenty-two. He had been a volunteer militiaman for five years. It was only two months ago he began military service. But he fought and preferred to die. He wanted to fight to the end.

María Elsa, a sister, joined us. She carried her AK47 rifle around her shoulder. 'I feel so sad. But we have to continue this war. Women have to take up arms to fight too. We have to take up rifles and get organized. Those Americans should come and see what the situation is here in Nicaragua.'

The mother, a tall, slim woman, came out to greet me, her eyes red and filled with tears, her hair dishevelled and tied up in a scarf. She held back her tears and said she was glad for a chance to speak with a foreigner. She wanted me to know how people were suffering at the hands of the Americans so I could tell others outside. Her hand shook as it rested in mine.

Many people stayed away from work that day. In the afternoon there was a funeral for four of the boys. It began late while CDS workers tried to get a bigger crowd into the church. Death is all too common in Condega and people tire of funerals. Inside the church people waited. No one talked. Women who had been hysterical the night before were now composed, standing by the flower-covered coffins. The wailing had given way to a calm, silent respect for the dead. It was not the first time the young parish priest had conducted a multiple funeral.

After a short service a Sandinista official from a nearby town spoke to the congregation outside the church. He said he was confident that Nicaragua had the resources to respond to the Contras. 'The whole population is going to be mobilized', he said. 'Our ability to defeat the enemy depends on the strength of each one of us; men, old and young, women and children. Condega is a revolutionary village whose people fought for the Triumph.[1] For the sake of the sons of this village we must have confidence.'

A large crowd followed the four trucks as they bore the coffins round the central square and up to the cemetery next to the Highway. Emotions were running high again, set free in the open air. The family I had met invited me to ride on their truck. I thanked them. 'We are honoured to have you with us', said María Elsa, the sister. She walked alongside the truck, her rifle over her shoulder, tears falling down her face.

At the top of the hill the crowd pushed through the cemetery gates and stumbled over gravestones to where the fresh graves had been dug and lined with concrete. A mistake had been made and the graves were all too short. The gravediggers had to send for more cement from Estelí the regional capital, an hour's drive away. Condega urgently needs a new cemetery.

As the crowd waited the hysteria mounted again. There was something menacing about the way the clouds raced across the sky at the top of the hill and the tombstones stood out against the light. People pressed around the graves, some throwing themselves on the coffins, moaning and fainting. The stench of rotting bodies was almost unbearable.

On the brow of the hill lay the wreck of a National Guard aeroplane which was shot down by Sandinista guerillas during the insurrection on its way to bomb Estelí. It has been placed there as a memorial to the liberation of Condega. A strong wind had blown it off its stand and it perches menacingly amongst the gravestones and their simple wooden crosses. It will stay there until someone finds the time or energy to put it back.

The rifle under the bed

Luisa the CDS worker pressed me to stay that night, and it was from then that I began my stay with the Centenos. Three generations of the family were gathered on the veranda discussing the day's events.

I was immediately made welcome and offered supper of beans, rice and coffee.

The radio was on for the news bulletin broadcast on a crackly frequency from the Sandinista radio station in Managua: the Americans have blocked another meeting of Contadora – a group of Latin American states trying to bring an end to the war in Nicaragua ... a government jeep has been blown up, killing a top agricultural expert ... the Government has offered an amnesty to Contras ... food prices are to go up ... austerity measures are being introduced to cope with the economic crisis brought on by the war. Everyone will be affected.

Reception was poor. Someone twiddled the knobs and stopped on the unfamiliar sound of a commercial for painkillers. This was Radio 15 September, the radio station of the Contras arriving loud and clear from powerful transmitters in nearby Honduras. The music is American. A hysterical voice proclaims 'This year is the year of the final offensive to liberate Nicaragua. Today the communist traitors in Managua. . . .' The radio was quickly switched off. Luisa's parents, Donatila and Antonio, are both Sandinistas. They have lost two sons to the cause. The younger one died recently after volunteering for the militia. Donatila, a matronly woman of fifty-seven, shook her head: 'I can't hear this thing. As it is I never stop worrying. I have a headache most of the time. Whenever someone is killed, I suffer. I feel the same pain as if it were my own.'

Luisa was nervous too. Her two small children hung around her chair wanting her attention, but she had her mind on other things. Her husband, a small farmer, had been away on his farm in the mountains for over a week, and she hadn't heard a word. 'I usually get some kind of message from a neighbour, but this time nothing.' Communications were difficult. Few cars make it through the zone and after dark movement is especially dangerous. There was no doubt that being married to a well-known Sandinista activist would make Luisa's husband a target for the Contras. Gulping down her plate of rice and beans, she went off to find a messenger.

The lights went out and her father, Don Antonio, fumbled for the oil lamp. There were no candles in the shops these days – another shortage. He is a thin, wiry man of sixty-three, and runs one of the town's four electric mills. 'You never know when the light goes out whether it is the Contras about to attack the place', said Donatila, nursing a sleeping grandchild on her lap. When the Contras attacked the nearby town of Ocotal, the first thing they destroyed was the brand new generator.

But, said Don Antonio,

Things were much worse before: we were terrified. By six o'clock everyone was in bed. There was a strict curfew and if the Guardia caught you going out you would be shot. We would close the door and turn off the lights. You couldn't talk like we are today, even inside the house. Sometimes they would go around breaking people's doors down to rob.

Luisa and her brothers and sisters are all involved in one way or another in rebuilding and shaping the post-Somoza Nicaragua. Some of them played a key role in the revolution itself. They wanted to tell me about it, but it would take a long time – about what things were like under Somoza, about how in 1978 they and other young people went into the streets in demonstrations, defying the bullets of the National Guard. About how the town helped the guerillas in the mountains and even took up arms themselves.

'The trouble is, we've all been so busy since the Triumph that no one has ever had the time to write anything down', lamented Miriam. 'Why don't you stay?'

As I lay awake that night dogs barked in the village. In the distance came the sound of artillery. In the early hours someone came into the room I was sleeping in, and reached under the bed for a rifle. They were going on a journey into the mountains. If you are a Sandinista it is better to go armed.

3.   The road to the north

I knew about the ambush near Condega the day it happened. I was in the north with a reporter from *Barricada*, the Sandinista daily newspaper. Mónica, the reporter, was Chilean by birth, but had lived in Nicaragua since the revolution and taken Nicaraguan nationality. A good-looking, confident woman of thirty, she had two children and was well-travelled. She knew Mexico, where she had worked with exiled Sandinistas during the 1970s.

In 1979, the year of the Sandinista victory, everything changed. She and other exiles returned to Nicaragua to begin rebuilding a country that had been devastated during the insurrection. Fifty thousand Nicaraguans had died. Homes, factories, schools and hospitals lay in ruins after bombing raids by the National Guard. The economy was bankrupt – to compound a huge foreign debt, Somoza and his friends had fled with some $1.5 billion capital. But despite all this, the mood of the country was ecstatic.

1979 was a bad year for the USA. In Nicaragua they had lost a client government in the shape of Anastasio Somoza, the last of a family dynasty that had ruled Nicaragua for forty-five years. Elsewhere popular uprisings had put paid to other friends: the Shah in Iran; Eric Gairey in Grenada.

What was particularly exciting about the revolution in Nicaragua – and what had attracted me to the place – was that it had succeeded where so many of its Central American neighbours were failing in their attempts to cut the umbilical cord that had tied them to the USA for over a century. Nicaragua was only a small country, more or less the size of England and Wales with a population of less than three million. The despotic Somoza family had lived like playboys, whilst the people stagnated in poverty and disease. Two out of three peasants were effectively landless. Over half the population were illiterate.

Reports from Nicaragua now told a story of a peasantry in transformation. The landless were getting land, the poor were getting education and health care, the people were participating in politics. This was no flash in the pan, no palace coup that had replaced one corrupt dictator with another. In November 1984 Nicaraguans had

voted overwhelmingly for a Sandinista government in the country's
first elections since the revolution.

Of course there were the inevitable criticisms of the revolution:
that it was set on the course of a marxist totalitarian state, that the
Government was suppressing individual freedom. Many of these
statements came from disaffected businessmen and the Reagan
administration in the USA, a fact which tended to reinforce my
interest in what seemed to be a profound process of social change.

Why I should want to make a break from my job actually to go
and stay in Nicaragua needs some explaining. It was not the first
time I had been to the 'Third World'. As a journalist working on
television documentaries I had often come into contact with people
and communities whose struggles tell of the price that is paid for
the wealth and power of the industrialized West. But the media had
its own set of priorities and its own deadlines. 'Analysis' on television
tends to reduce most conflicts to three or four superficial sentences.
After a few days of intensive searching and interviewing, the TV
crew would be back on a plane home, congratulating themselves on
getting such 'good quotes'. Not only was there no time to get to
know the people properly, but the TV presentation of their story
would lose all measure of the people themselves and the complexities
of their lives and reduce most communities to stereotypes.

It was a relief to leave all that behind for a few months in 1985
and arrive in Managua, the capital of Nicaragua, one sweltering
evening in January. Here, I resolved, there would be no outside
deadlines to meet, only my own need to have certain questions
answered. What did it feel like to live through a period of violent
social change? How much power had the revolution given people?
How quickly were attitudes changing in this most impoverished of
Latin American countries? Had the popular enthusiasm we read
about in 1979 survived in the face of economic crisis and war?

Managua: city of contrasts

Getting around Managua was not easy. The city centre had been
destroyed in the earthquake of 1972 and was never rebuilt, due to
its location on an earth fault. It remains desolate and overgrown. A
few damaged buildings and shacks remain between patches of open
scrub and rubble. All the important offices are scattered throughout
various *barrios* that make up this sprawling city of one million

people. Shops are hidden away in new shopping centres on the
outskirts. The telephone system is erratic and unreliable. The heat
was oppressive and the dust entered every pore of the skin.

Equally strenuous was the public transport system itself. The
wide, battered buses came infrequently and not before long queues
had formed. A mad scramble ensued to push oneself on board.
Meanwhile from the other end of the bus another wrestling match
would be taking place by those who needed to disembark from the
solid mass of people within. Sometimes the best way of succeeding
in this was to bend down to the height of a child and push one's way
through people's legs. Nicaraguans remained totally calm in the
midst of this confusion. There was no shouting and cursing, just
silent pushing.

Apart from a few black people and pure indians from the small
populations on the Atlantic coast of the country, most Managuans
are Spanish-speaking *mestizos*, meaning 'mixed'. Like the majority
of Nicaraguans they are descendants of Spanish colonizers and the
original indian inhabitants of the country. Their hair is dark – the
women usually wear it long, even down to their waist – and their
skin a golden brown, though some seem to have retained the paler
complexions of the Spanish.

Managua is on the Pacific side of Nicaragua, a country divided by
terrain and climate into two distinct areas. About 90 per cent of the
population lives in the more fertile and accessible Pacific region with
its lakes and volcanoes. When the Spanish arrived in the sixeenth
century, they contented themselves with 'colonizing' the indians
of the Pacific, which in practice meant enslaving and eliminating
hundreds of thousands and destroying their culture and language.

The indians living in the tropical rain forests and along the inac-
cessible river banks of the Atlantic Coast, survived intact, together
with the Creoles who arrived there from the Caribbean as freed
slaves. They were wooed by the British and were used as pawns in
the British imperial rivalries with Spain. Many remained hostile to
the *mestizos* of the Pacific, whom they called the 'Spaniards' –
and the hostility continues today in the form of a rejection of the
Sandinistas. I saw few Atlantic Coast people in Managua.

It is a city of contrasts. Just a few yards from the plush suburb
where I was staying, with its luxurious bungalows and well-watered
lawns, stood a poor *barrio* where children played barefoot in dirt
tracks that passed for roads, and mothers laboured to cook their
tortillas on clay ovens at the back of their rudimentary wooden
shacks.

In every public place women had set up braziers offering food or drinks, their barefooted, half-clad children scampering around in the dust beside them. Some of the street vendors would enter the crowded buses, baskets of pastries on their heads, and calmly sell their wares. These are the inhabitants of the shanty towns and shacks, the makeshift *barrios* that have grown up all around the capital over the past few years. They are people whose lifestyles have changed little since the revolution.

The drift from countryside to town is common to all Third World countries, but in Nicaragua, as I was to learn, the tendency had been accelerated by war and economic crisis. A third of all Nicaraguans live in Managua. Part of the lure of the big city was the chance to get higher prices for food·on the thriving black market.

In the Oriental Market – a teeming bazaar-like confusion of wooden shacks, down by the lake – all manner of imported items sell at hyper-inflationary prices, alongside an abundance of food in short supply. For the government this was a major headache. Inflation was out of control and speculation was making a mockey of their cheap food policy. In 1986 some Nicaraguans were reported to be using barter, or buying and selling directly in dollars.

For people struggling to survive in Managua, life seemed a frustrating process of queueing and waiting and pushing onto buses, timing the household washing with the availability of water and trying to fit the family budget round a devaluing currency. Dollars changed hands on the street at more than ten times the official rate of exchange with the cordoba. As a foreigner I was constantly pestered by offers to buy dollars – usually from small business people. The government has since had to devalue the cordoba officially to one per cent of its value at that time.

Under Somoza Managua had been the mecca in which Nicaragua's small middle class could prosper. Those with funds probably sent their children abroad to be educated. A job in the civil service was a real advantage. After the earthquake in 1972 Managua's middle class had to start from scratch. Despite the millions of dollars of emergency aid that poured into the country, little reached the ordinary citizen after Somoza and his friends had taken the lion's share. The earthquake in which the middle class lost their white stuccoed bungalows and villas, and were forced to move into breezeblock *barrios*, created great discontent with the regime and precipitated its downfall. For the older generation, the agony of the earthquake is now compounded by a resentment at the hardships of the revolution. Managua has a discontented petty bourgeoisie.

The contrasts were extreme. The Intercontinental Hotel – one of only two buildings which survived the earthquake – stands on a hill just above the open wasteland in the old centre of the city. The hotel swarms with foreign journalists and their TV crews, visiting delegations and businessmen. Life inside continues pretty much as in any five-star hotel in any part of the world – except for water shortages. Opposite the hotel stands a restaurant in which government ministers, top officials and bureaucrats are entertained by their foreign guests, or sometimes by each other. Prices are fixed at international rates, making the menu far beyond the reach of the average Nicaraguan. Those lucky enough to have dollars can savour their hors-d'oeuvre in the knowledge that in three mouthfuls they have devoured the average landworker's weekly earnings.

With my dollars and my foreign passport the world was my oyster – from fancy restaurants right down to a 'Dollar shop' available to diplomats, foreign journalists and even wealthy Nicaraguans (or at least those who could get hold of a pass). There in a streamlined international supermarket, complete with piped music, I could purchase every imported luxury item I might miss in the Nicaraguan shops – from genuine Levi blue jeans down to portable ghetto blasters and Estée Lauder make-up. Two of its most popular products were Andrex toilet paper and Camay soap. The shop was run by the Government and brought in a few extra dollars. As a symbol of social equality in the new Nicaragua, it left something to be desired.

Nicaragua mobilized

But if the legacy of underdevelopment stared you in the face, the drama of the revolution was evident too.

My lifeline to the rest of the world lay in managing to secure copies of the daily newspapers offered by small, barefoot boys to passing motorists at traffic junctions. It was a random business. *Barricada*, the Sandinista paper, was the hardest to get hold of. If I missed the street sellers in the morning, chances were that even their offices had run out. *La Prensa*, the paper of the right-wing opposition, was more widely available. Since the events of 1979 it had moved steadily away from the revolution and by 1985 was openly supportive of the Reagan administration's policies. In July 1986 *La Prensa* was banned after it officially endorsed the Contras.

Soon after I arrived, the newspapers carried large government advertisements calling on young men to register for a new round of the draft. Thousands of people in Nicaragua carry weapons or belong to the volunteer militias – a legacy of the insurrection in which the people of the poor *barrios* rose up against the might of the National Guard. Every year the 'people's militias' come to Managua from all over the country to celebrate another anniversary and to reaffirm their commitment to defence. They are peasants, students, women, housewives – young and old.

The concept of the people in arms dominates Nicaragua. But the Contras were forcing the Government to create a more highly skilled force of 'irregular warfare battalions'. Outside the new health centres across the city, boys began queueing for medical checks – some were enthusiastic, others sullen and apprehensive. Casualties in the war were high.

Near the military offices, the road was always busy with groups of young men and women in fatigues coming to register, to collect a pension, or to execute some official business. The military hospital nearby had a constant stream of visitors and patients. Many wore bandages or walked on crutches.

The war monopolized the headlines. Every speech and move made by President Reagan in the Central American drama got front-page coverage. In the pro-Sandinista papers, Latin American efforts at peace negotiations (Contadora) and Nicaragua's case against the USA in the International Court of Justice got equal prominence.

La Prensa was leading a campaign of opposition to the draft. I heard many older people attack the Sandinistas for sending boys to die at the front. It was the continuation of a public row that had accompanied the introduction of military conscription in September 1983. The most influential of its opponents was the hierarchy of the Catholic Church. But the majority of Nicaraguan voters had given their verdict in the elections of November 1984. The Sandinista Party, the FSLN, had won 67 per cent of the vote. Managua was still plastered with graffiti and hoardings – official and unofficial election slogans. 'Viva el FSLN', or 'The only vanguard FSLN'. Some were for opposition parties too.

Outside the ruined cathedral in Revolution Square, thirty-eight-year-old Daniel Ortega, former guerilla and prisoner of Somoza, was installed as president shortly before I arrived. A colleague on the *junta* which had governed the country until then, Sergio Ramírez, became vice-president. The elections were endorsed by observers as being the most free in the country's history and a number of Western political figures attended, as well as Fidel Castro, the Cuban president.

The square was where hundreds of thousands of Nicaraguans rallied on 19 July 1979 to celebrate their victory over Somoza. It continues to be the venue for many of the major rallies of the mass organizations. When the crowds assemble to reassert their revolutionary determination and feel the strength of their numbers, slogans echo round the shell of the old cathedral and the pillars of the national assembly building – once Somoza's palace.

I walked there through the waste ground of the old city centre one evening and found it strangely peaceful. When the sun sets it lights up the stucco façade of the cathedral in a blaze of yellow warmth. The wind blows up dust and tears into the flags. Opposite are two shrines, one to a founder of the FSLN, Carlos Fonseca, who was killed in 1976, another to General Sandino. A torch burns to commemorate the fifty thousand who died in the insurrection. This is one of the Sandinistas' few concessions to monuments and formalities. People sit silently here. A mother with a child gazes across the square.

The war of the red berries

There is another war going on in Nicaragua at present – a war of production. Everyone is encouraged to volunteer for this battle. Not only has the price of Nicaragua's major export crop – coffee – fallen on the international market, but half the crop is threatened by Contra activities in the coffee zones. In offices of every organization there are posters advertising the delights and revolutionary duty of helping the harvest and thereby the *patria*. Whole ministries had been closed down and their entire staff despatched for a six-week stint on the hillsides.

I joined a group of hospital workers for a weekend at the harvest. They came from the Children's Hospital: nurses, orderlies, doctors, porters and a large group of student nurses. The health workers' trade union, FETSALUD, where I registered, reminded me of the control room in a strike headquarters at home. Trade union membership has mushroomed since 1979 and to my surprise I was treated like an official guest by two women employees who held a queue of new members and their problems at bay whilst they proudly explained the union's history and role.

On the Friday evening after work the volunteers gathered in one of the few remaining buildings in the rubble of the city centre and waited for over two hours for transport They were entertained by a good-humoured rotund young man in army fatigues and a Sandinista t-shirt, with the red and black scarf round his head. Alvaro worked in the hospital accounts department and was a Young Sandinista. In scout-masterly fashion he gave instructions and exchanged jokes with an appreciative audience of giggling student nurses. In the end only one lorry arrived so many of the volunteers never made it to the coffee-picking. As an *internationalista* I was among the privileged.

It was an uncomfortable journey, clinging to the sides of a pick-up truck, being thrown hither and thither over pot-holes in the road. No amount of discomfort could subdue the excitement of the young people packed like cattle in the back. I noticed a preponderance of women, but there were people of all ages, even children.

The lorry bounced over a dirt track into a forest where the trees were taller than any I had ever seen. By then it was several hours after dark and the headlights threw a beam up into the exotic tropical vegetation. Finding a place to sleep proved somewhat of a problem and the lorry-load of volunteers were turned away from two farms which were already overflowing with pickers. We were finally sent on foot down two kilometres of pathway, lugging our sleeping bags and blankets before feeling our way into an unlit barn where bare boards were to be our beds.

This was the standard accommodation traditionally available to Nicaraguan landworkers and their families during the coffee harvests. The bottom tier of wooden boards was divided into compartments in which families were housed. On top were two further tiers with no privacy at all. And that was it. No mattresses, no light, very little ventilation, just two doors at each end of the barn. Outside, one single cold tap was the extent of the plumbing; to shower you filled an old oil can with water and poured it over yourself in a cubicle. There were three toilets for all seventy of us.

The food (the usual country fare of rice and beans) was provided by the management of the coffee estate. It was a privately-owned farm (60 per cent of the land in Nicaragua is in private hands), but the owners had come to an arrangement with the government to supply harvesters for a fixed fee. In the past, poverty and starvation would have driven the thousands of seasonal landworkers to spend two or three months at the harvest. The revolution and its agrarian reform had dried up that supply. But Government had a shared interest with private landowners to maximize the crop for the sake of Nicaragua's dollar earnings.

In the old days, the more workers picked, the more they earned. The principle had now been extended and adapted to fit in with the volunteer spirit. The more you picked, the greater the accolade and praise you earned for your contribution to helping Nicaragua. Picking coffee is a gruelling and backbreaking task – trying to keep a foothold on steep muddy inclines whilst balancing large flat baskets round your waist into which you drop the berries is an art which it takes some time to master. But here there were no skivers, no shirkers. Men, women and children set to with determination and good humour which kept up even during the tropical downpours of rain which left you soaked to the skin and shivering in the wind. To get to the coffee we had walked nearly two miles at six in the morning. On the way back there were women and men limping with pain and gasping with thirst and heat in the afternoon sun. But no one complained.

And in the evening spirits revived. To the delight of the wide-eyed, half-clad children of the resident farmhand, a guitar was produced and songs sung. Alvaro and other young men (members of the Sandinista Youth) led the songs and told the jokes. Several of the volunteers buttonholed me to tell of their experiences of the revolution, or to ask me what people abroad thought of Nicaragua and 'the process', as it is called. 'It is a beautiful thing, our revolution', said Alvaro, as we gazed across the hills to the twinkling lights on Lake Managua in the distance, 'Why do people want to destroy it?'

Two days with *Barricada*

With Alvaro's queston still ringing in my ears, I set off with Mónica in a government jeep for the north – a journey that was to bring me to Condega.

Mónica wore green fatigues for the journey. There are times when it is useful to wear uniform, especially if you are writing a feature on Contra activities. You might need information from the army for whom declaring yourself as a Sandinista would help. For a moment she hesitated over my jeans and t-shirt – she could lend me a uniform the right size. But no, on reflection it would be better if I wore my own clothes.

With Mónica's AK47 rattling around in the back, we were soon climbing up the Pan American Highway into the mountain range that runs up the centre of the country, fanning out across the whole of the north-west. I felt a pang of excitement at leaving the sultry climate of Managua and entering this rugged country at the centre of the conflicts. Mónica knew this region well, having lived there for six months as a political worker in rural communities. The region which contains the departments of Estelí, Madriz and Nueva Segovia had suffered one of the highest casualty rates of the war, alongside the neighbouring areas of Matagalpa and Jinotega.

Estelí, the administrative capital of Region One, was brimming with army vehicles and young conscript soldiers. It is situated on a plateau from which a circle of blue mountains can be seen all around. Its single-storey shops and dwellings reminded me of the Wild West. Nearly all the males wore fatigues – a sight I was to get used to in the coming months. There was evidence of another war too – the war of liberation. The buildings in this town still bore the evidence of the fierce fighting that had engulfed the town during the insurrection.

From Estelí we continued up the Pan American Highway to Ocotal and San Fernando. It was a whirlwind tour. We met *campesino* victims of Contra attacks, refugee children and orphans, Contras who had surrendered under an amnesty, *campesinos* working in the fields with their rifles at the ready, women and children, party workers responsible for running towns, army officers, and people from the mass organizations. We visited the wrecks of schools, grain silos, homes and government installations, and saw the damage inflicted in hit-and-run attacks. The whole region appeared to be seething with anger and determination and tragedy.

It was in the Condega district that we began to feel the presence of the Contras. At the Frente office Eunice and two women welcomed us – all enthusiastic and young full-time party workers in their twenties. They greeted Mónica as an old friend and talked excitedly about the efforts of the community to rebuild the damage.

The next day we accepted their suggestion of a trip into the mountains of Canta Gallo to see for ourselves how the co-operatives were surviving. Eunice came too, in army camouflage drill and with rifle. The heavy gear seemed incongruous on her slim figure. The weapons were checked and put at the ready. A male party worker came along as guard and sat at the back of the jeep as it jolted over the narrow, rocky tracks that serve as roads, ascending gradually into the wide expanse of mountains. Around us the dense bush, and then trees and scrub, stretched as far as the eye could see. Even the coffee estates and the dwellings were hidden from view, swallowed up by the rugged terrain which turns from green to blue as it layers into the distance.

It was on the return journey, as we drove out of the last settlement on the mountain range, that we were warned of the Contra ambush taking place just over the brow of the hill – an event that was to convince me I should stay in Condega. A man came rushing over, rifle in hand, and flagged down the jeep as it sped towards the main road. He was breathless. There were quite a few Contras, he said, and not many *compañeros*. They needed help. For a moment everyone froze. What shall we do, asked Mónica. Stay or get out? There was no question of using telephones or radios. These did not exist. Eunice took charge immediately. We would return to Condega and alert communities on the way back to get help. The jeep drove along a back route at a furious pace. The party worker and another comrade sat in the back, their rifles pointing out of the open doors. In the front seat Eunice loaded her weapon. At every community along the way we stopped for her to inform the local militia.

It wasn't until we reached Condega that our pace relaxed. Everything looked so normal. We slowed down to the crawl of the farmers' trucks that bumped their way down the dirt tracks. People smiled and waved their greetings. We parked and went for lunch.

The Centenos

The day after the funerals I decided to accept the Centenos' invitation to stay in Condega. It was not that Condega was exactly typical of Nicaraguan towns: in the elections Condega had returned a higher than average vote for the Sandinistas. But to find a 'typical' Nicaraguan community was impossible. Each region and place has its own idiosyncrasies. What attracted me to Condega was its sense of unity, which seemed to be rooted in the history of the place. Unlike in Managua, people were coming up to me to tell me about the revolution and how their lives had changed. Being in the centre of a coffee zone, Condegans had direct knowledge of land reform. And as it was the main market centre for a host of small communities, I would have good contact with the remoter places in the mountains.

At the Centenos' house Luisa's mother Donatila was the centre of the household. A large, warm-hearted woman, her dress was permanently smeared with charcoal from the open stove at the back of the house. Shortages of Calor gas had forced many Condegans to abandon their modern gas cookers in favour of makeshift wood-burning ovens.

The L-shaped brick bungalow consisted of a collection of rooms built around a veranda and back garden, where all the day's activities take place. Like all the houses in Condega, it has a corrugated iron roof. When the rains come the din on the roof is deafening and the back yard turns into a muddy swamp.

Families are close in Nicaragua and three of the Centenos' children were living close by with their own families. It was often Donatila's food they came to eat, when commitments in the town had left them no time to cook. There was always a large pot of beans on the stove, some rice, and, with luck, an egg. It was a diet I had to get used to quickly, because I ate little else during my stay. Not so long ago, they said, they could get hold of milk and bread quite easily in the town. Not now though.

The house sometimes felt like a railway station. During the day most of Donatila's grandchildren were around or came there for meals after school. They charged in and out from the street, hung around the veranda and churned up the dust in the back yard, with its hens, pigs and fruit trees. At night they collapsed exhausted onto one of the shared camp beds.

As the visitor I was given a room to myself. It had red flagstones on the floor and a simple canvas camp bed. It was the only room in the house with a wardrobe in which precious items like clean sheets, medicines or jewellery were kept. Next door was a proper WC and a makeshift shower in which water trickled down from a pipe fixed into the roof. Condega has no proper sewage system and each house has its own cesspit. Clothes are washed in a concrete sink which stands in the yard. There is no hot water and washing is time-consuming and backbreaking. The dirty water runs into the dusty ground, sending chickens and children scurrying out of the way. The soap comes in large grey blocks from the Sandinista Defence Committee, the CDS, but it is used sparingly because of predicted shortages. Cooking oil is already scarce and toilet paper a luxury item.

The first sound every morning was that of the electric mill next door, which provides the bulk of the family income. As early as 4.30 a.m., queues of women and children form outside the house. They carry plastic bowls of maize or coffee beans and wait patiently while the antiquated machines churn up the beans for breakfast. Their biggest problem is overheating, especially early in the early morning rush. Those trying to fit in another hour's sleep would be rudely awoken by a high-pitched screech from the machine as it juddered to a halt for a breather.

The mill goes on humming until at least mid-day. On market days old *campesino* women arrive on horseback from the isolated hamlets outside Condega. They tether their horses outside the house while waiting for their ground maize, which is usually laboriously ground at home by hand.

A refugee from El Salvador worked the mill until lunchtime, in exchange for free board and lodging with the Centenos. He was the first to grab the newspapers when they arrived, searching for news of the latest guerilla victory in his country. Later in the day, he laboured over his school books in preparation for night school. Already in his mid-forties, he hoped to reach secondary school level – an education denied him until the revolution of 1979.

In the evenings, when the toddlers were in bed, there was usually some calm. Donatila might actually sit down and write a letter. She was proud of her writing learnt at night school after the revolution. Neighbours and relatives would drop in for a gossip. Luisa and her sisters, Alicia and Miriam, all working in various branches of the revolution, would sit on the plastic chairs on the veranda and report on the day's events. There was always a heated discussion and comparing of notes.

The war was pretty much the centre of people's thoughts. Don Antonio had usually found out the latest news of the Contras and their activities in the district. This was not just of academic interest but a matter of survival. In 1984 Contras had attacked the town of Ocotal less than twenty miles away and destroyed grain stores, the radio station, the generator, light industry and homes. Condega lived on tenterhooks.

4.   The silhouette of Sandino

My second encounter with the Condegan community came a week after the funeral. A public meeting was held in the community centre. A former FSLN guerilla commander, Comandante Pichardo, would be there and most of the Centeno family were going. I was curious to learn who was who in the town. The kitchen was cleared in record time and Donatila changed into a clean dress.

The CDS, and particularly Luisa, had a big hand in organizing the occasion. In the regional headquarters in Estelí where Luisa worked, the old hand-cranked duplicator had churned out notices which willing hands had folded carefully in half. They were driven up the Pan American Highway to Condega and taken round to every household in the town. The front of the leaflet carried a stencilled silhouette of Sandino. In the late 1920s Sandino had held US marines at bay in the nearby mountains of Las Segovias. Fifty years later he inspired the Sandinista Revolution.

The silhouette was familiar. Sandino's figure, complete with ten-gallon hat and breeches, peers out from the walls of countless buildings in Nicaragua. There must be a factory somewhere which produces thousands of such stencils for use by anyone needing some pro-revolutionary graffiti.

The meeting had been called to commemorate the anniversary of Sandino's assassination in 1934. It was a deed masterminded by Anastasio Somoza García, the ambitious head of a new American-financed army, the National Guard. At a stroke Somoza wiped out his most formidable opponent and cleared the path for his own bid for power.

It was hard in these revolutionary times to keep in mind how the mere mention of Sandino's name was capable of landing one in jail during the long reign of the Somoza dynasty. For the Condegans who packed into the church hall that evening, it was still a novelty to be able to recall such events. Indeed most of them only began to learn about Sandino after 1979. Since the revolution the new Government had set a great deal of store by the reconstitution of Nicaraguan history. There are institutes of Sandinista studies in Managua and widely-available volumes of Sandino's writings, not to mention the countless organizations whose names recall the first Nicaraguan nationalist to defeat the USA.

Everyone, however, knew that the main message of this meeting would be political, not historical. It was not often that Condega had the chance to question a commander about government policies. We arrived late and trooped into the brightly-lit hall. Heads turned in mild curiosity at a foreign face, though by then my presence in the town had been widely noticed. My being with the Centenos gave me a stamp of approval.

The benches which not so long ago had borne seven coffins were arranged in rows for the audience. Two tables at the top served as a platform for the speakers: Eunice, Condega's FSLN secretary, this time dressed in civilian clothes; the Comandante, a small bespectacled man in his thirties, whose military uniform carried the insignia of his rank; Evelio, the CDS regional secretary; and an earnest young man whom I was to meet later, Dachsun Cattin, the local CDS worker. And at the end of the row sat a tall man barely thirty with, most unusually, blond hair. This was Enrique, the Argentinian parish priest, tonight dressed in jeans and t-shirt.

With the exception of Enrique, these were people who came into politics during the struggle against Somoza as guerilla fighters first and foremost, and not as intellectuals. As FSLN militants, their goals are now to defend the sovereignty of Nicaragua, to consolidate the popular revolution and to transform the economy, eradicating injustice and the legacy of underdevelopment left by Somoza.

The FSLN began as a small guerilla force, not as a party. Its leaders are guerilla commanders, not professors. Its philosophy is based on the writings of Sandino and a kind of populism, while its authority in the country derives from having led the insurrection that defeated Somoza. Even today it is not a large organization. Its National Assembly in 1986 had ninety delegates of whom a third came from the army. It sees itself as an organic force amongst the masses whose first task is the defence of revolutionary power. Its programme is committed to a mixed economy, participatory democracy and non-alignment.[1]

The audience, the majority of whom were women, was on average older than the people on the platform. There were mothers, housewives, people who ran local CDS shops – *expendio popular* – through which subsidized food was distributed. There were peasant-farmers who had just returned from a long day on their land, members of nearby farming co-operatives, workers from the slaughterhouse and the tanning factory across the road. Some, like the Centeno parents, were members of the Sandinista base committees. Others were active in the CDS.

Everyone wanted to talk about the Government's new austerity measures. Ministers and comandantes had appeared on television to explain why food subsidies were being withdrawn – a measure which was already making itself felt in the shops. These were not five-minute appearances, but long speeches of half an hour or an hour, in which precise details of the country's economic plight were recounted. It was the first time food prices had gone up significantly since the revolution and there were widespread complaints. However sympathetic the audience was to the revolution, they needed good answers for the critics.

Anyone expecting to hear about class struggle and socialism at this meeting would have been disappointed. Its themes were patriotism, production and defence of the nation. Nicaragua's economic crisis was not of the Government's making, said Dachsun, who spoke first. International prices for its exports had fallen. The price of a jeep had gone up, while the price of coffee had fallen. After the revolution, the country had tackled basic demands for health, water, electricity, education and housing. But this meant that the problems had been postponed. Dachsun was nervous. It was not often he had to make a speech in front of a comandante.

Defence had to be the number one priority. Production had to be reorganized and stimulated for the war which was already eating up 40 per cent of the national budget. Subsidies on food would have to stop. This would mean that sugar could cost a lot more (there was a ripple of shock from the audience). There would be new taxes and war on speculators. People would be encouraged to work, to join the farming co-operatives.... 'We must find out what people think about these measures. The CDS have to be in contact with the masses. We must talk about the supplies, the prices, military conscription, the police', he said.

And so on. Speakers reminded the audience of the destruction the contras had wreaked locally – on grain silos, on co-operatives, on people. Price rises on the open market were listed, showing how speculators had to be stopped.

There was some outspoken comment from the floor. One woman asked why her brother's only son had been called up into the army when it had been expressly stated that only-sons would be exempted. It had hit the family hard. A man pointed out that it would be easier for him to increase production in the coffee harvest if he could get hold of a pair of shoes at a price he could afford. Another man complained that some of the conscripted youth hadn't been home for more than three months. When would they get a break?

Not all these points got direct answers. Eunice took a tough line with those who complained of hardships. There were some 350 boys who had evaded the draft in Condega, she admonished. Yet in the countryside most of the youth had willingly gone to fight, leaving a shortage of manpower for production.

> If we here have to eat just rice and beans and if we only have one pair of shoes, we will do so, so that the soldiers can eat properly and go and fight. The more young people go to fight, the quicker we will resolve the conflict and the fewer deaths there will be.

The Comandante spoke last, and the audience listened intently:

> Our revolution was very ambitious. The romantic ideal we had before we had power was that power itself would resolve all the problems. As romantics we built schools, but without the trained teachers to teach in them. We built health centres, but without the doctors. Our cultural level is very low. But people sat back and thought that the state would solve the problems.
>
> We now have to reorder the economy, to sacrifice things now for the future. You might need a hundred houses in Condega, but it would be better to invest that money in coffee production. We can't go for the easy way. During the Second World War Russian workers worked an eighteen-hour day. We must face the tasks gladly.
>
> It hurts to send our youth to fight, but we have to destroy the enemy to reach the future. It's that or letting the enemy come to burn our houses. We can't let the martyrs of Canta Gallo fall in vain.

With this stirring appeal the entire hall rose to its feet to sing the Sandinista national anthem. Sobered and inspired people filed out of the building, while CDS activists got to work signing people up for duties in the village, capitalizing on a new sense of confidence.

The legacy of empires

The nationalism that swept Nicaragua in the early twentieth century was rooted in centuries of foreign domination and oppression, first by Spain, later by the USA.

In 1522 Nicaragua became a province of Spain's Central American empire, ruled from Mexico by a governor appointed in Madrid. It has been estimated that at the time of its conquest Nicaragua had over two million inhabitants. These were indians who lived by cultivating maize, beans and cotton and raising chickens. To the Spanish the indians of Nicaragua were easy fodder for transportation to work the silver mines of Peru and Panama. By 1537 nearly half a million men had been captured and shipped out as slaves. Those who showed any signs of resistance died in brutal massacres. Many died of hunger. By the 1570s Nicaragua's population had been reduced to an estimated mere forty thousand people.[2]

Condega features in the early Spanish records as a Chorutegian potters' village. According to documents from 1554 its citizens paid large tributes to the local concessionaire, Juan Gallego. By the 1580s Condega was destitute: its inhabitants were unable to escape the fate of the majority of their countrymen. In 1586 a Franciscan monk, Friar Alonso Ponce, travelled through the village and wrote that it was in 'complete decay, having only eight houses'. Along with hundreds of thousands of indian Nicaraguans, its inhabitants had died or been forced to leave.

The situation improved slightly two centuries later. Archbishop Friar Agustín Morel de Santa Cruz affirmed that Condega's population were mulattos and lived by growing cotton. He counted 140 families living in fifty-five straw houses. A century later, in 1851, a North American traveller, J. S. Bradbury, described Condega as 'one of the most beautiful villages of the state. It has a church and many well built houses.'[3]

Not that Nicaraguan indians were passive in the face of Spanish rule. The violence was countered by local insurrections and revolts amongst the indians which continued well into the twentieth century.

When the Spanish empire collapsed in 1821, it was not long before the USA took its place. US entrepreneurs were hungry for raw materials and the Government protected their adventures in Central America and the Caribbean with military force. Under the Monroe Doctrine of 1823, Britain – once the leading trading power in the Caribbean region – agreed to keep out.

In 1853, just thirty years after Nicaragua's 'independence', the country was being mortgaged as collateral for loans provided by the banking friends of an American filibuster, William Walker. He had invaded the country and reimposed slavery, making himself president. Walker did not last long. Thereafter the USA used the weakness of two rival Nicaraguan ruling elites, one conservative, the other liberal, to get its own way. The elites in turn vied for American backing by selling their country's sovereignty in a series of treaties.

The vast mass of Nicaraguans could barely maintain themselves above subsistence level at this time. In the Atlantic zones many worked for American companies, producing rubber, gold and bananas. In the north, coffee was rapidly becoming the major export crop, and thousands of peasant-farmers were losing their land and being forced into wage labour as plantation hands on private estates. The coffee-owning class – landowners and traders – lived an almost European lifestyle.

From the beginning of the twentieth century the USA thought nothing of direct military invasion to impose its will in Nicaragua. Until Sandino, this usually achieved quick results. When a liberal president, Zelaya, began to seek alliances with other foreign powers, the USA sent in the marines (in 1909). They backed a conservative uprising that they had largely engineered and had Zelaya deposed. The conservatives gave the USA control of the country's finances, in return for help in policing their Government against the mass of peasants.

US marines invaded for a second time in 1912 to quell another liberal uprising. Two years later they had secured a treaty granting them exclusive rights in perpetuity to build a canal linking east and west, and a naval base.

By 1917 Nicaragua was virtually a US protectorate. All its fiscal revenue was handled by a US-run High Commission, ensuring that American bankers got their loan interest payments before all else. They also began pushing for the creation of an American-trained army.

Better rebel than slave

By the 1920s a new wind was blowing in Central America, stirred up by the Mexican Revolution and the upheavals of the First World War. It was above all the son of a small Nicaraguan farmer from

Masaya, Augusto C. Sandino, who was to give Nicaragua its first taste of the new breeze.

Born in 1895, Sandino left Nicaragua in the 1920s to work in an oil company in Mexico. In 1926 the Mexican Government incurred the wrath of the USA by nationalizing its oil and forcing US companies to take out fifty-year leases. It was an inspiration to Sandino, who like most Nicaraguans resented US domination of Central America.

When the Mexicans showed some sympathy for a new liberal rebellion in Nicaragua, alarm bells rang in Washington ('a direct challenge to the United States', said the US under-secretary of State). Marines invaded for a third time with two thousand men and air support. No one expected the liberals to hold out for long. Sandino, now aged thirty-one, gave up his job and returned to Nicaragua with the express purpose of recruiting a patriotic army from the gold miners and peasants of the north to fight the marines. Within a year he had some 300 men under arms and had won back several towns from the control of conservative forces.

Sandino's nationalism was far more radical than anything Nicaragua had known previously. When the liberal generals surrendered, wooed by an American plan to give them a share in government, Sandino was incensed. He denounced General Moncada for treason and issued a circular to all government officials in the Segovias region. 'I am not willing to hand in my arms, even if the others agree to do so. I prefer to die with the few who follow me, because it is better to be killed as a rebel than to live on as a slave.'[4]

Sandino's refusal to disarm took the USA by surprise. In Ocotal, just north of Condega. G. D. Hatfield of the US Marine Corps announced: 'Augusto Sandino, erstwhile General of the Liberal Armies, is now an outlaw, in rebellion against the Government of Nicaragua.' From this point onwards Sandino's army fought US marines on its own, relying principally on their support amongst the peasant-farmers of the north.

Sandino called patriotic Nicaraguans to join his army in order to free Nicaragua from US troops, and so restore its dignity and sovereignty. The ideological motivation of the army was rooted in an ardent patriotism and disgust at the Nicaraguan rulers. Sandino wrote:

> The army defending Nicaragua's sovereignty has no commitments to anyone. It is bound by the sacred principle of loyalty and honour. It doesn't yield to conventionalities or accept

outside interference, because it defines its image by its actions.
If the Constitutional President of my country were ousted by
Yanqui force, and villainously betrayed by the man to whom he
confided command of the army, the brave handful who uphold
the legality of his election with their blood would still hold in
one hand the symbol of the nation and in the other a rifle, to
defend the nation's derided and humiliated rights.[5]

The army grew quickly in size, attracting workers and peasants.
The international slump in coffee prices after 1929 brought Sandino
more recruits. There was unemployment and famine amongst peasants and agricultural labourers. Landlessness was growing.

Sandino's men had only rudimentary arms – many carried only
machetes – but the 'Army in Defence of the National Sovereignty
of Nicaragua', no more than six thousand strong at its height, held
down the marines for several years. When US marine firepower
defeated him as it often did, Sandino was able to retreat into the
hills. There, unlike his adversaries, he could count on an intimate
knowledge of the terrain and a growing number of sympathizers
from amongst the peasantry who provided a brilliantly effective
intelligence network.

The man who knew Sandino

In Condega the American marines fighting Sandino built an airstrip
down by the river and *gringos* wandered in and out of the village
mingling with the population. By and large they put over the picture
of an outlaw who terrorized the *campesinos* – a picture that even
Don Antonio says he never questioned until the 1970s. But in the
surrounding mountain communities of Canta Gallo to the east of the
town, where today Contras are laying ambushes and attacking co-
operatives, Sandino had supporters. Some *campesinos* were recruited
to fight in his army or to supply information or provide food. A few
of these old men now live in Condega, and I was urged to visit a
certain Don Leandro Córdoba, to hear for myself about General
Sandino.

I found Don Leandro Córdoba, now aged ninety, and his wife, in
a small brick house up a steep hill, which they share with grandchildren and relatives. That evening there was no electricity in the
town. I began the climb up the hill, stumbling over loose rocks and

into the dried-up furrows made by previous rains, wondering how they would feel about a pale-faced stranger knocking on their door after dark.

A young woman opened the door just a crack. It was pitch black inside. Don Leandro was in bed, but they would call him. 'Come in', she beckoned. There were no chairs, but I could faintly make out a camp bed in each corner of the room. A folding chair was brought in from outside and a candle placed on the dirt floor – there was no furniture on which to place it.

Excited whispers could be heard from outside, children stifling a giggle. It seemed not just Don Leandro, but the whole house would arrive for the occasion and the process of preparing the household for the night would go into reverse. An old man was helped through the doorway from outside. I scanned his face for signs of disapproval and inconvenience and suggested I returned another day. No, he insisted enthusiastically. Of course we can talk. I obviously wasn't the first such visitor he had had.

I was shown outside to a wooden eating area where at least the moon and stars could provide some light. As he settled down on a bench, children appeared out of the dark and sat down, wriggling around in anticipation. He enjoyed talking about Sandino and didn't need any questions to spark him off. In the half-light I could make out his face – smiling, and surprisingly healthy.

At the time of Sandino's rebellion, Don Leandro was living in Los Planes, a tiny rural community in Canta Gallo near Condega, working a plot of land growing maize, beans and sugar. Sandino's men would pass by asking for food. Don Leandro remembered one occasion:

We killed pigs and chickens whenever they came by. One day they sent a message to go over to Sandino with three hundred tortillas. I agreed but I was afraid of the planes which went around attacking Sandino. So I asked a boy to accompany me and he spurred on the donkey with its load till we got to Los Perrerros where there was a camp. I couldn't tell how many soldiers there were there because it was in a coffee plantation.

I asked for the General and the guard led me through. Someone said to him, 'This man belongs to the conservatives. He is one of those that helps both political parties at the same time.' The General asked him, 'What class of man is this honest man?' 'A worker', he said. 'OK no problem', the General said, and saluted me. I was very nervous. You know how deep down one gets nervous. 'Yes you are going to work with us', he said. He said he was fighting to get rid of the slavery we were living in. I was delighted because I had always been an opponent. I'd always fought for change. That was my struggle.

With the help of his wife and other young peasants in his village Leandro Córdoba collected the provisions and despatched tortillas to Sandino's troops. He became a trusted messenger.

Sandino's stock-in-trade became his attacks on military garrisons and ambushes of US military convoys. For the marines the war in Nicaragua became a nightmare: 'rains, mosquitos, swamps, swollen rivers, wild animals, the horror of falling into an ambush, fever and always the invisible enemy'.[6]

The USA reacted to this new type of opponent – a guerilla army – with savage aerial bombardments destroying whole towns and villages (but often leaving their enemies unscathed in their trenches). The brutality of their methods and the forced evacuations of peasants from villages backing Sandino served to harden support and respect amongst the peasantry for the legendary guerilla leader.

Don Leandro had little time for the marines, whose treatment of the *campesinos* in the area was notorious. He told me his own story of arbitrary arrest:

They arrested me one day when I was on the way to a friend's house. I stopped in a place to play billiards and they arrived there and took hold of a man and started beating him up. I was watching them and didn't understand why. So I left in search of my friend's house. But they called me back. So I came back, saying to myself, they are going to kill me. They had killed a lot of people that I knew. An American who spoke a bit of Spanish asked me what I was doing. I told him I was just looking and playing billiards and that I didn't know the man that they'd arrested.

He gave me a shove and tied me up and threw some water over me. They made me sit down on the floor and started doing a lot of things to me. But a friend who knew them and worked with them intervened on my behalf and they let me go.

At the height of the war Sandino's guerillas were organized in twenty-one columns over ten of Nicaragua's sixteen departments. Sandino described his combatants as 'not soldiers but armed citizens'. His war against the marines earned him international acclaim, even in radical circles in the USA. In a development that was later mirrored during the Spanish Civil War, volunteers from other Latin American countries formed an international brigade and came and fought for Sandino.

Even the peasants employed by the US marines had divided loyalties. When the marines came to Don Leandro's village, he was tipped off by a Nicaraguan peasant who drove the donkeys: 'I spoke to the boy and asked him what shall I do? If these Yankees discover I'm helping Sandino they'll kill me. So he said it was better I go to Condega. So I came here and didn't go back until they left.'

In Condega Don Leandro dared not show where his sympathies lay. The marines based there once tried to recruit him to fight one of their battles: 'I told them I didn't know how to work a gun and I would get killed, but they insisted and took me down to the river and trained me.' Don Leandro chuckled at the thought of fooling the Americans. They took him out into the mountains for a battle. But he was let off the hook at the last minute when they met a convoy of wounded American marines: 'They stopped us. There were three Yankees dead on a donkey and some carrying stretchers. Four were wounded. So we grabbed hold of the wounded ones and helped them bury the dead. They took the others away in planes.'

By this time Sandino's army virtually controlled the north of the country, running it as a state within a state. In these liberated zones co-operatives had been formed and peasants and soldiers received basic literacy classes. At the beginning of 1933, after 176 fruitless encounters with Sandino's forces, the marines were withdrawn, unable to secure a military victory.

Sandino had refused to lay down his arms unless the canal treaty was torn up and land redistributed in favour of the peasantry. But with suppplies of ammunition running out, he was forced to negotiate with Somoza, the head of the new National Guard. On the verge of a ceasefire, on 21 February 1934, Sandino met President Sacasa for dinner to clinch the deal. Somoza's men struck as he left the presidential palace.

For Don Leandro, Sandino's death was the cue to return to his village, and it was another forty years before he was to hear of the Sandinistas again. The National Guard wiped out over three hundred of Sandino's soldiers in the north, beginning a period of savage reprisals against the vestiges of guerilla resistance.

5. Don Antonio and the question of land

I took suggestions from anyone in Condega as to whom I should meet, and where I should visit. There was no shortage of advice. Whenever I sat down to talk with the people running the key organizations in the town, I found myself compiling another long list of names. There were the Catholic lay delegates, the co-operative members, the midwives, the youth, the conscripts, the trade unionists, the Frente workers. ... All were people who had something to tell me about the history of Condega, people who – it was felt – had contributed to making the place what it was.

I wanted to start with the landworkers and the peasant-farmers. Farming was after all the main source of income in the district, and the question of land had been crucial in the revolution. I noticed a large map stuck on the wall in the Office of Agrarian Reform. It was a well-thumbed map of the Condega district covered with a mass of red and blue shapes. The shapes indicated the land that used to belong to Somoza and his friends, and which was taken over at the time of the revolution. It was a massive area. Red stood for land that is now run by a state enterprise; blue for the peasant co-operatives formed after 1981.

The map told the story of how the revolution has come to Condega. Gone are the wealthy Cubans exiles who owned tobacco farms on the Highway. Gone too are the private owners of the coffee processing plant up the road. Along with the big cattle ranches and the slaughterhouse, they are all now in state hands. Gone are the few big landlords who, by muscling in on the small farmers, had gradually taken possession of all the best land in the district. Their coffee estates and cattle ranches have been distributed amongst the landless.

The yearning for land was a key factor in the radicalization of Nicaragua's peasantry in the 1970s. Around Condega few of the small farmers could survive from the produce of their own little plots of land. The full-time landworkers on the coffee estates were joined at harvest time by thousands of men, women and children needing to supplement their meagre family income.

Don Antonio Centeno was the man from whom I began to learn about the life of landless peasants in Nicaragua. Most of his life he had laboured on the coffee estate at Darailí in the nearby mountains of Canta Gallo. I had plenty of opportunities to talk to him and he loved an audience. Discussions always revolved around the revolution and how his life now compared with the old days. There was nothing, no amount of hardship, of price increases, of shortages, that could compare with the brutality of life on the coffee estates, the greed of the ruling elite of Condega and the hypocrisy of the authorities.

For his age – he was over sixty, old by Nicaraguan standards – he was remarkably active. He had a slim, sinewy body, his wiry hair still dark, though even at home he preferred to hide his receding hairline under a stetson. Sometimes he would go off for a day and a half, travelling on the country's dilapitated bus system to far-away towns in search of a new bolt or part for the mill. The old machines in the room adjoining the house looked ancient, but somehow they kept going.

Religion was a favourite subject. He was a devout Catholic, like most of his generation and the majority of Condegans. A row was currently raging between the hierarchy of the Catholic Church and three Catholic priests who had posts in the Sandinista Government. They had been told to relinquish their posts, or give up the priesthood. Don Antonio said: 'These are real Christian priests in Nicaragua. They were appointed because they exposed their lives for the revolution. They are not in it for the money. For me these are the real Christians.' He saw revolution as an act of Christianity – resulting from the realization of the poor that they could struggle against injustice. In the early 1970s, there had been Christian discussion groups in Condega and people had begun to re-read the Bible for its message of struggle against injustice.   He talked of the priest who was massacred by the National Guard for his support of those fighting Somoza. He berated American-financed fundamentalists who opposed the use of arms to defend the revolution. Don Antonio fumed: 'We are Christians, but not the type of Christian who refuses to carry arms. I carry a weapon to defend myself from attack, not to attack others.'

It was one of Don Antonio's biggest disappointments that the Pope, who had visited Nicaragua in 1983, had not endorsed the revolution and had snubbed bereaved mothers who asked his blessing for their sons killed in the war: 'The holy Pope for me doesn't have a Christian quality. He has a lot of power. But if he were a Christian he would use the Church to stop all the wild aggression that exists in the world and he doesn't.'

In many ways, Don Antonio was Condega's most enthusiastic ambassador for the revolution – not because of his own part in it, so much as his memory of what went before and how things have changed. When his sons and daughters joined the Sandinistas to fight Somoza, he disapproved at first, dreading Guardia raids and their random shooting at demonstrations.

Later, in 1978 – Somoza's last year – he was one of the first members of the United People's Movement, which brought together Christians, the middle classes and the masses in joint opposition to the dictatorship. After 1979 he was one of the first volunteers for the town's militia. Whenever the town needs defending, he is up out of his bed and, rifle in hand, has made it to the Frente office while others are still struggling with their shoes.

He is an active member of the Sandinista base committee in Condega and regularly hosts meetings in the house. Old *campesino* men in their stetsons and women dressed in their best clothes sit in a circle in the back yard. The atmosphere is serious. It is easy to forget that, for these people, the freedom to participate in politics has only recently been won.

The curse of illiteracy and ignorance has plagued them all their lives, and many older peasants are shy about speaking up in larger groups. They discuss the reaction in the town to the latest price rises, the international situation, Reagan's latest ultimatum to the Nicaraguan Government. They often defer to those with greater knowledge – for instance, to the younger generation. But Don Antonio plays a leading role at these meetings; he does not lack confidence.

At the end of the day I could count on finding him around, sitting on one of the old plastic chairs on the veranda, looking at the newspaper. He couldn't read properly, but managed to get the gist and made it his business to keep abreast of the news. One topic of conversation would be bound to get him going, and that was Somoza and the dictatorship that ruled Nicaragua for forty-three years.

Somoza's grip

In 1931 Sandino fought a big battle near the estate on which Don Antonio worked as a young boy. Some twenty marines died. It is one of his only memories of the man whose ideas he now admires. In those days it was a different story.

Born in 1921, to a woman with many children, Antonio was given away at the age of six to the owner of a coffee plantation. He was supposed to be a foster child, but the landlord lost no time in putting him to work, expecting him to labour like a man. There was no education for farm-hands and very little contact with the outside world. Sandino's reputation on the estate, as put about by the landlord, no doubt, was of a cruel merciless murderer who terrorized innocent people. Antonio, then aged thirteen, remembers celebrating when Sandino was killed: 'it was good because it meant the end of the war.'

Life on the estates around Condega was harsh. The landlord later 'gave' Antonio his own patch of land. It was a meaningless gift, for the landlord demanded that he hand over the maize he had grown to the estate. Like thousands in his position Antonio ran into debt and had to give up his land:

> I was a paid labourer. It was the hardest work you could imagine. We couldn't afford tools and could hardly eat. I worked seven days a week. Later I was paid a bit more for experience, but my children would go to school or to work without eating. Sometimes I would leave home on a cup of coffee and remain without food till 2 p.m. I couldn't tell the boss because he would tell me I wasn't fit for work.

Donatila worked on the same estate, as a cook. During the harvest she was expected to cut coffee too, even when heavily pregnant. Food had to be bought from the landowner's shop. They would buy food for fourteen days and run up a debt that they could never pay off.

Meanwhile, Anastasio Somoza García had become president of Nicaragua. Through the National Guard he wielded an unprecedented power over the country and began amassing a huge personal fortune. The crux of wealth in Nicaragua lay in ownership of the land. And land was Somoza's main target. Nicaragua in his hands was transformed into a private farm producing exports for sale in the USA and the West.

Somoza had few scruples. During the Second World War he simply confiscated the property of Germans and Italians and added them to his estate. His stock-in-trade was to bankrupt the small farmers. Using the denial of credit (he owned the bank) he would run them into debt and force them to sell cheaply. Forty per cent of small landowners were dispossessed and forced out of their homes. He instituted graft as the common way to do business, taking bribes and payments from foreign investors and Nicaraguans alike.

The small cattle ranchers around Condega soon felt his influence. Somoza laid down that no one could move cattle without a permit. When these did not arrive in time (Somoza controlled the issuing of permits), he forced the ranchers to sell their stock to himself at a low price. The landless remained desperately poor and ill fed. On the coffee estates near Condega pay never exceeded four cordobas a day and remained at that level, despite massive inflation during the war which sent the price of maize up 700 per cent.

The USA had long treated Nicaragua as a source of raw materials. Gold, coffee, bananas, meat and sugar were extracted – sometimes directly by American companies. By 1940 the USA was earning nearly $9 million a year from gold-mining and other investments. To help their friend Somoza the Americans were happy to plough a little back under the 'Good Neighbour' programme. There was some spending on health and they agreed to finance the building of the Pan-American Highway which runs through Condega. More than anyone it was Somoza who benefited from the road. His construction companies took the profits and, as an outside observer remarked in 1950, the route of the road had been specially planned to run past his own estates.[1]

In 1939 Somoza was received with full state honours by President Roosevelt. It is said that on seeing the list of prospective state visitors, Roosevelt asked his Secretary of State 'Isn't he supposed to be a son of a bitch?' The Secretary of State replied, 'He sure is, but he is *our* son of a bitch.'[2]

The Guard was the crux of Somoza's power. Paid for and trained by the USA, it manned Nicaragua's army, its police force and prison administration. It controlled the local magistrates and, by buying informers known as *orejas* (ears), administered its own 'justice'. It collected taxes, granted business licences and ran the trade in liquor and prostitution. Eventually Somoza gave the Guard control of the railroad and the postal service. Some 2 per cent of the population depended on a salary from the Guard.

One of their most important tasks was to deal with opponents of Somoza's rule. In 1944 students and middle-class people took part in street demonstrations in a wave of protests. They were dealt with ruthlessly. There was practically no means by which people like Don Antonio could protest against their lot. There were no landworkers' unions. The Conservative Party had members in the area, but they were closely monitored by the National Guard and Somoza's agents.

After only ten years in office, Somoza was thought to be worth around $120 million. 'In approximate terms Somoza is the proud possessor of fifty-one cattle ranches and forty-six coffee estates within Nicaragua and is by far the largest coffee producer.'[3]

When his terms of office ran out in 1947, Somoza manœuvred himself back into power by a military coup, thereafter appeasing rebellious conservatives by offering them a share in government. His use of absolute state power put an end to Don Antonio's indifference towards the dictator:

> When he staged a coup against Argüello I changed.[4] He was already pushing himself forward. We could see that there was no law.
>
> There was no liberty. The pressures were terrible. Every member of the Guardia was a law unto himself. They killed, robbed, raped and there was no one to complain to. They were the law and against the law. Anyone who complained would be killed. They stole cattle and sold them to each other. No one could do anything.
>
> They would treat a _campesino_ like a dog and a _campesino_ would treat them as if they were tigers. You just couldn't go up to a military man and address him with a problem. They would be as likely to rob you of what you had in your pocket, and arrest you. And if you spoke out about it, they would kill you.

In 1956 Somoza García was assassinated by a young poet and intellectual from Leon: Rigoberto López Pérez. But with some help from its friend, US President Eisenhower, the dynasty was able to continue. Power passed to Somoza's American-trained sons – first Luis, then later Anastasio II. The process of personal aggrandisement continued. The family empire expanded and diversified, using American regional aid to move into paper, fishing and meat-processing. The slaughterhouse in Condega became a highly mechanized affair, employing some 400 workers.

American companies investing in Nicaragua had a field day. They were given tax incentives, exemption from currency restrictions, could transfer all their capital and profits out of the country and export freely without taxation. Credit arrangements were available through Somoza's bank.

From the mid-1950s the economy was coming out of slump but few people in the Condega area noticed. Cotton overtook coffee as the country's largest export. Over 180,000 subsistence farmers lost their land to the cotton lords and added to the army of seasonal workers travelling Nicaragua to eke out a living as paid harvesters.

In the northern coffee areas the process of land concentration was speeded up. I heard countless stories from Don Antonio of people who had been dispossessed in this period. One came from a Catholic lay preacher who is now a member of the National Assembly:

> I remember in La Dalia there was a family called Gutiérrez. They had half a *manzana*[5] and lived by cultivating coffee and selling it. The landlord started buying up the land around them, snatching it and leaving them in the middle. Once he had them surrounded he said to them: 'either you sell me your land and leave , or I'll finish you. I forbid you to drive animals through my lands.' This meant that the Gutiérrez couldn't take their coffee out for market.
>
> Landowners would take land off the *campesinos* by force. They arranged with the local Guardia to have them arrested by accusing them of theft. At other times they would buy the land at half price.[6]

People and poverty

Ironically, Condega itself at that time was said to be benefiting from the economic boom of the 1960s. If you had happened to pass through the town in 1968, you might well have have looked at a tourist brochure about the department of Estelí and read the section on Condega. This describes Condega as a town in an 'indisputable process of urban improvement and considerable commercial activity. Its population of 3,500 is served by a supply of drinking water, three doctors, one dentist, twenty-two groceries, six larger shops, a health centre and a modern school.'

A whole paragraph is devoted to the parish church, the exterior of which 'contrasts favourably with modern churches elsewhere which inspire neither piety nor devotion and are little different from a railway station or a customs shed.' Under 'human values' there is a list of Condega's prominent citizens. They include two engineers, a colonel, a doctor, two generals of the National Guard and the former mayor who built the 'park' in the town's central square.[7]

Walking through the dusty streets with their symmetrical layout, passing the town houses and the headquarters of the National Guard, observing the men outside in their spanking new uniforms made in the USA, you probably would not have seen anything to contradict the impression given of a thriving, well-ordered community, its population happily producing tobacco, rice and maize.

The author of the brochure obviously didn't take the trouble to speak with Don Henry Vargas, a local reporter for *La Prensa*, who tells a different story:

> There were three big landowners. One was Sebastian Pinel – a big cattle rancher who made his money in the meat business. He used to run racehorses. He paid the peasants what he wanted and it wasn't much. Juan Moncada was the most powerful merchant in the town. He controlled all the trade in beans and maize. He was a total bandit. He paid the peasants a mere 20 cordobas for their harvest. He used to lend them money. If they couldn't pay him back, he would take everything they had – even their house. We didn't confiscate many houses in the village after the triumph, but his was one.
>
> The coffee estates were owned by Filemón Molina. He spent the year travelling between Europe and Mexico and returned only once a year for the coffee harvest. The tobacco farms were owned by Cuban [exiles] who commuted from Miami. The slaughter-house and the tannery were owned by one Paulo Rener, a senator who lived elsewhere in Central America. Another landowner was a sergeant in the National Guard who was also a powerful figure.
>
> The medical situation was very bad. There were three doctors but they looked after the rich families. In the mornings they had surgeries for the people. But their charges were very high. The medicines which came to the health centre would be stolen and sold for profit. Even the doctors used to steal the medicines. If people came to the surgery, they would tell them to come back to their private clinic for treatment. . . .

Don Antonio had moved his family into Condega where they managed to survive by constant labour. He too begs to differ with the anodyne words of the brochure:

The older children had to work on the tobacco farms but even
then there wasn't enough to eat. For half the year we would go
off for the harvest, all of us. What we wanted was that the
children wouldn't suffer, that they would have something, a
little to eat.

   To call a doctor out to where I lived cost about 200 cordobas.
That was nearly a month's pay. If you had the means you could
save yourself. If not you died. When my mother fell ill, my fourth
child, Alicia, was just a toddler. I had to sell all my mother's
land plus the four cows she owned and her pigs to raise the money
to send for a doctor. There were health centres but they were
useless. They couldn't even get rid of parasites in the health
centre.

There were in fact only six dentists and fifty-three doctors in the
whole region at the time – one for every five thousand people. Health
centres existed only in the towns. In practice only a fifth of the
population in the region ever got any medical attention. In the
countryside around Condega if you were sick, you died.[8]

   But, with the help of the National Guard, Somoza could count on
a docile quiescent population. Don Antonio was no exception:

I lived submerged in my work. I worried about my children. I
didn't get involved. Unions were forbidden. I knew there was no
point because such people were the first to die. And what for?
What was the point in thinking about this?

   Every time a government changed we had hope that there
would be change, that there would be work. But every time there
was a change of government the oppression got worse. Somoza
was rigging the elections, we knew that. So we didn't bother to
vote. We didn't like the situation but all we could do was be
silent. Nothing else.

In Condega few people could read and write. Half the population of
the region was illiterate. In the isolated rural areas illiteracy was
close to 100 per cent. There were only 311 schools in the region so
only 11 per cent of the population had access to education.[9]

   It wasn't until the mid-1960s that a secondary school was started
in Condega. It was left to an American Capuchin priest, Andrés
Weller Colby, to make the first moves. He started in a private house
with twenty-five students but even this was expensive and only
affordable by the better-off. In the early 1970s they acquired a
proper school building and began attracting students from the whole

area. Amongst them were the younger children of Don Antonio who by now had managed to raise a loan and buy the house and mill where he lives today. Little did their parents know that the school was to become one of the first recruiting grounds for the Frente Sandinista.

6. Luisa

Popular Health Day

The loudspeakers started blaring at four in the morning. It was Popular Health Day. Not a soul in town would have been able to sleep through the noise. Stirring music, then an urgent voice, bade citizens a hearty good morning and summoned volunteers to make their way to the CDS office. The message was repeated every ten minutes for over an hour. One of the loudspeakers was situated right outside my door. I was consoled only by the thought that all over Nicaragua people were being given a similar rude awakening.

By 7 a.m. I was squashed up in a jeep travelling across muddy tracks towards the rural vaccination centres around the town of Jalapa. Inside were Ministry of Health officials, a doctor from the hospital, a party organizer and Luisa Centeno, daughter of Don Antonio, who had brought me into the Centeno household.

At the age of sixteen, back in 1974, Luisa was one of the first of a handful of young people in Condega who joined the FSLN, the Frente Sandinista. They began to work secretly in the town to win support for armed resistance to the Somoza regime. Now she is a mother in her late twenties, but her spirit is just the same.

Louisa had insisted I go to Jalapa with her. She was gradually becoming a kind of unofficial tutor to me, making sure I had access to what was happening. She had heard there was going to be a wedding in Jalapa that weekend. Maybe I could take some photos? (My camera had become an item of intense local interest in Condega. Ever since the funerals people had been coming up to me in the street asking for their photo – as if it would pop out of the camera there and then.)

We arrived in Jalapa one Friday night after a long journey through border mountains close to Honduras. Around us stalked the Contras, but unseen because the road was busy. Over there, Luisa said, nodding in the direction of the border, they still had all the health problems Nicaragua used to have not so long ago. 'People arrive at the hospitals there almost dying of hunger, without shoes on their feet. I saw it myself when I went there. You don't see that kind of misery here now.'

The CDS office was buzzing with people comparing notes, checking on the numbers for the following day's campaign. Its success depended on volunteers turning up for a water-tight schedule so that the precious vaccines could be transported under cool conditions up rivers, across ravines, over mud tracks to the makeshift vaccination centres, in schools or homes. The Sandinistas are particularly proud of their achievement in eradicating polio and malaria, which were previously endemic in the country.

The popular health days themselves are organized by the Sandinista Defence Committees, for which Luisa works as a regional co-ordinator. With a membership of over half a million, the CDS are the biggest of the mass organizations which make up Nicaragua's 'participatory democracy'. Anyone can be a member of their local committee. It begins at street level. The Centeno family, for example, belong to a block CDS which has some fifty members. Their co-ordinator joins others in a neighbourhood committee. Neighbourhoods have co-ordinators in municipal committees, and so on. In Condega there are around seventy-eight committees in five neighbourhoods. In the entire district here are another 176 – all part of a network of eight thousand committees across Nicaragua.

The job of the CDS is to defend the revolution politically, ideologically, socially, economically and militarily. On a day-to-day level this means organizing the night patrols in every town and village (called revolutionary vigilance) and overseeing the distribution of subsidized basic foods and supplies.[1] But it is the big campaigns which people like best and which get the most volunteers. For weeks beforehand Luisa was working on the plans in the regional CDS office in Estelí.

I called in there one lunchtime. The building was once an elegant modern house in the central square but now stands as a monument to the bombs that Somoza dropped during the insurrection. Where there was once a leafy foundation in the interior courtyard, there is now the drip of putrid water around broken blocks of concrete. Luisa's office is at the top of a flight of damaged concrete steps, which half-way up gives way to a tangled mass of metal. Somehow they have withstood the busy thoroughfare of the past few years.

Luisa has a strong face, her thick dark hair is cut short, and she is almost boyish in appearance. She makes few concessions to femininity. Her job requires her to wears her own clothes. But I think if she was given the chance, she'd probably wear green fatigues all the time. Green has become a kind of Sandinista uniform in the north. She insisted later that I take a photo of her wearing them.

Her enthusiasm for the revolution is infectious. She is virtually *married* to it, getting up every morning to hitch a ride into Estelí, returning late at night. She talks in a firm voice as if she were addressing a crowd. Her denunciations of imperialism, and the reverence with which she talks of the 'Frente Sandinista', giving it its full title, might sound like political jargon to a cynic. But Luisa, a devout Catholic, is fired with an emotion and conviction that I encountered in many young Nicaraguans. Their vocabulary is strident and denunciatory, but the more you get to know about their lives, the more you understand the meaning invested in their words. It is a vocabulary which, in its own way, reflects the drama of their lives.

On our tour of vaccination centres around Jalapa, our jeep pulled up outside remote schools and shacks where the volunteers – teenage school girls and teachers from the communities themselves – would come to greet us, smiling proudly in their colourful clothes and chatting excitedly about the progress of the campaign. Inside, mothers and children queued for sugar lumps. Others arrived barefoot with large families in tow. Some had come several miles on foot. Keeping the vaccines cold was a major problem. They were packed with lumps of ice inside orange-coloured cool boxes, like the ones you might take to the beach. By the end of the day, most of the ice had melted and they were swimming in water.

Luisa was pleased with the results. *Barricada* had done its best to prepare the day with plenty of publicity and articles on the health achievements of the revolution. But, in the absence of proper roads, and with low levels of literacy, rural people still had to be visited in house-to-house calls. The volunteers had sometimes encountered reluctance and opposition to vaccination. The Contras were telling *campesinos* that the vaccines would turn their children into Communists. But more often than not the reluctance was the product of ignorance.

The ever-present CDS volunteers did not give up. They kept lists of all local residents and made another house call on those who'd failed to turn up. 'Sometimes people say their children have diarrhoea or a cold, so we check out the children and if there isn't a problem we talk to the mother again and encourage her', said a lively sixteen-year-old, who had been up since 3 a.m.

At a tobacco farm a large crowd of noisy women and ragged children were waiting for their pay packets to arrive. It was a state enterprise – nationalized after the revolution, but increasingly in the hands of a female labour force. Here the entreaties of the volunteers fell on somewhat stony ground. They looked decidedly uninterested – probably from exhaustion. They had worked all week, and since six that morning, and their priority was getting their money. Something like half the male population of the area was mobilized in defence duties, leaving a majority of women to work the tobacco farms.

The military hospital

The Contra ambush still continued to haunt me. On our return, Luisa took me to visit one of the wounded soldiers. It was the most direct way she could show me the suffering the Contras were causing Nicaragua. The victim was married to a woman who worked in the Centenos' household.

There were no vehicles available for the twenty-kilometre journey from Estelí south to La Trinidad, so we hitched a ride from a farmer transporting tomatoes. At the entrance to the modest one-storey building which serves the whole region as a military hospital, Luisa handed in a revolver concealed in her handbag – something all CDS officials can carry in case of attack.

The wards were full of war casualties from all over the north; boys without arms, without legs, with bandaged hands and limbs. When we found Luisa's friend his face was black and swollen and swathed in bandages. They had just amputated his arm – badly damaged by shrapnel. He was conscious and spoke angrily about the battle, before falling asleep again. His young pregnant wife stood at the end of the bed, terrified. Not all the patients were war victims. One old man had caught his hand in an agricultural machine. Another boy had shot himself accidentally – a common occurrence in a country where nearly everyone has their own rifle. He laughed and joked at his bandaged hand which doctors had managed to save.

One patient in particular stuck in my mind: Xavier Rodriguez García, a twenty-three-year-old conscript whose leg had been shot to pieces in combat with the Contras. He lay stretched out with a blood-stained red and black Sandinista scarf spread over his chest. He was one of the only survivors of a three-day battle and had lost several of his friends – there had been no artillery support available. He smiled at me through his evident pain and asked what I thought of Nicaragua and the revolution. It was the kind of question I found difficult to answer – there were just too many impressions to deal with. I asked him why he was fighting: 'We have to get peace, though war is very hard. But it's for our children and the future.' The Contras? They were 'Nicaraguans who speak Spanish but think in English – like Pinochet', he said. 'They are the same as the National Guard of the past.'

Xavier's coherence took me by surprise. His courage was humbling. Did his parents know he had been injured, I asked? 'No, it's only a small wound. There's no point. They'd only worry', he said, dismissing the idea with a wave of the hand. 'I want to get back into the fight as quickly as possible. Our war is not just fought by the gun, it's fought by the morale and spirit of the people. It's an inevitable process.' Xavier was a member of the Sandinista Youth. As he spoke his face twisted in pain. A yellow liquid oozed from his bandaged leg into the sheet. Adjusting his Sandinista scarf, he posed for a photo, smiling.

A woman's liberation

We walked home from the highway through the darkened streets of Condega. Several people, spotting Luisa, came up to ask her advice about their problems. Each one she spent time with, questioning, advising, encouraging, promising to do what she could.

Many people had told me about the participation of women in Condega – how they were the mainstay of the revolutionary organizations in the town. Seventy per cent of CDS members are women, for example. Women were even involved in guard duties on buildings and factories in the town. Luisa's confidence and the responsibility she took on was something I tended to take for granted after a few weeks. What was surprising therefore was to hear her talk of having an inferiority complex in the past.

> My personality has changed since the revolution. I used to be nervous and very shy. I used to think I wasn't capable of becoming anything. It was the system. The dictatorship said a woman was inferior to men and had to stay at home looking after the children.
>
> Now I feel I've got rid of some prejudices. I can now go into any place and speak as I like, without being self-conscious. I can go up and speak to any *campesino* or he can come and bother me

at home with his problem and I will invite him to sit down and offer to help. These are big changes.

She had begun working with the CDS in Condega almost the day after the triumph in July 1979. It was unpaid work – really just a continuation of her role in the civil defence committees during the insurrection. She began as a block co-ordinator, then moved up to become a full-time worker for the municipal CDS.

The participation was enormous. People were very active in clearing the streets, reorganizing their lives. In Condega we didn't even have a hospital. We got the money to build a proper road into the mountains, we built four health centres and seventeen schools. I went up into the mountains for the literacy crusade up until three days before my son was born.

What she enjoyed most was working with the *campesinos* in the rural areas.

I prefer a thousand times to work with the *campesinos*. They are more astute. I was learning from them, not teaching. They would say for example that they wanted to construct fifteen houses with toilets. We would have to co-ordinate with the town council to provide cement and wood. They did the collective work.

Luisa was married to a small farmer. She had known him since the mid-1970s when she recruited him as a driver for the Sandinistas. Politically they seemed to be poles apart. He once told me he was a capitalist. I was interested in how her marriage had survived the disruptions of her job.

In the past he would never have allowed me to attend a meeting of men on my own. Men get jealous. They think that when a woman goes out, all she wants to do is find a man. But in reality it's the revolution. I do have problems sometimes. But I say to him, look at what we are trying to do. The FSLN wants to maintain family unity. I ask him to come with me. Sometimes he's convinced. Other times he gets angry. He says he's the one who gives the orders. I have to do what he says. He's worried that others will say I wear the trousers at home.

Things have changed a lot now. I spent three months in Cuba. Before he would have left me for that. I attend meetings of reservists and the territorial militia. He sees this now. In the past he would never have allowed it. No way. I couldn't even go to the cinema without him.

There were other problems too. Her eldest boy needed a heart operation but Nicaragua did not have the resources or the skills for this. Many of the wealthy private doctors and specialists had left Nicaragua after the revolution for more profitable pastures. Only the Cubans might be able to help. She waited anxiously for news.

Although she never said so, I felt her new job – basically a desk-job in the regional offices – was unsatisfying. Luisa wanted to be where the people were, where the battles had to be fought ideologically. For the CDS was more than just an organization of volunteers. It was the organization through which the Sandinistas remain in contact with the people – the eyes and ears of the revolution, as some have described it.

People missed Luisa's presence in Condega. It was one of the results of a shortage of skilled and experienced cadres in the revolution that, time and time again, a local leader was transferred out of his or her community into administration at a higher level.

Anastasio Somoza Debayle and the first protests

The story of Luisa's transformation from a deeply religious, shy fifteen-year-old into a clandestine leader in Condega, and now a Sandinista official with regional responsibilities, is not unique in Nicaragua. The role of women in the revolution is a remarkable phenomenon. At the time of the insurrection of 1979 there were thirty thousand women under arms. Thousands more took an active part in the uprisings in the towns and villages.

When I arrived in Nicaragua, the FSLN had been criticized for its failure to tackle issues that Western feminists have on their agenda (see Chapter 14). Yet in Condega it was women like Luisa who built the first cells of the organization in the early 1970s, and who now carry on its work at local level.

It began in the secondary school. Luisa attended after a shift in Don Antonio's mill.

> We all had to work. I used to have to get up at three in the morning to work the mill – most of the poor people in Condega had to get up at this time to get to the countryside to work. It was really hard. I sometimes went to school on just a plain tortilla and coffee. Sometimes my family couldn't even afford to buy me pencils.[2]

Along with other members of the Centeno family, Luisa was active in a charismatic Christian movement. She was one of sixty lay preachers – or delegates of the word – in Condega. They visited Condega's rural communities to bring the message – in those days a traditional one: 'My family are strong believers and I loved the bible. It wasn't a political thing. But I saw the relevance of the life of Jesus for Nicaragua.'

The movement of lay preachers had started in the 1960s as a way of compensating for the scarcity of priests. Local people, once trained, could preach in their own and neighbouring communities. It was a time of change for the Church. In 1973 Condega had acquired a new parish priest who arrived fired with a new radical interpretation of the bible being developed in Latin America. This interpretation, loosely known as 'liberation theology', sees Jesus Christ as the leader of the oppressed masses of the Roman Empire, a martyr to the cause of liberation and the war against injustice. The Christian must be committed to work for social change, encouraging the poor and needy by their vision of a better world.

Both Luisa and her elder sister Amanda attended the 'Christian base groups' which the priest set up in the church hall. Bible lessons increasingly focused on the conditions of life. 'He made you think', said Amanda (see Chapter 10).

By 1974 young people in Nicaragua had become acutely aware of the activities of Anastasio Somoza II. To the economic exploitation by the Somoza family was added a new factor: a brutal repression of the increasingly vocal opposition to the dictatorship.

Anastasio Somoza Debayle had come into office amid a hail of gunfire. On 22 January 1967, with the election campaign in full swing, he had ordered his men to fire on a huge demonstration outside the presidential palace. The opposition to his candidacy had rallied 60,000 to protest at his misuse of power. Over 600 people were killed outright and opposition leaders rounded up and jailed. Two weeks later with the opposition parties in disarray, he was declared president, claiming 70 per cent of the vote. Thus began a period of twelve years in which Somoza ruled by a policy of state terrorism. He broke up any forms of legal opposition, and with US help used counter-insurgency methods to deal with growing radicalism amongst the peasantry.

To the young people in Condega the corruption of the president and his friends was more than plain. The earthquake which destroyed the centre of Managua in 1972 and killed over 10,000 people was a turning point. As international aid poured in for the 300,000 homeless it was diverted into profiteering rackets for Somoza's own companies and the National Guard. Medical and food aid was cornered for sale on the black market. Rebuilding contracts were siphoned to Somoza's friends and denied his enemies. Somoza's monopoly of the construction industry was reinforced.

But the earthquake and the boom that followed also created a more militant working class, willing to protest against falling wages, longer working hours and an attack on living standards. It generated open criticism of Somoza's wealth and power, even from business circles which previously had kept their mouths shut. While Somoza flaunted his riches in the style of a casino king (white suits with silk sashes, fat cigars, an entourage of glamorous women, a playboy lifestyle) the average wage for a farmworker was about £400 a year.

Somoza ran Nicaragua like his private farm. He owned the national airline, controlled a quarter of the farmland, owned a daily newspaper, a TV station, a bank, the Mercedes concession (most government cars and taxis were Mercedes) and nearly fifty of the most important companies in the country – many of them monopolies. He was thought to be worth about £300 million himself.

Nicaragua began to seethe with unrest. In August 1974 in Condega the Christian base group meetings began to discuss the role of Condega's mayor, a Somoza henchman. It was Luisa's sister, Amanda, who suggested a plan of action. Her suggestion was to break through the atmosphere of repression that had gripped the town. 'People said the mayor is no good, he doesn't do anything for us. I said, well, if he's not good, why don't we get rid of him.'[3]

At the secondary school a group of students responded eagerly to the plan. Some of the students involved were children of members of the Conservative Party, others active Christians. They had already started publishing a school magazine which carried poems and satirical articles on the life of the peasantry, subtly raising political issues in a historical context.

On 1 September 1974, defying warnings from their friends, twenty-four students, the majority of them women, took over the church and demanded the resignation of the mayor. Not only were the National Guard taken totally by surprise, but the move was immensely popular in the town. 'We had the support of the local population who brought us food and money. It was the first time people in this town had mobilized against the Somoza dictatorship and his representative, the mayor', said Luisa. At one stage during the twenty-four-day occupation a thousand people gathered outside the church to show their support. When the National Guard raided homes in the town and arrested students, their friends left the church and marched to the barracks to free the detainees.

The occupation failed in its objective but it was a political triumph, breaking through the fear and silence of Condegans. Neither did it go unnoticed by the Sandinistas.

1974: the FSLN comes to Condega

Shortly after the occupation of the church, Luisa was approached by a fellow pupil and asked to join a clandestine group of young people who were fighting against the Somoza dictatorship: the Sandinista National Liberation Front. The Front was not something which people talked about openly. Luisa's elder sister Amanda was approached at roughly the same time, but neither of them spoke about it and neither was aware of the other's involvement.

> When I was approached, I didn't know what the Frente was. When I heard people talk of it, they spoke in hushed tones. Some people had heard of it as a guerilla organization which had fought battles with the National Guard. It meant fear. People were terrified to mention it.

At the Institute in Condega, two teachers had become involved with the Frente and were quietly involved in recruiting some of the pupils. One, Orlando Aguilera, taught mechanics. Another was a woman, Rosana Espinoza. Luisa's contact was another pupil.

> I belonged to a cell of three members. We were not allowed to know about any other members. There was very strict compartmentalization and discipline. We started working in the town. My job was to find safe houses for the leaders of the Frente and also to raise the consciousness of the population. But we never said we were members of the Frente. I accepted the condition that nothing should be told to my family.

The FSLN had been in existence for thirteen years. It was founded in 1961 by a group of three former university students. Their inspiration came from the assassination of Somoza in 1956, the Cuban revolution of 1958 and a determination to liberate Nicaragua from a dictatorship that the Conservative opposition had been unable to fight and which was the expression of Nicaragua's domination by the USA. Carlos Fonseca (whose shrine I visited in Managua) was one of their most outstanding members. The group was soon joined by survivors of Sandino's war and set about a serious study of his writings. (They have all since been killed, except for Tomás Borge, Nicaragua's current Minister of the Interior.)

From that time on they held fast to two basic principles of Sandino: the need for armed struggle in the mountains, and the need to build the support of the local *campesino* population. But the FSLN also directed its message to the growing working class and rural workers who were beginning to organize in the sugar and cotton mills and on some coffee estates in the north.

In the 1960s the FSLN existed principally as a small group of armed men hiding in the mountains near the Río Coco in the northeast. They had little success in winning support from the Miskito indians who lived there. When they clashed with the National Guard in 1963 they were severely defeated. They hardly grew at all in the next few years.

In 1967 the group was trying again in the Matagalpa area, east of Condega. Here they had more success and built close links with the local *campesinos*. They made daring bank raids and launched harassment operations on the local National Guard. In August, however, the Guard detected their camps at a place called Pancasán, and wiped out thirteen of their leading cadres. Three hundred peasants paid with their lives for the sympathy and tortillas they had offered the guerillas. 'Pancasán' was a serious setback, yet it put the FSLN on the map in Nicaragua, giving it publicity, provoking solidarity actions from students and workers, and providing the impetus for the creation of support networks in universities and the major towns.

After their setback, the FSLN revised their strategy and for a while abandoned the idea of dramatic military action, in favour of 'prolonged popular war'. By the 1970s workers in Nicaragua's major towns were also joining the FSLN, and the student movement grew. Students were sent out into the mountains to train as guerillas and build up networks of support amongst the peasantry. In the towns they built on the growth in working-class activity after the 1972 earthquake. But using their extensive network of informers, the National Guard was often able to infiltrate the FSLN's urban cells. Many Sandinistas were imprisoned and tortured.

It was not until December of 1974 that Luisa and other pupils at the secondary school really began to believe that the FSLN could be effective. Just after Christmas a column of guerillas surrounded a house in a wealthy neighbourhood of Managua, taking hostage a group of leading Somozist politicians and diplomats who were attending a reception. The condition for their release was the freeing of Sandinista political prisoners. The action took Somoza totally by surprise and he was forced to agree their terms in full. The Sandinistas were able to broadcast a statement on radio and television, and in the press; they were given their $2 million ransom and were provided with a plane to take the entire group of fourteen political prisoners and themselves to Cuba. They included the man who later became Nicaragua's President – Daniel Ortega.

To crown Somoza's humiliation, he had to make pay increases to industrial and agricultural workers and even to members of the National Guard. Crowds lined the road taking the prisoners out to the airport shouting 'Viva el Frente, Viva Sandino.'

The National Guard closes in

Needless to say, Somoza took his revenge. He decreed a state of siege, introduced martial law and press censorship, and set up military courts. Using the cover of censorship he launched a series of raids on peasant communities in the north, desperate to root out any support for the FSLN.

The effects of the state of siege were felt in Condega, as Luisa recalls:

> They used to kill people here. We would find dead boys in the river. And we would ask Who has done this? We knew it was the Guardia but we didn't have the courage to say it out loud. I remember there was a curfew in those days. After 6 p.m. no one could leave their house.

As Somoza's reprisals against *campesinos* further north took hold, leading Sandinistas came to Condega to build a base of support in the nearby mountains. These people are now household names in Nicaragua: Mónica Baltodano, Omar Cabezas, Bayardo Arce; all of them were guerilla leaders during the insurrection and are now Comandantes of the revolution.

Luisa began travelling out to the countryside using the cover of her work as a lay delegate.

> Our work was to go out into the communities. We all used pseudonyms. I used to go and see the leading FSLN members

who lived in a safe house belonging to my sister Alicia. We ran messages for them to the countryside. I used to put them in the pages of notebooks or in my socks. Officially I was going there as a lay preacher, so I had a reason to be travelling. I had the job of recruiting someone with a car so we could get there. That's how I recruited the man who became my husband.

I remember once we were travelling with one of the commanders, Mónica Baltodano, when I suddenly realized we were being followed by a National Guard. I couldn't take her to the safe house, so I had to think of somewhere else quickly. There was a Christian woman I knew who was quite revolutionary, so, although she didn't know anything about Frente, I took her there and introduced her as a fellow Christian from León. I said that my family were unfortunately unable to put her up because their house was full. Thank goodness she accepted this.

The consequences of discovery by the National Guard were well-known: torture and possibly death. So the protection of the organization and its members sometimes involved strong-arm tactics:

One day the priest, Wésther López, called me over and told me he'd just received a visit from a man who said I was working with the FSLN. The priest told him it was impossible – he knew, whatever the truth, to say anything would be fatal. The man was someone I had been trying to recruit. But I had not known that he had a heart condition. After I had talked to him about joining he'd got bad in the night and his wife told him he must refuse to collaborate.

The next day I went to see the man at six in the morning. I told him that if he denounced me, he would die.

When the Frente captured an arms store of the National Guard in the nearby town of Ocotal, Luisa's job was to deliver one of the weapons to a house in Condega:

I had to bring the weapon from a certain place on the road to my home. I don't know what kind of weapon it was, but it was in a bag of sugar and was very heavy. At first I got very nervous. The trouble was I had to walk right past the Guardia post. My knees were shaking. I had arrived almost opposite the post when I went into a shop and bought a packet of chewing gum because I was dying of fright. When I got to the corner I passed the bag to my contact. I was convinced I was followed home. But no.

A member of Luisa's cell was killed during this time. But still she continued, knowing the risks:

> I once had to visit Somoto with a friend to deliver a message. We got into the bus – I was quite nervous but I calmed down. When we got to the crossroads between Ocotal and Somoto, the Guardia were there, stopping the traffic. I had put the message in a packet of chewing gum. So when they made us get off the bus to search us, I got out another packet and began to chew gum quite normally. The other packet was hidden. I even offered one of the Guardia some gum.

In Condega itself it was not easy to recruit members to the FSLN in those days: 'people were terrified by the regime. It was not like later when people stood up and were prepared to die.' But in the countryside the FSLN's patient efforts were beginning to bear fruit:

> It was the youth who responded, even children. I remember the boy who recruited me was only sixteen. He had started when he was only fourteen. He died in an action but he would have been a commandante, I'm sure. In the countryside the conditions made people respond. A poor person earned between eight and ten cordobas a day. They didn't know how to improve their wages. But they couldn't afford to study without money.
>   We had leaflets and we discussed their problems, such as their social problems – to push them. We approached people as human beings concerned for other human beings. It wasn't like political parties. It was real comradeship. The Frente put it to people that we have to have comradeship and fraternity.

By the end of 1975 twelve to fifteen families were involved with the Frente in Condega. But the National Guard were closing in and had begun to take interest in the *campesinos* in nearby Canta Gallo who had begun working with the Frente. At five in the morning on 8 December the Guard struck in Condega:

> We were all asleep and we heard their vans draw up and banging on the door. They burst in through the mill. We told Amanda to get out of the house the back way, but they grabbed her and threw her into the van. A boy was in the van too. It was he who told them about Amanda. But he couldn't be blamed, he'd been tortured. Of course when I saw him I was terrified because this boy was in my cell too. I hadn't realised he worked in Amanda's cell. In fact I had only known she was a member for three

months. I was terrified he would denounce me too. And what was more we had a leading commander, Mónica Baltodano, hidden away in my sister's house across the road. But they just took Amanda.

With her sister arrested, Luisa had to act quickly. Few people, however well-trained, could be expected to withstand torture.

The Frente told me to go to the mountains to escape, but I felt I couldn't do that. With my sister arrested, it would have been a dreadful blow to my mother and family if I had gone off to the mountains [as a guerilla]. I just didn't feel capable of doing it. But I had to get out. I knew what they had done to a number of *campesinos* they had arrested. They had pulled out their nails and tortured them with maggots. So at about nine in the morning I left the house to go to relatives in a village. The river was flooding and a friend who was with me had to rescue me. I lay low until it was dark and then we started walking. It took us all night to get to my relatives, keeping out of sight all the time.

Amanda meanwhile was taken to Ocotal, a town twenty miles to the north:

I was privileged not to be tortured [too much]. All they did was put electric plugs on me. I was hooded and told that I'd be kept like that for a long time. Every time someone passed me they would hit me. The Frente had given us guidance in case of torture – it was that we had to hold out for three days to give the others a chance to mobilize. I thought I'd hold out as much as possible because I had to think of the survival of the organization and its work. It would take a step backwards. Also because my family was involved.[4]

In fact Amanda never cracked and was released after a week. When she returned to Condega, two of her brothers, Toñito and Armando, had taken asylum in the Mexican embassy and from there went into exile. Now she was suspected of being an FSLN collaborator it was unsafe for her to stay in town so she too went into exile. Another sister, Alicia, joined her there with her husband, their safe house in danger of discovery.

When they had gone, Luisa returned quietly to the town. Though her family was implicated, she managed to avoid suspicion. But she lost contact with the Frente and remained out of contact for over two years.

7. Families in the Contras' firing line

Bertilda

The tiny community of Los Potreros near Condega does not feature on most maps of Nicaragua. Although it is little more than five miles east of the Pan American Highway as the crow flies, the journey is awkward and uncomfortable.

Fording a river impassable in the rain, a jeep took us through a tobacco farm and immediately began to climb up a dirt track. Deep furrows in the sand sent us lurching from one side to another. The hills are close together with deep ravines in between and tropical foliage on either side. We met a solitary peasant carrying a bundle of clothes.

The track hugs the hillsides until all but the strongest vehicles have to stop. From there begins a trek on foot, down into a ravine, onto stepping stones over a stream, through a gate and then a slow, steep ascent up a mountain side, slipping and stumbling over loose rocks. The two women and three young militia men who agreed to take me there made light work of the climb. It was a journey they had made virtually every day of their lives until recently, for the little cluster of peasant dwellings at the top of the mountain was where they were all born and raised. It was there, before the revolution, that the boys of the Frente would pass and be given food and lodging. It was there, after the triumph, that families formed a co-operative to work nearby land and were given funds to build a school.

I had heard Bertilda's story, but something urged me to go there myself to see with my own eyes what the Contras had done. Grey clouds hung low over the hillside, making the red rocks of the mountain give off an eerie light. There was something oppressive about the way the hills huddled together, deadening the echo in people's voices. The enclosed feeling grew as we approached. There would be no sounds from the houses today.

The wooden school building was boarded up. Sacks of maize had been pillaged and the bark lay strewn over the green in front of a semi-circle of shacks. Though the shacks had new roofs, several of their walls had caved in. Bullet holes could be seen all over the planks and branches which made up the walls. Weeds were beginning to grow up in the back yards.

Bertilda, a slim *campesino* woman in her thirties, picked her way through the ruins of her kitchen and made a half-hearted attempt to clear some of the mess. She didn't attempt to go into the neighbouring shacks where her cousins had lived. They were a revolutionary family. They had pooled their land and worked it collectively. The men and boys were in the militia. Bertilda herself was active in health brigades and had campaigned for the Sandinistas during the elections. Her uncle ran the CDS shop which supplied the community.

But she could no longer call this home. A gang of a hundred Contras had attacked the community and killed her uncle, cousin and his six-year-old boy. They had laid siege to her own house and bombarded it with bullets while her son and a cousin fought them off from inside. Bertilda, meanwhile, sheltered the children in the house, clinging onto the terrified two-year-old, and reloaded magazines for the boys. She was lucky to be alive. As they reatreated the Contras captured all the unarmed men they could find.

She pointed to one of the boarded-up shacks next to the school: 'That was where the boys lived who were kidnapped', she sighed. 'They were all in the militia but they did not have their weapons. We have still not heard a word about them. We think they may just be dead because they would never agree to fight on the side of the Contras.

Bertilda was one of the most serene and courageous women I had encountered in Nicaragua. She was not an educated person, but had an ability to articulate the tragedy that had befallen her family in a way which transcended anger and pain. The day I first met her, she and her wounded son were staying with relatives in Condega, just days after the Contra attack. She sat next to her son – his knee and shoulder swathed in bandages – and calmly recounted what had happened, stooping every now and then to bathe the shrapnel wounds in his legs and mop his brow. The simple brick house with its dirt floor was full of relatives of all ages. They sat and stood in awe, listening, not for the first time, to the story. No one said a word, not even the toddlers. Bertilda just talked.

It was a Saturday at 6.30 in the morning. I was washing a cup to give some coffee to my sons when I saw them beating up a boy who was outside chopping wood. I shouted to my son 'Son, don't go out, because the Contras are coming.' There was a struggle and we saw them tie up the three militia boys who were running to get their weapons.

I shouted to my son and his cousin to get their weapons. By this time there were about seventy Contras in the community. They were looking for the three houses belonging to my family. They surrounded us.

I went and sheltered under a mattress with four children. I had to tie up my two-year-old girl so that she wouldn't run away. My uncle and my cousin were shooting back from their side.

My son's rifle was blown out of his hand and he was wounded in the shoulder. Then I remembered we had another rifle, so I got it for my cousin. I loaded five magazines for them and dragged myself along the ground to give it to them. My son carried on with one hand. His trench was some sacks of maize and beans.

At the end the Contras began throwing grenades and mortars and trying to destroy the house. They were shouting to my son and nephew to give themselves up, but they shouted back 'Que se rinda tu madre'.[1] The Contras fled in the end when our militias arrived back from a patrol.

They managed to kill my uncle and his son Ramón, who was in charge of the militias. They died fighting. And Ramón's son, who was only six, they assassinated in his bed when they went in to loot the house. He was asleep and they shot him.

When I went out onto the patio I could see pools of blood of the people who'd died. The Contras weren't satisfied with killing them. Afterwards they bayoneted their arms and legs all over. They did it as if they were slicing up a pig. They chopped them up and left them, torn into shreds. And then they started to loot the house. They took ham, bread and all kinds of things.

Afterwards they killed my pigs, beasts, hens and whatever got in their way. They left a little pile of corpses and animals.

Outside the home where Bertilda's cousin died his young widow, Nicola, could hardly speak for tears. She just pointed to the spot where she found her husband's body. The two women sat down on the wooden patio of what was once their home, silent. They had tried to save her six-year-old son. They put him on the only horse the Contras had left alive to take him down for help. But he died on the way. Bertilda remembered his words to his mother before he died:

He said to her, 'Mummy my body's fallen asleep and a man shot me. Isn't it true that my daddy said that the comrades don't shoot?' He must have seen the man in military uniform and thought it was a comrade. 'No', his mother said, 'It's the Contras who shot you and they shot your daddy too.'

   He asked to be taken to his father and stroked his face saying, 'Look they made a hole here', when he saw his arm. We asked if he wanted some coffee, but he wanted some water. I could see that he wouldn't live because his backbone was all destroyed.

While we talked Bertilda's relatives – three militia boys – patrolled the woods around. Every now and then they would shout to each other, checking for their safety.

María

Not long afterwards I met María, an educated, self-assured woman of twenty-four and mother of two. The day before she had made a miraculous escape from a Contra attack on her home. She talked rapidly and nervously. Her face was white. María belongs to a slightly younger generation of secondary school pupils than Luisa. In the insurrection she took up arms and joined the guerillas based in nearby mountains. 'I don't scare easily, I know what fighting is all about', she told me the day after the attack, trying to control her nerves.

   We drove back to the village where she lived. She was keen to talk and to visit her house again, but frightened that publicity would only bring the Contras back again. The house had been well built, of brick and concrete, but all that remained was a shell and a few burnt-out bedframes. The corrugated iron roof had caved in over charred rafters. The Contras had set fire to the whole lot. A child's plastic doll lay on the debris in one of the rooms, its face and limbs mangled by heat. María's little boy ran to pick it up and refused to let go. His mother kept on shaking her head in disbelief, 'I am just so lucky to be alive.'

My husband was away that night. I was asleep. At about 1 a.m. I heard someone shouting from outside, 'You son of a bitch, *piricuaco*. Give yourself up, we've got you surrounded. We're going to burn your house. Bring out your wife and kids. We're going to talk to you. We want you alive, we're going to execute you.'

You think really quickly in those situations. I went out and asked them what they wanted. They said they were from the FND. 'Do you know the Contras?' he barked at me. 'We are fighting to defeat communism in Nicaragua.' They said they were in the final offensive. They had already taken Condega and Palacagüina and Estelí. ...

I told them there was no one here ... when they asked who was the owner of the house, I invented a name. I told them I was the housekeeper and was looking after the house with my husband for the weekend.

They told me to bring out my husband. So I went and fetched the young boy who looks after the animals. This fooled them because he looks like a peasant and they knew that the man they were looking for wasn't a peasant. They started to interrogate us. They were threatening us and used insults. They said they would kill us if we didn't co-operate and tell them where the ammunition was and the rifle.

They wore camouflage uniforms. One was about twenty-seven and the other must have been about eighteen, though he said he was fifteen. He said he was from León. They explained that they were Nicaraguans and not Americans. They said they were peasants but one looked more like a lazy town bloke. The other one looked like a student. He was quieter. He hardly said a word.

They looted the whole house. They took clothes, the electric iron and some books and the tape recorder. They had a look at all my husband's papers. Fortunately all they found was a pile of bills. I just kept repeating that we were the housekeepers, we didn't know where the rifles were, that there weren't any here.

The children were paralysed; too terrified to be able to cry. After about ten minutes one of the Contras began machine-gunning the house. They made us open the doors and then they shot incendiary bullets into the room. Things were catching fire.

I asked them not to burn down the house because it was rented and they'd just be hurting someone else. They refused. He was a *piricuaco*, that the *piricuacos* have money, they are rich, etc. They clearly believed this. They are so far from reality. But you couldn't argue with them because of the way they spoke. Then they threw us out. They said, get lost, go to the outhouses on the farm and don't come out.

I was terrified because I never thought I would come out of it

alive. I know what they do. I've seen a lot of cases of people with
their throats slit. That's what I was worried about; that they'd
slit my throat and my children's. I could see that they had
bayonets. I was really worried about the bayonets. That is what
they normally do with people. A friend of my husband's had his
nails pulled out and his eyes. They do terrible things.

For hours after the Contras had gone María and her children stayed
in the barn. Her husband arrived in the morning to find the house
burnt down and, to his amazement, his family still alive.

Following the CIA manual

In Condega what concerns the population is not so much the threat
of a regular army engaged in set-piece battles with the Sandinista
forces, but the insidious work of groups of mountain-based rebels
who live by looting and pillage, terrorizing the rural communities,
forcibly kidnapping their menfolk, and aiming their attacks at specific targets designed to destroy the structures of the revolution and
wipe out the people who have committed themselves to change.

The figures bear out their concerns. By 1985 already some ninety-
seven civilian communities had been attacked, and nearly three
thousand civilians killed by the Contras. Over seven thousand children had been officially registered as war orphans. The Contras had
destroyed fourteen schools, and forty-one health centres. Over eight
hundred adult education centres had had to close, along with 359
schools. Eighty state-owned enterprises had been attacked.[2]

If anyone doubted the reports of atrocities committed by the
Contras they had to look no further than their financiers and teachers, the Central Intelligence Agency. During 1984 the CIA circulated
a manual amongst the Contras, 'Psychological Operations in Guerilla
Warfare', outlining methods of undermining the Sandinistas, including sabotage, murder and intimidation. Chapter 3 of the manual
states that 'to conduct armed propaganda in an effective manner
the guerrilla should destroy the military or police installations and
remove the survivors to a public place, set up ambushes in order
to delay reinforcements in all possible entry roads and kidnap all
government officials and agents.' Section Five advises Contras to
'neutralize carefully selected and planned targets, such as court

judges, district judges, police or state security officials, Sandinista Defence Committee leaders, etc.'

If these were the officially-sanctioned methods, the unofficial ones were worse. According to Edgar Chamorro, a former spokesman for the Nicaraguan Democratic Force (FDN) – the major Contra group operating from Honduras – the manual was designed to raise standards because of an excess of random killing, rape and looting.[3] 'Witness for Peace', an American Protestant watchdog body, collected a list of Contra atrocities during 1985. Apart from murder, these included: the rape of two girls in their homes, the torture of men, cutting off arms, cutting out tongues, gouging out eyes, castration, bayoneting pregnant women in the stomach, scraping the skin off the face and castration of a seventy-year-old man, pouring acid on the face, piercing the shoulders and breaking toes and fingers of an eighteen-year-old boy.[4]

During my stay in Condega I was told of several incidents where these methods had been used. In one in December 1985, forty-one-year-old farmer Eleuterio Matute was murdered at his home some ten miles away at Cruz de Piedra. He was a CDS co-ordinator, a health brigadier and a volunteer member of the militia. Like so many Sandinista activists in the area he was also a Catholic lay delegate. According to witnesses the FDN came around midnight and, posing as the army, called him to come out and go on watch with them. When he did not respond they broke a window, threw a grenade through the door and opened fire into the house. Eleuterio's wife and the younger children made it out of the house and hid in a ravine. The next morning they found the bodies of Eleuterio and a sixteen-year-old son. Eleuterio's abdomen had been slit open from the breast-bone down. He had been punched with a knife or bayonet many times in the chest and his tongue had been cut out. The examiner who inspected the body said the heart had been taken out.[5]

'Violations of the laws of armed conflict by the Contras cause great suffering to the Nicaraguan people', says the 1987 Report of the Americas Watch Committee, a widely respected human rights monitoring group based in the USA. 'They still engage in selective but systematic killing of persons they perceive as representing the Government, in indiscriminate attacks against civilians or in disregard for their safety, and in outrages against the personal dignity of prisoners.'

Both Bertilda and María confirmed this statement. Bertilda's uncle had supported the Sandinistas from the early 1970s. In those days they were punished for their support by the National Guard; today by the Contras.

> The Contras knew who they were going to attack because they stopped at three other houses in the community first where there are no weapons and didn't say or do a thing to them. They asked for food and ate it and were OK when they arrived. They must have had people with them who knew us. This person knew which people were organized and who the revolutionary woman was. A lot of people realized that my uncle used to help the revolutionaries secretly. I knew the commanders myself and they knew me. They all used to work with my family. It was us they wanted to kidnap and assassinate. This was the cause: the hatred that they bear towards my family.
>
> They can't stand people who are organized, people who work in co-operatives. They want to destroy them so we are worse off every day. In Los Potreros we had a co-operative. It was the first time we had anything. We, the poor people, in Somoza's time, didn't have the opportunity. If we didn't have anywhere to work, we didn't eat. We'd have to beg food off the rich man. These days no. Before my community had no land. Now we're growing potatoes, tomatoes, maize and beans. We earned back what we borrowed from the bank and my uncle had already repaid them and our debts are quite small. So I imagine that this is the motive of the Contras. They don't want people who are working and who are liberated, because they still want to keep us the way they did before.

María's husband worked for the Ministry of the Interior and was well known as an investigator in the area.

> He used to visit families of the Contras at home and get them to convince their relatives to give themselves up under the amnesty. He even had a nickname among the Contras. We knew this made him a target. People used to say to me, why don't you come and live in Condega, but we had our farm here, so we had to stay.

Fundamentally people in Condega see the same forces at work in the Contras as they saw in the old National Guard of Somoza. In the countryside the Contras are even called 'La Guardia'. This confused me at first, but their identification of the USA as the backers of both forces is absolutely correct. Between 1950 and 1975 nearly five thousand members of the National Guard passed through US military training programmes. In roughly the same period Nicaragua received $23.6 million in grants and credits under the US Military Assistance Programme.[6]

In return for such support, the National Guard and the Somoza family could be relied upon to support US regional policies. In 1954 Somoza invited CIA agents and Guatemalan exiles to use Nicaraguan territory in the overthrow of Guatemalan President Jacobo Arbenz. In 1961 Nicaragua was used as a landing stage for the Bay of Pigs invasion of Cuba.

From 1964 special Nicaraguan elite forces were set up and passed through US counter-insurgency and training programmes. The National Guard became the key participant in the Central American Defense Council which specialized in regional repression of internal threats to the Central American dictatorships. In the final years of the dictatorship a Nazi-style supreme elite force, the EEBI, was set up armed with M-16s and Israeli Uzi sub-machine guns.

Made in the USA

The Contras were born in 1981, the year President Reagan was elected. His special adviser, Vernon Walters, worked with CIA officials to bring together groups of disgruntled former National Guard officers in Honduras under the title Nicaraguan Democratic Force. A grant of $19 million from the US National Security Council helped pay Argentinian military advisers who did the training at first to conceal US involvement.

From 1982 the Contras made their presence felt across Nicaragua. From their bases in Honduras, the site of eleven US military bases, the Contras made nearly eighty acts of combat inside Nicaragua that year. Here they were sustained at first by family links and dependent relationships formed with peasants in the most isolated communities of northern Nicaragua – a place where there were historical ties with the National Guard.

Revelations in the 'Contragate' affair have shown that the US administration has not only been the main source of financing for the Contras (which was an open secret), but also has directly controlled their operations via the CIA and the National Security Council's Colonel Oliver North. When Congress banned Reagan from direct funding, he mobilized right-wing private sources to step into the breach. As early as 1983, over 150 CIA officials and some sixty Spanish-speaking military personnel were stationed in Honduras, the command and control centre for the Contras. The CIA admitted to Congress that the agency had 'now assumed day-to-day control of counter-revolutionary activities, including pin-pointing targets, plotting attacks and conferring with rebel field leaders.[7] In 1983 they managed 600 armed attacks, in 1984 nearly a thousand.

The FND was the largest grouping, but there were others too. In Costa Rica a former Sandinista commander, Eden Pastora, and businessman, Alfonso Robelo, set up ARDE, a rival group. In the northern Atlantic Coast, disaffected Miskito indians were brought together to form Misura under Steadman Fagoth, and Misurasata under Brooklyn Riviera.

The leading office-holders in the FDN were appointed by the CIA.[8] Its military chief, Enrique Bermúdez, has impeccable Somozist credentials. He joined the National Guard in 1952, attended the US training school in Panama, was part of a Nicaraguan contingent in the occupation of the Dominican Republic in 1965, and in the 1970s became military attaché of the Somoza Government in Washington. The FND chief of staff is Emilio Echaverry; he joined the National Guard as second lieutenant in 1961, and is a specialist in counter-insurgency, trained by the US and the Argentinian army. Of the forty-eight top chiefs in the high command of the FDN, some forty-six are former National Guard officers. Four of the five military commanders, six of the seven regional chiefs and nearly all the task force chiefs were trained by the National Guard.[9]

The CIA and the Argentine army provided training and funds thought to be worth around $30 million, and the FDN grew slowly to reach a force of 10,000. Their funds were boosted by an estimated $5 million collected from right-wing organizations, such as the Korean leader of the Unification Church, Myung Sun Moon.

At one time the USA denied that their support for the Contras was connected to their dislike of internal Nicaraguan politics. President Reagan insisted that annual funding was aimed at halting the (alleged) arms flow from Nicaragua to El Salvador. From 1985 the USA dropped this pretence and the President stated his goal quite openly: to bring about the overthrow of the 'Russian-backed' Nicaraguan Government.

By then the US Government had invested more than $80 million in the Contras, now thought to number between twelve and fifteen thousand. President Reagan began to lobby Congress directly for military aid for the Contra 'freedom fighters', citing the threat of a 'Communist cancer' in Nicaragua as grounds. His task was made harder by revelations of drug-dealing and gun-running by Contra leaders, and a rift between the key figures. Nonetheless in June 1986 Congress voted a grant of $100 million – $70 million for military hardware and $30 million for non-lethal aid. Two days later the World Court of Justice at The Hague ruled that

> the United States of America, by training, arming, equipping, financing and supplying the Contra forces or otherwise encouraging, supporting and aiding military and paramilitary activities in and against Nicaragua, has acted, against the Republic of Nicaragua, in breach of its obligation under customary international law not to intervene in the affairs of another State.[10]

There have been several direct US attacks on Nicaragua too. The Court also condemned the US for launching direct attacks on two Nicaraguan ports, a naval base, two towns and Managua's airport in 1983 and 1984, for directing overflights of Nicaraguan territory, for mining the two main Nicaraguan ports, and for declaring a general trade embargo on Nicaragua in May 1985.

Urged to clean up their image abroad, the various Contra groupings formed a Unified Nicaraguan Opposition, whose civilian leaders had little connection with the discredited National Guard. Adolfo Calero, former CIA agent in Nicaragua and manager of the Coca Cola subsidiary, was named as Commander-in-Chief. He was joined by Arturo Cruz, former president of the Nicaraguan central bank and for a while a member of the Sandinista junta. By March 1987 Cruz had resigned. Little changed in the military leadership however.

For the people of Condega the US connection is the key to the Contras. Bertilda spoke for all of them:

> As far as Ronald Reagan who finances these people, these vampires, is concerned, what I would ask this man is that he leaves not just my family alone, but all Nicaraguans. We saw the weapons they were using. They were made in the USA, even the bombs they used. If they did not give them the money, these people could not come here to Nicaragua to assassinate a family, just because they are organized and working freely.

I thought of something she had told me about the Contras who attacked her family:

> They left a hat with a slogan on it about Christ. But how can we believe that these are Christians. They speak about Christ but they are just assassins. They are not even Nicaraguans because

they are helped by Reagan. Without help, they wouldn't be able to do anything.

I saw Bertilda again a few weeks later, making her way to the market in Condega. There had still been no word from the four cousins who had been kidnapped. The attack had left a total of sixteen children under six years old without breadwinners. She seemed more distraught, more angry, anxious to speak about her ordeal again.

The family were unable to return to Los Potreros; instead, they had been offered a shed on a tobacco farm as temporary shelter. Twenty-eight people were camping inside, sharing camp beds, hanging up their clothes to dry on the rafters. A makeshift kitchen had been rigged up outside. The rainy season was just starting and the ground outside was a river of mud. An old well served them with water and as a shower.

Bertilda went to Estelí to meet some visiting US Congressmen and give her testimony. Shortly afterwards she was refused a visa to visit the USA with a Nicaraguan delegation. She shrugged her shoulders as if to say, 'Well what do you expect?'

8. El Jocote: the enemy in our midst

El Jocote lies on the extreme eastern boundary of the district of Condega. To get there you take the road to Yalí, passing by the communities of Santa Rosa, the mountains of Canta Gallo and the coffee estate of Darailí. It was near El Jocote that the seven young soldiers were ambushed. For months it had been a place in which Contras were harboured and from where they launched attacks and ambushes on nearby roads and in the mountains.

For a while the nurse in Condega was too afraid to make a visit there. She had a feeling that she could not trust the people who were her hosts: 'They told me I was OK with them, but at the same time there were Contras in the village and no one warned me. I had to get out, quick.' The school teacher had stopped giving classes. She had been dragged out of her house and warned she would 'learn what was good for her' if she came back. Parents had started saying they didn't want their children to go to school. Impromptu visits by outsiders are not recommended. If the army is warned in advance, they can give protection.

At the entrance to the village, just past a bend in the road, are the remnants of a concrete bridge blown up in an earlier attack. Wooden planks take vehicles across. The little peasant shacks perched across the hillsides either side of the road house no more than 700 people. The houses are far apart from each other. People watch from their porches when a vehicle passes. It is a rare event. Down a little track a new brick building has been constructed. From inside comes the sound of chanting, then a hymn. It is Sunday and the born-again Christians gather here for most of the day. Their pastor, a young man, stands on a platform reading from the bible. A few heads turn as I enter. The congregation – a small bunch of women, children and a few men – repeat the words after him:

Así como los padres de Jesús entregaron sus hijos a dios, nosotros tambien tenemos que entegrar nuestros niños y nosotros a dios.

As the parents of Jesus presented their son to God, so we too have to present our children and ourselves to God. . . .

The phrase, taken loosely from St Luke chapter 2, is as far as that day's lesson appears to be going. The pastor picks out members of the congregation to repeat the phrase off by heart. Not many of them can read. They stumble each time. When they get it right there is effusive praise. As a reward there would be another hymn. Then back to the phrase – 'Así como los padres de Jesús entregaron sus hijos. . . .'

The people of El Jocote are small farmers. Their contact with the revolution has been limited. If the literacy crusade came in 1980, not much came afterwards. This small community has no health centre and just one school. There is no collectively owned land and, apart from the farmers' union (UNAG),[1] few of the mass Sandinista organizations have a presence here. Communication with Condega and other urban centres was always difficult, but petrol shortages and poor bus services has made it even harder.

Historically El Jocote and its neighbouring hamlets had few ties with the Sandinista guerillas. It did however have some connections with the National Guard, which set it into conflict with the nearby Canta Gallo peasants. What is more, the El Jocote valley lies on the edge of the mountains of Jinotega and Matagalpa – a region in which the Contras had done more damage than anywhere else. In the months before my arrival, some twenty young men from El Jocote went off with the Contras. Villagers gave food and lodging to the men in blue. Some were forcibly recruited against their will.

In a small shack in Condega I met fifty-year-old Ambrozio Ruíz, who had worked a small farm in El Jocote:

> The Contras arrived one night and threw me and my sons out of our beds. They stole money and threatened to kill us if we didn't go with them. They called me a collaborator. There were a number of other peasants kidnapped too. Altogether there were about 500 Contras in the group. One night we were put up by peasants in La Rica who are very friendly. In the one month I was with them there were four battles. The made me stay with them as cook, but they didn't give me arms. I couldn't leave. They said I wouldn't get further than fifty yards alive. My son had been kidnapped once before. He spent eight months in a training base in Honduras. When he was sent back to Nicaragua armed he gave himself up under the amnesty. Now the Contras have him again. They took him away. I suspect that he's not alive any more. That's what I fear. The people of El Jocote say they haven't seen him. They usually know.

They humiliated me all the time. You can't argue with what they say. They said they belonged to a task force in The Segovias. They are Nicaraguan peasants from all parts. There must be Guardia amongst them too. In Plan de Grama they kidnapped two girls. The chief slept with one of them. The other died in one of the battles. In El Tule they picked up more people. I'm sure some of them came voluntarily.

Ambrozio Ruíz escaped from the Contras but was too terrified to return to El Jocote. He had left his farm with his twenty-five-year-old daughter, but shortly afterwards she was kidnapped too. They found her body some weeks later. She had been raped. One of his sons, a member of the Frente, had died too in an ambush whilst heading a brigade of militia men.

Ambrozio was, as might be expected, in a highly emotional state. In Condega too he was desperately frightened. We talked in a wooden shack near the river. He talked in low tones, looking around for unwelcome ears. A man in dark glasses sat in the room listening all the time. The woman he was staying with kept out of the way. 'They are here in Condega too, you know, the Contras', he whispered.

How the Contras recruit

The bulk of Contra forces have been Nicaraguan peasants, recruited from isolated areas of the north. Illiteracy, poverty and a total lack of infrastructure characterize these areas – 'places where we had no effective presence, we had no effective involvement with the people to clarify their doubts and fears and promote their organization', Agustín Lara, political secretary for the region, told me. 'They are isolated sectors at the mercy of all types of confusionist and coercive activities.'

The Contras' tactic was to try and frighten these people into drawing back from what little involvement some had with the revolution. Their propaganda broadcast from Honduras on Radio 15 September said that the Sandinistas would take their land away and would subject them to religious persecution. It was a familiar message, identical to Somoza's anti-communist rhetoric.

Every effort was made to link the FDN's goals with the Catholic hierarchy. 'The Christian Guerillas', proclaims one headline in the FDN magazine, *Comandos*. 'The Pope is with us', says another, over a large photo of the Pope, and underneath 'Christ is the liberator.'

The message of the Contras coincided with a concerted and well-financed drive by US born-again Christians to recruit support across Central America. Their conservative fundamentalist message is the opposite of liberation theology. It stresses passivity, concentrates on the after life, and countenances against participation in what they see as Sandinista 'communism'. Their ideology is strikingly similar to that of the Contras.

In El Jocote and nearby hamlets, donations from the USA have paid for brand-new brick evangelical churches. Villagers spend their evenings in 'cults' which are a cross between a musical evening and a born-again rally. Religion in their hands takes on an almost social function, which the Catholic Church was never able to provide in these remote areas. The Catholic priest probably visits El Jocote no more than twice a year, and is certainly not able to stage a nightly happening. The fundamentalists pull villagers into an all-embracing daily routine, cocooning them in a set of ethical rules and regulations, enforced by dire threats of God's retribution.

But to persuade the peasants in these isolated places actually to join the Contra forces was never simply a matter of propaganda and persuasion. And, though they are a mercenary army, financial inducements were not particularly successful either, partly due to corruption in the higher ranks of the Contras. Outside the few places with historical connections with the National Guard, the Contras were forced to resort to recruiting through a combination of psychological terror, playing on the deep obscurantist mentality of subsistence farmers, and physical fear. 'You don't argue with an armed man,' said one woman in El Jocote. Threats were made against anyone who associated with the social, medical or educational reforms the revolution was bringing. Isolated activists in such places had to be very committed to stand their ground. Many died.

By the middle of 1983, incidents of direct coercion, such as forcing peasants at gunpoint into Contra columns, began to be commonplace. By early 1985 the Government estimated that some two thousand *campesinos* had been kidnapped. If the Nicaraguan peasants could not be torn from the revolution voluntarily, then they could perhaps be physically separated from it by force. Abductions served a dual purpose. They swelled the ranks of the Contras and they sabotaged the production of food for the Nicaraguan economy by removing the labour force.

Agustín Lara explained what happens:

The Contras arrive in a community, select a group of men, take them off to Honduras, train them, arm them and bring them back into the country and try to compromise each one of them individually with criminal activities which then strengthens their dependence on the rebels.

The reaction and behaviour of the *campesinos* is not one of support for the counter-revolutionary position, but rather one of survival. When you ask why they got involved the majority say that they had no choice but to agree.

This acquiescence or ambiguity is also shown by some non-activist *campesinos* when the Contras come to attack Sandinista targets. It is not a sign of support, simply survival. Such a fear has smoothed the Contras' path in many instances. Bertilda's neighbours, for example, according to her cousin, Reynaldo, do not agree with the Contras.

But what happens is that they are frightened of them. Because you have to treat the Contras very carefully. To be OK with them, you are forced to be a Contra yourself. Because if you say something against them, their job is to assassinate you. As soon as someone says that they don't agree with the assassinations they carried out in our village, they would immediately have their head cut off.

María's neighbours kept away when the Contras came to kill her family.

The neighbours were listening. But they didn't have any weapons. But after the Contras left, no one came to see what had happened. Even the woman next door who is always in and out of my house. I was here in the kitchen waiting until my husband arrived at 5 a.m. in the morning. He thought I would probably be dead. My neighbour said the same. She didn't come because she thought everyone must be dead.

The neighbour came into the house whilst we were talking there and asked, rather sheepishly, how things were.

In many other instances Contra attacks had prompted communities to seek to join the militia and arm themselves for future defence. I met a group of *campesinos* near Ocotal who had escaped after the most horrific treatment in a Contra camp. One of their party had been castrated. They had stayed with forty-three other kidnapped peasants in the camp, living in rags. 'With these methods, how are they going to defeat us?' asked one man. People don't just fear them, they hate them. The men guarded their land and homes round the clock from a militia post, their support of the revolution strengthened by their experiences.

In El Jocote itself I met some former Contras who, under a government amnesty, had applied for permission to return to their farms. The Sandinista army had set up a post in the village and these men needed their protection. Their stories were all similar. Gustavo is twenty-nine. He was kidnapped during a wake where men and women were mourning the death of a four-year-old child.

About fifteen Contras arrived in the evening. They said 'Good evening'. I didn't know any of them. They had on blue uniforms and carried Falle rifles. They took about thirty-seven people with them from the village, walking. After eight days we were in Honduras. We were hungry and cold. All they gave us to eat was rice. There were about 120 people in a training camp. We couldn't ask for anything. They were not violent with us, but there was not enough to eat. We wanted to escape but they guarded us all the time. We slept under bits of plastic. They showed us how to arm and disarm the rifles. We had to sleep at the top of the hill, while they lived below. It made us feel bad. There was a fundamentalist sect there. They took us to the church and talked about the word of God. They were Jehovah's Witnesses. There was a service every day. The Contras gave money to those they trusted. They paid 100 pesos a day.

Gustavo got away when he was sent back into Nicaragua. 'I'm afraid they'll come back. If they get me now they will kill me.' His hands shook as he spoke. We were hidden behind one of the shacks under a tree and talked in the presence of an FSLN worker. 'All we want to do is to work in peace. The revolution is helping us with loans. We are happy now we have schools and land. The commandante who came to talk with us told us they would leave us to work and grow basic grains.'

Roberto Pineda Rivas is only fifteen. He was abducted from El Jocote together with his father.

They stopped us in the path, it was dark, and they told us we had to walk with them. There were about sixty Contras. They separated me from my father. We had to walk for days and days. Sometimes they gave us a bit of meat. We had to drink river water so I had diarrhoea. Sometimes I had a bit of tortilla. I was

really hungry. They ate the same as us, but they must be used
to it. We slept on the ground. I was afraid. I knew they'd kill me
if I tried to get away. I just thought about going back home.
There were no battles. They sometimes bought arms from people.
When they came back round near here I plucked up courage to
come home.

Roberto's father was still with the Contras. His mother, María-
Luisa, who came with him to meet me, had five children and only
the fifteen-year-old Roberto to work on their small patch of land.
'Someone told the Contras that my husband collaborated with the
army. I haven't found out who it was. I think it was friends of ours.
I feel frightened in this place because you don't know from one
moment to the next who people are,' she said. We were talking in
the presence of the Frente worker, and María-Luisa was choosing
her words carefully. 'The Contras are against the peasants. Some
people go with them because they don't like the people who are
in power and because they like the life. They are just in it for
themselves.'

Later, when I talked to her alone, she said that the army's presence
had not been welcomed by everyone in the village. They called the
army _los Compas_ (short for _compañeros_) and there are some who feel
there is little to choose between _los Compas_ and _la Contra_. Families
with personal ties to the Contras would tend to see _los Compas_ as
the enemy. 'Before people felt better and freer. Now people are
afraid,' said María-Luisa out of earshot of the Frente man. It seemed
that the recent price increases and military service had given the
Sandinistas a bad name. 'Fathers don't want their sons to go. There
aren't any youth here at all.' I began to have my doubts as to
whether her husband had been forced to join the Contras.

The people of El Jocote are not popular in Condega, nor with the
nearby communities of Canta Gallo. They are held responsible for
the Contras' ability to infiltrate the area and stage their attacks – if
not directly guilty of complicity with the attacks themselves. People
reacted with suspicion toward the Government's amnesty, fearing
it would make the district more vulnerable. The town's magistrate,
Orlando Navaretto, explained why:

> In El Jocote everyone is Contra. There are whole families
> collaborating. The army arrested quite a few of them and
> announced why publicly. They released them into the village and
> they are integrated there again. But they're still involved with
> the same thing. Ideologically they are still with the Contras. It's

one of our fears that the individuals who go with the Contras
and later come back to the community have not really changed.
We are suspicious of them. Some have infiltrated themselves
into the army to have more control.

The amnesty and the DGSE

The government amnesty brought back some 1,500 *campesinos* to
their homes. Its declaration in January 1985 coincided with a serious
drop in morale within the Contras – a response to the Government's
military offensive. It was designed to help those who had been
kidnapped and were unable to escape, those who feared reprisals if
they returned to their homes, and those who feared they would face
unemployment and insecurity if they returned home. It promised
that those who gave themselves up would be given productive work
on the land.

In the Estelí area, 150 of those who responded were held for
debriefing in the headquarters of the state security directorate in
Estelí. It is a building concealed behind a rock, high up above the
Pan American Highway going south out of the town. A constant
stream of army vehicles passes up and down the road. Half-way
along is the regional command, at the north end the helicopter
launching pad.

I went there to meet them with Mónica, the *Barricada* reporter.
For a place of temporary detention for Contras the building seemed
surprisingly relaxed. The General Directorate of State Security
(DGSE) is a kind of secret service and special branch rolled into one,
and deals principally with internal threats to the revolution – in
practice it is a kind of political police. It is rated as important as the
army in terms of defeating the counter-revolution.

Unlike most countries, the Nicaraguans make no bones about
their state security system, the motto of which is 'Security of the
State is Security of the People.' They even produce a pamphlet
explaining their role in the 'undeclared war' launched by the White
House, and listing a number of now well-established attempts by
the CIA to sabotage Nicaragua, along with successful thwarting
operations by the DGSE.[2]

Contrary to my expectations the place did not exude an atmosphere of heavy security. There were no iron doors. It seemed as if

anyone could just walk out if they so wished. The building had open sides and views on both sides of the hill across the wide plateau of Estelí. A couple of miles away, a few military tents were visible in the regional headquarters. And in the distance was the rugged blue mountain range, locus of the war itself.

We were shown first into the canteen. It was lunchtime. The staff, young men and women in green fatigues, indistinguishable from members of the militia or the army, were devouring large plates of rice, beans and meat. The food was served behind a counter by large, smiling peasant women. Everybody ate fast. There were no special tables reserved for higher ranks.

And there too, sitting at the same tables, were a large group of men and boys in somewhat dirty civilian clothes. Some wore baseball hats, popular amongst the _campesinos_ of the north and often taken to be 'Contra'-wear. Some were in their early teens with bare feet and large crucifixes round their necks. They looked just like any other poor Nicaraguan peasants of the north: farming people with rugged hands and mud-sprayed, broken boots. Some had the distinctive indian features, common in the remoter parts of the north. They too were eating large plates of food and going up for second helpings. Some chatted amongst themselves. Others leant against the walls looking on sullenly. They looked preoccupied, busy with the business of surrendering – or perhaps thinking about their return to their families?

I was somewhat taken aback that the staff appeared to have no fear or compunction about mixing with them, despite their past. The emphasis with all Nicaraguan prisoners of war and former Contras is on rehabilitation and politicization, not with punishment.

A group of five were chosen to tell us their story. The officer who debriefed them sat in the small bare room with us. He let them speak, interrupting occasionally to ask them to clarify something or to add a detail they had omitted to mention. It was a similar story to the men from El Jocote. The five men lived in Los Pinares, a small hamlet not far north of Condega. The FDN arrived one night and kidnapped the six men from the community. One of them, a Sandinista, resisted and had disappeared, they presumed him dead. A total of forty men were kidnapped that night and marched through the night in close formation to a camp in Honduras. 'We weren't allowed to speak. They treated us like enemies and said they'd kill us if we escaped,' said Julio Sánchez of Los Pinares.

There are an estimated thirty-five Contra camps in Honduras and the bulk of the Contra forces are maintained there, holed up in an area they call 'new Nicaragua' with the silent complicity of the Honduran Government. The men slept in the open air and were given only rice and noodles to eat, and not much of that: 'We were so hungry that we ate blades of grass.' For three months they were kept in the camp, somewhat apart from the other 300 inmates. Their commanders in the camp in Honduras ate tinned American food and slept in proper huts with their women. The men were given uniforms and old weapons and trained rigorously – on empty stomachs. They were told that the Contras were soon getting more money from the USA, for modern weapons. They were humiliated and jeered at by the men who had captured them.

Along with the training routines came political lessons. The men were told they had to fight communism which was making their country hungry, that it was God's war, and that the country would soon be 'free'. 'The Contras hate peasants,' said one man. 'They say they are Nicaraguans but if they are, then they are like the Guardia.'

One of the most striking things about meeting the amnestied Contras was the almost universal absence of any political or ideological motivation either in themselves or in the Contras they talked about. The camps in Honduras appeared to be kept together by coercion, a small amount of money, and above all a fear of recrimination back home. By mid-1986 Sandinista military intelligence estimated that the FDN had recruited only 259 Nicaraguans into the Contras so far that year. Most recruits come from the most isolated peasant communities. Their understanding of the larger conflict and their ability to grasp more complicated fighting tactics are limited. Another thousand were thought to have joined from Honduran refugee camps (where young male refugees reportedly come under a great deal of pressure to join).[3] 'They threatened to kill our families if we refused to fight. We felt hate for them. They are never going to win like that,' said another man from Los Pinares. I agreed that they were incapable of winning, but it was clear they could do a great deal of damage.

State of emergency

The state of emergency declared in October 1985, which brought criticism from both inside and outside Nicaragua, was primarily an attempt to deal with Contra networks inside the country. Discontent at the economic situation had provided the Contras with their strongest card against the Government. 'When someone is losing he either surrenders, negotiates or launches a counter-offensive,' said President Ortega.[4]

The emergency suspended various guarantees of the basic statutes passed in 1979, and gave the Government powers to detain without charge in cases of counter-revolutionary activities. The right of habeas corpus was suspended in such cases. It also restricted the right to freedom of movement, of information, of meetings and demonstrations, of association and organization, and the right to strike. Many of these clauses had been in effect since the passing of 'state of exception legislation' in March 1982. 'We are annulling the licence of the false prophets and the oligarchs to attack the revolution,' explained Commandante Jaime Wheelock.

Two days later a group of men were presented to the press accused of a terrorist plot to blow up a low-price supermarket for workers, an electric sub-station, an Aeroflot office and other targets. In Jinotega 130 people were detained, including peasants, merchants and import-traders, and accused of forming a network of messengers and recruiters and of organizing ambushes, distribution of propaganda, lists of people to be assassinated and planned explosions.

Many religious activists were among those briefly detained. They reported being warned against promoting evasion of the military draft. Most of the hundreds arrested were detained for relatively brief periods and released without charges. The Americas Watch Report accused the Government of abusing their new powers by the short-term detention of many political leaders, priests, pastors and lay religious activists. In the first six months of 1986, some 1,500 people were arrested under suspicion of involvement in Contra networks.

El Jocote and neighbouring hamlets were prime targets of the DGSE in the emergency. Fourty-seven mostly elderly men from El Jocote and El Bramadero were detained and held without charge in the prison at Estelí. Comandante Pichardo, of the Ministry of the Interior, who allowed the Americas Watch team to visit the men, said they had been arrested on suspicion that they had provided food, shelter and intelligence to an FDN contingent operating in the area. The men told Americas Watch that they had been coerced into doing so. All but four of the men were released in April 1986, five months after their capture. Three others were due to be tried, and one was still being investigated after ten months.[5]

The length of their detention (Americas Watch knew of only a 'handful of cases' where people spent more than four or five months in pre-trial detention) bears witness to the strength of local feeling in the Condega district against the Contras' base in El Jocote. State security in the Condega district, although centrally co-ordinated, operates in close conjunction with local communities and people.

Outside certain target localities, however, few people were affected by the state of emergency. There was no increase in police activity and life carried on as normal. But 'free expression' in Nicaragua today has inevitably suffered as a result of the Contras' activities. It is easy with such tensions operating on local communities, and where lives are at stake, for all political dissent to be written off and labelled as 'Contra'. It is not the Nicaraguans who are to blame for inducing this climate, but the USA.

There is no civil war in Nicaragua, but there is a polarization between those whose commitment to the revolution has been strengthened by Contra activities and those who have remained somewhat removed from the political process of change and reform. The situation is exacerbated by economic hardship brought about by the US decision to isolate Nicaragua commercially and financially (see Chapter 20).

And there are inevitably some, though very few, disturbing cases of individual retribution by Nicaraguan officials. (Americas Watch reported twelve such incidents in 1985–6.) One occurred in the hamlet of Guayucalí, near El Jocote, in the month the emergency was declared. Reverend Juan Pablo Pineda, pastor of the Pentecostal Church, was arrested by a Lieutenant Rene Lagos, the commander of the military post in that village. Lagos shot and killed Pineda the same day at the command post. His body was found two weeks later, showing signs of torture and several bullet wounds. It was also decapitated. The Protestant Aid and Development body (CEPAD) in Managua reported that Lagos was arrested and taken to Ocotal. He escaped but was recaptured and brought to Managua. Within two months he had been sentenced by military courts to twenty-five years in prison.[6]

It is significant, though, that Americas Watch, anxious that their findings should not be distorted by the Reagan administration, in 1987 saw fit to affirm that:

> The government of Nicaragua does not engage in a pattern of
> violations of the law of war. Nor does it engage in systematic
> violations of the right to life or to physical integrity of detainees,
> which are the clearest cases of non-derogable rights. Nor does it
> engage in a deliberate pattern of forced disappearances of persons,

a practice that would violate those and other non-derogable rights. Some cases of such abuse do take place in Nicaragua.... Our information indicates however, that they do not reflect a governmental policy to commit them or to tolerate them.[7]

9.   Moisés Córdoba: *campesino* of the Frente

The man sent to El Jocote to try and win the *campesinos* to the revolution was Moisés Córdoba, the son of old Don Leandro, Sandino's messenger.

Moisés Córdoba was not an easy man to track down. Nobody at the Frente office knew his movements from one day to the next. Or if they did, they weren't saying. I made several trips in vain in the heat of the day to his house on the edge of Condega. The family live in a brick house, but the sum of their worldly possessions appeared to be three dilapidated fold-up chairs, some kitchen utensils and a pile of oranges in the corner on the dirt floor.

I knew Moisés's story would be interesting. He was one of the first peasant revolutionaries of the 1970s, fought with the guerillas during the insurrection, and could tell me something about how the Sandinistas built a base of support in the Canta Gallo mountains near Condega in the 1970s. It was against *campesinos* like Moisés that Somoza unleashed a wave of terror after his humiliation at the hands of the FSLN in December 1974.

On my fourth attempt, I was lucky. Moisés, whom I guessed to be in his late thirties, sat in the back yard in full military gear eating his breakfast. He had just arrived and had three hours to spend with his family before returning to El Jocote. He had not even bothered to unstrap the magazines round his chest. He seemed by nature quiet and mild-mannered, and had a big smile which revealed a gold tooth.

His wife darted about the rudimentary kitchen, preparing a meal, sharing his jokes and complementing his stories. A good-looking woman, she is one of his strongest fans – her bright eyes glow with admiration for the man who rarely takes off his uniform, and never stops work. She is an energetic and nervous woman. Her three children were born during the family's exile in remote caves in hiding from the National Guard at the end of Somoza's regime. Now, seven years after the triumph, she is reliving some of those same fears – this time caused by the Contras. She admits to insomnia and permanent headaches from worry.

Moisés was the youngest of Don Leandro's eleven children. None of them had any education but to a certain extent politics was in their blood. They belonged to the Conservative party, which opposed Somoza, and were constantly harassed by the Guardia as a result. Moisés had of course heard about Sandino's struggle against US marines from old Don Leandro, his father – 'he always said that sooner or later we'd have to get results, to start a revolutionary war'.

They considered themselves lucky to own even a small plot of land: two-thirds of rural Nicaraguans had nothing, or not enough land to support themselves. Others paid a steep cash rent to absentee landowners. Disease and sickness was endemic. Infant mortality stood at 130 per thousand births. Children died of undernourishment, diarrhoea and common diseases such as measles. The average calorie intake was only 1,800, just over half the recommended minimum of 3,000.[1] Few people could afford a doctor, and in fact there were only five clinics in the whole of the country.

Moisés's family (the average size of a family was around seven) shared a single-room shack in Los Planes, Canta Gallo, divided by a thin partition. It had dirt floors, no electricity, no toilet and no drinking water. In the hamlet there was no school. Condega's parish priest and some of the lay delegates were the only visitors who could read or write.

It was impossible not to be in debt. Local money lenders charged 50 per cent interest, and often borrowing was the only way a *campesino* could purchase cooking oil, sugar, salt and gas – let alone tools. Everyone, men, women, old folk and children, supplemented their own production of beans and maize by seasonal work on the coffee estates. They would earn something like sixteen cents for a twenty-pound load. And during these three months or so, they, like 400,000 or so other Nicaraguans, would share one of the wooden barracks with hundreds more like the ones I slept in near Managua. In exchange for providing food for the pickers – beans, rice or tortillas – the landowner would deduct three hours' pay.[2] To cap it all the landowners enforced their regime through local judges, *juez de mesta*, who doled out fines on average of $10 each and the National Guard whose uniform and weapons conjured up terror in a *campesino*'s mind: 'The oppression was terrible. The Guardia would help themselves to what they want,' Moisés remembered.

Where men and mountains meet

By 1975 the underground cells of the young Frente members in Condega were beginning to provide the Sandinista guerillas with the links they wanted in the mountains nearby. Some of the FSLN guerillas had been in hiding and training in isolated camps in the mountains for two or more years – taking their example from Sandino in the 1920s. The motto of a leading member, Henry Ruíz, was 'In the mountains we will bury the heart of the enemy.' According to some estimates there were as few as sixty rural guerillas in the FSLN at the time. Another forty members were based in towns and over 200 suspected members were in prisons.

The Centeno family, which had relatives all over the area around Condega, were particularly active. Toñito, the oldest son of Don Antonio, had worked as a foreman on the San Jerónimo coffee estate. He knew all the plantation hands and *campesinos* in the area and offered to make introductions for FSLN cadres.

In August 1975 two of the guerillas, disguised as medicine pedlars, accompanied Toñito Centeno into the mountains of Canta Gallo. One was a mechanics teacher from the Condega Secondary School, who had had to disappear from the school in a hurry to avoid arrest. The other was a former León university student, Omar Cabezas, now a commandante and a director in the Ministry of the Interior. In his autobiography Cabezas described their reception:

> Those poor people nearly died when they were told we were from the FSLN, because it was not long since the Guardia had massacred a lot of people in the mountains. So our presence there was synonymous with disaster for them – because from the start we meant commitment, misfortune and death.[3]

An old *campesino* who befriended 'the boys' at this time is now a frequent visitor to the Centenos' house. Gilberto Zavala, now in his seventies and living in Condega, allowed them to camp out in a coffee field some 200 metres from his house. He, like many in the area, had been a member of the Conservative Party, but 'since the Conservative Party did not reflect their interests, they became Sandinistas'.

The acclimatization for the guerillas, mainly young students, was long and painful. All contact with their family and friends was suspended. They lived hidden away in jungle conditions, dependent on local sympathetic peasants for food and safety from the National Guard, always ready for an unexpected Guardia raid which might result from an informant's tip-off or the arrest and torture of a sympathizer. Gilberto's wife was terrified that the Guardia would discover her 'lodgers'. The boys gradually won her confidence by showing her pictures of their children and mothers. Next they persuaded Gilberto to take their messages down to the commanders in Condega.

Today, Gilberto Zavala is a thin-faced, rather formal old man. He, like so many others of the Canta Gallo peasants, the early members of the FSLN, are respected older citizens. They are not now in the forefront of the rebuilding of Nicaragua, as that responsibility lies with much younger people. They have the time, however, to sit back and think about what has happened to them in the past ten years and put it into some kind of perspective. They take a fatherly attitude to the revolution, expressing concern about some things, pleasure at others; sometimes they are critical of the way the younger people in charge handle problems, yet full of admiration for their commitment.

The day I met him, Don Gilberto had come to ask Don Antonio's advice. He was under pressure to give up his house and go and live in the co-operative. 'I can't do anything for the co-operative at my age. I'm past it now. I've got my land near here and I don't want to give that up.' He nodded to me and looked slightly embarrassed about discussing such a matter in the presence of a foreigner. The irony of his situation struck me immediately, for the question of land had been the key motivating factor of the *campesinos'* support for the Sandinistas.

When he met the FSLN, Zavala worked as field worker in the estate and was in dispute with his relatives over a small piece of land that had been left to him.

Omar Cabezas and the mechanics teacher used to spend the day hidden – at first in some rocks near a stream and later in Don Gilberto Zavala's granary. At night they would go to the peasants' houses and, drinking coffee after coffee, hold long discussions about their economic situation, their lack of land, the landowners and the reasons for their poverty.

The first thing we would ask was whether the land on which they lived was theirs. The answer was always no, it belonged to the rich folk. Or they would laugh, as if making a joke, or they would hang their heads ... because for the campesinos the land was a dream. A dream of their fathers and of their fathers' grandfathers.... So if you came and asked them if they owned

the land, they just laughed. Because the land had never belonged
to them. Naturally we steered our political discussions toward
the reason the land was not theirs.

We were trying to awaken the campesino to his own dream.
We wanted to make him see that though the dream was
dangerous – since it implied struggle – the land was their right.
And we began to cultivate that dream. Through our political
work, many campesinos began partaking of that dream.[4]

In Moisés's hamlet, Los Planes, the twenty-five families there had
only a hundred acres of land between them. Many *campesinos* had
lost their land in the enclosures and had to grow their crops on
land loaned or rented by the landowners. In harvest time they had to
sell their crop to the landowner too. All the imported essentials,
tools, salt, aspirins, etc., had to be bought from the landowner's
shop.

Moisés, who had a small plot of land, remembers the 'boys''
arrival:

Omar arrived with a friend of mine, Toñito Centeno, and one
other boy. They started to talk to me about the revolutionary
struggle. They explained that they were members of Frente, that
they were preparing conditions to destroy the Somozist
dictatorship. They asked me to collaborate and help them with
food, somewhere to live and weapons. And I agreed.

Moisés's father, old Don Leandro, could not believe his ears when
he heard that Sandinistas were in the area again – it had been a good
forty years since he collaborated with General Sandino's army. He
agreed to meet two guerillas.

My son told me that there were some men who wanted to speak
to me. I told them to come at night. I was amazed. I was very
frightened. Omar came – he used a pseudonym, Juan José, and
we sat there talking. He believed, as I do, that we could get rid
of these Yankees and take power.

According to Omar Cabezas the meeting with Don Leandro was
an historic occasion:

He told me how he was Sandino's messenger, told me about Pablo
Umanzor, General Estrada, Pedro Altamirano. He knew and
worked with all of them. He told me about it as if seeing them
right there, he remembered details. When he saw our weapons
he asked, 'What did you do with the other weapons?' I didn't

understand that he was linking me with the old Sandinistas he knew and was asking me about the weapons in the way someone might ask what have you done with the weapons we used yesterday. That moment for him, in which he had aged by forty years, was just an instant.

I had never felt more of a child of Sandinism, a child of Nicaragua, than in that moment. I was a young student who got to know Sandino through books. I had arrived at Sandino by studying Sandinism, but I hadn't got to the root, the true paternity of all our history. So when I met that man, I felt like his child, a child of Sandinism, a child of history. I understood my own past, I had a country. I wanted to hug and kiss him.[5]

The support from Moisés and Don Leandro was a turning point for the FSLN, whose reception by the *campesinos* had been coloured by their fear of the National Guard. It set in train a period of close collaboration between the Frente and the peasants of Canta Gallo that continues to this day.

Moisés was made responsible for the work. Using the freedom that his position as a lay Catholic preacher gave him, he could make contact with other peasants without rousing suspicion.

Political work was directed through the Church partly because political meetings were prohibited. I would tell the people that just saying you are a Christian is not enough. You have to act, help the sick and infirm, fight for justice on the land, demand justice if the Guardia attacks an innocent man. We started organizing the peasants. We did community work, repairing paths, school books, helping orphans and old people. Doing this we were not in danger. The people knew what it was about. We would go openly to other communities and explain. The priests directed us. They didn't know that the Frente was involved. Without their collaboration and help things would have been different. They condemned the injustice and talked of organizing. . . .

We set up lines of communication, and began to form small columns of guerillas. I chose who to ask to join us because I knew the area. All the peasants who joined were young – between twenty-six and twenty-eight. Many came from Conservative Party families.

At first my wife didn't know what I was doing. I used to tell her to make me six meals, that I had some workers who didn't have wives to cook for them. Then at night I'd take them to my father's house, where the boys were. Later on, when she knew what was happening, she helped us. We set up four camps and did military training, stealing our weapons from the Guardia. We attacked informers who worked with the Guardia but they never found us, though they would cross the area looking. The oppression was terrible.

Don Leandro's age prevented him from taking much of an active part, though he used to run errands: fetch new leather soles, matches or cartons of cigarettes for the boys when he went to Condega.

When I came back they would ask me excitedly, 'How is Condega?' And I would say, 'You should see it, man.' I'd watch them with a .22 rifle, the type you go deer-hunting with, and I'd ask, 'What do you think you're going to do with this old thing?' And they'd say, 'You wait, old man, you'll see. These things will kill.' 'Maybe', I'd say, but I always had the hope that they would win.

1976: Canto Gallo under siege

Towards the end of 1975, the network of Guardia informers was beginning to draw closer to the new base of FSLN support in the countryside. The unending cycle of peasant poverty and the power of the National Guard made it easy to bribe people to become informers or to torture a statement out of a peasant.

The Guardia struck first in Condega, where the FSLN commanders were in hiding. The arrest of Amanda Centeno in December 1975 and the flight of several members of the Centeno family meant the writing was on the wall for supporters in Canta Gallo. Don Pilar Monsón, another of the older citizens of Condega who fought with Sandino, and a frequent visitor to the Centenos', was one of the first to be arrested in Canta Gallo.

Twenty Guardia arrived and denounced me for holding a camp in the mountains. I used to go around with Omar Cabezas selling cheese. He taught us how to use weapons. The Guardia surrounded my house, beat up me and my son and took me away. They took me to Managua and I was a prisoner for two and a half months. Every day they tortured me with electric wires. They pulled out my nails one by one.

Shortly afterwards, the Guardia arrived for Moisés:

> It was half past one in the morning. A group of about 300 Guardia
> arrived at my house. I had military boots, a uniform and a
> revolver hidden below a seat. They broke the door down, rammed
> machine guns into our stomachs. My youngest girl was ill with
> a temperature. They took the two boys and threw them out.

Old Don Leandro was not spared, despite his age:

> They came to my house. They'd got Moisés. They'd tied up two
> cousins with their wives and wrecked the house. I pretended to
> be a feeble old man, more feeble than I was. They didn't do
> anything to my wife, but took me. There were five of us. They
> walked us at gunpoint to where the road was where they had
> lorries. They tied us up and took us to Yalí, threatening us all
> the way. There they asked where was the revolution? The
> guerillas? I said I hadn't seen them. I was lying at first. But of
> course they were torturing the boys, burning their legs with
> electric wires. They didn't torture me. I think they felt sorry for
> me and thought such an old man wouldn't survive it. Then they
> took us to Jinotega and then to Managua. They separated us
> then. Moisés was in one place and the others went somewhere
> else. I didn't know where Moisés was.

The crackdown was part of the state of siege declared by Somoza
after the FSLN attacked Chema Castillo's house in December 1974.
By 1976 counter-insurgency troops were combing every inch of the
mountains, using aircraft to bomb likely areas for hidden camps.
Peasant huts were burned out and their crops destroyed. Women
were raped. There were six concentration camps set up in the north.
In April 1976 over a hundred families disappeared from three
hamlets. Their bodies were never found. Altogether, some three
thousand deaths are estimated to have occurred during the three
years of the state of siege. Moisés and Don Leandro consider themselves lucky to have survived. Moisés was tortured. 'They put hoods
on us and gave us electric shocks to our heads. Our hands were tied.
I was hooded for five days and had nothing to eat. They gave shocks
to my whole body, my genitals, my hands, my mouth.'
Don Leandro remembers his time in prison in great detail:

> I didn't think for a moment I would survive. We had no contact
> with anyone. I was put alone in a cell in Managua. All I could
> hear was the screams of the people they were torturing. I didn't

tell them anything. Once they brought me to a journalist, blindfold. I don't remember his name. He asked me why I wasn't answering. But I knew what it was like and the Guardia were there. So why was I going to answer him? 'Is this your name?' he asked me. I said 'If you say so.'

They took me to the court to take a statement. I told the court that we came from the mountains, that the boys sometimes came by and asked for food and we gave it, that the Guardia would come by the same way and we gave them food. That's the way we are, I said.

When we got to the Modelo prison we were warned that there were a lot of prisoners and we shouldn't take any notice, that they'd probably signal to us, but we should just carry on up. They opened the door and we went in and some Sandinista prisoners came up to us shouting, 'Long live Sandino.' We had to keep our mouths shut. Because they were prisoners they were free to speak. We weren't. When we got to the top we recognized some people we knew from Santa Ana. They were so pleased to see us. There were even some women prisoners. We were pleased too. Until then we had had to share a tortilla between four of us with a spoonful of beans. We were starving.

Some 600 peasants were jailed. Don Leandro was released after fifteen days.

The repression kept the guerillas pinned down in the mountains during 1976 and most of 1977, unable to launch any effective actions. One of the biggest blows to the fledgling organization was the death of its founding member, Carlos Fonseca Amador, who was killed near Zinica by a Guardia foot patrol in November 1976.

But despite the repression, few of the FSLN camps were detected, owing to the foresight of the *campesinos*. As Moisés explained,

They wanted to know where the Sandinistas were, how many people there were. I told them that they sometimes passed by but they didn't have camps. Because in fact after we were arrested one of my cousins went to find the place where the camp was in Los Planes. He and others pulled down branches and roughed up the ground so there would be no sign of anything going on there. He threw all the cigarette ends and cigarette papers into a hole. So when the Guardia went to look for traces they didn't find a thing.

There were protests in several towns, including Condega, at the treatment of peasants in the north. Moisés is convinced that the protests helped him and others win their release towards the end of 1976. He owed his life, he said, to the intervention of a lieutenant of the Guardia. Somoza operated a specially trained death squad called the 'Black Hand' who were responsible for the murder of many political prisoners. They came for Moisés, but the lieutenant intervened and told them he was due to come up for investigation by a special commission so they shouldn't take him away.

The regime in prison was brutal:

> I lived for six months on a spoonful of beans a day and a quarter of a tortilla and water. It was forbidden to study or read in jail but in fact we had international support. People were sending money so we could buy books. I learnt to read and write.
>
> When they released me I returned home to Canta Gallo. Omar Cabezas came to see me. When he saw the wounds and lacerations all over my body he started to cry.

Moisés did not stay long in his old home. With some seventy other families, he and his wife went to live in caves in a more isolated part of the mountains. They stayed there for over two years, building up a political network and military base.

Moisés in El Jocote

Today, more than ten years after he joined the Sandinistas, Moisés is again in the hot seat. The Frente's decision to send him to El Jocote had come after a number of other options were dismissed. El Jocote was not a strategically important village, simply a major irritant. In Condega and outside, people demanded that something be done about the Contras there. The question was discussed by a regional committee of both the FSLN and the army and, as with most problems, there were disagreements as to the best solution.

When I first arrived in Condega I was told of a plan to evacuate the hamlet and move the inhabitants into nearby settlements, where they would be given land and encouraged to integrate into co-operatives and Sandinista communities. This policy was being tried in remote mountainous areas bordering Honduras, where the army wished to create a free fire zone to repel large-scale Contra attacks. It sounded to me like forced removal, though Eunice, the Frente secretary, explained it as an altruistic move to give the landless land. In the event, this plan was dropped, after vigorous opposition – not just from the inhabitants of El Jocote, who protested to the farmers' union (UNAG), but also from the residents of the settlements themselves. They feared this would only bring the Contras closer to their own communities.

By sending Moisés into El Jocote, it was hoped that villagers could be persuaded to drop their support for the Contras. Moisés knew the mentality of the small subsistence farmers and had a calm way of talking to people. Above all he understood the revolution and the benefits it could bring. It was, however, a dangerous assignment and a lot of lives depended on his success. He was accompanied to the village by a small company of conscript soldiers, and set up his headquarters in the village school, where attendances had been dropping in response to Contra propaganda. From here they set out to befriend the villagers, and earn their trust, and by their very presence deter the Contras from using El Jocote as a base.

I travelled out to see him there with his wife one Sunday morning. The nurse had decided to make the trip to visit some of the midwives in the village. Moisés's wife had cooked a hot meal and came in her best dress, laden with a basket of food. She didn't often miss an opportunity to see her husband. The trip had involved complicated arrangements and the army had been alerted. Time was needed for Moisés to persuade people to talk to me. No, he insisted, it would not be possible for me to accompany him on his visits outside the village; perhaps I didn't understand how dangerous it was.

The road to Yalí was deserted. Right up until El Jocote, ours was the only vehicle. The countryside and the mountains glowed in the sunshine, yet the silence was eerie. In the village very few people showed themselves; for Nicaraguans this was most unusual, as they are usually the most friendly and welcoming of people. A few conscripts hung around near the school entrance. Moisés was just coming off night patrol, his green uniform positively dripping with ammunition.

His mission had been to some extent successful, as several people had already returned to the hamlet since he had arrived. But it was an uphill struggle.

We explain to the people the distorted politics of the enemy. The Contras told them there would be a Contra victory this year. But in fact they were defeated. They tell them that the Sandinistas are communists and that communism will take away

their religion and their sons. The Contras put a terrible fear into
the people. There is collaboration, but it is forced. My work is
to fight the political backwardness and the lies, and to persuade
people that man is not on earth just to work, but for something
more.

Within a month of his arrival the school had reopened. Moisés
reported proudly that villagers had attended a meeting of the farmers' union and complained bitterly that the activities of the Contras
were preventing them working in peace in their fields. They
demanded action from the Frente to get the Contras out. But the
ambiguities remained – as he knew only too well:

> People are half with the enemy but we now have a political power
> in the zone. We got forty-two people to go and cut coffee. That
> was a big change. The community is doing communal work like
> tackling the drinking water. They've been making chairs and
> tables for the children at school.

It had been a mistake of the Frente in Condega that they had
neglected places like El Jocote, he admitted. But would his salvage
operation be sufficient? As a result of a drop in support from subsistence farmers, the Government had decided to shift the emphasis
of land reforms away from co-operative farming and give more
farmers land for individual cultivation. Prices for beans and rice
were increased to stimulate production. It was depressing, though,
to think that as fast as the Sandinistas made friends in such places,
the effect of the economic crisis and the war in Nicaragua threatened
to undo his work. Condega had no money to bring material benefits
to El Jocote – a health centre, for example, new housing, clean
water – and it was these reforms that would most convince the
campesinos that the Sandinistas were their friends.

10.   A tale of two priests

Religion and the revolution

Unlike the Eastern bloc states with which Nicaragua is so often erroneously linked in the Western press, the history of the Sandinista Revolution is one of close collaboration between revolutionaries and Christians, in particular those of the dominant Catholic faith. Liberation theology, not marxism, was the popular ideology of the revolution. It was the idea of Christian struggle against injustice that inspired people to come onto the streets and risk their lives, not a socialist blueprint.

The Sandinista leaders see no contradiction between Christianity and revolution. The new Government came into office pledging total religious freedom:

> We affirm that our experience shows that when Christians, motivated by their faith, are capable of responding to the needs of the people and history, their beliefs drive them to revolutionary activity. Our experience has shown that there is no irreconcilable contradiction between the two.
>
> No one is to be discriminated against in the new Nicaragua for publicly professing or propagating his or her religious beliefs. Those who do not have a religious faith also have this right.
>
> For the revolutionary state religion is a personal matter, the responsibility of the individuals, churches and the associations that are organized for religious purposes. The revolutionary state, like every modern state, is a secular state and cannot adopt any religion because it is the representative of all the people, believers as well as non-believers.[1]

Today there is no monolithic view on religion within Nicaragua or within the FSLN. The party contains people of varying opinions. The National Directorate supports a middle course of mixed economy, political pluralism and non-alignment. And although it contains some people who hold an orthodox marxist view of religion as a reactionary force, these are in a minority. Even the few marxists on the National Directorate are split on the question. Those who disapprove of religion keep their mouths shut. Other marxists expect that the country's development will gradually reduce the relevance of religion.[2]

In Condega I came across no marxists, but plenty of Christian Sandinistas. The Catholic church is still one of the busiest buildings in the town. On Sundays the cheerful hymns of a specially written Peasant Mass, commemorating God as the God of the poor, can be heard all around the square. On the great religious festivals, such as Easter, people come into the town from miles around to take part in the traditional celebrations. Colourful processions go on all week: old men solemnly bearing larger-than-life statues of the Madonna and Christ (who is considerately given a peasant stetson to shade his head from the sun). Little shrines are erected on every street corner and the procession stops at each one to pray.

Most of those who began their political lives in the 1970s as young members of Christian base groups are now leading cadres in the organizations of the revolution – working in education, in the CDS, in agriculture or as party officials. In the Centeno family the five who were lay preachers have done precisely that. For Luisa this does not mean she has dropped Christianity.

> I am as committed a Christian as before. I love the bible. I always have. It wasn't a political thing, though I saw its relevance to the political situation we were in. I can't attend services as I did before because my duties in the revolution take up most of my time. But I'm as committed as before.

Some Christians, people like Don Antonio for example, are troubled by the Church hierarchy's attacks on the revolution, which for them is giving the poor of Nicaragua their first opportunity for improvement. They have reacted by abstaining from religious practice.

Other Sandinistas are both active churchgoers and active Sandinistas. Sixteen-year-old Karina, Don Antonio's grand-daughter, is a very active Christian.

> I put the revolution and religion on an equal level. Religion teaches you to think about your neighbour and help your neighbour. It also teaches you to work with the revolution because the revolution is for everyone. There is no contradiction between the two.
> Some of my friends say that I shouldn't be so active in the Church if I am a young Sandinista and that the Church is

reactionary. But I want to do both. But these days you hardly see young people in church. Sometimes I can't attend, either, when there are Frente meetings.

Father Enrique

Father Enrique Oggier became parish priest of Condega in 1983. He is about thirty; a tall, slim Argentinian who goes about in jeans and t-shirts. He is a popular figure, unequivocal in his support of the Nicaraguan Revolution. His last post was Mexico. Nicaragua, he feels, is tackling the problems that Mexico has to live with. He believes that many of Nicaragua's foreign-born priests in this region feel as he does. 'The revolution encourages churchmen to be involved. The people are still very religious. My role is to encourage them to face life's pressures. We try and bring something to the revolution.'

He is a regular guest on the platform at CDS and public meetings of the town. He observes his parishioners closely. 'There's still a great lack of consciousness, but slowly the message is getting through.' The spirit with which the *campesinos* face up to adversity seems to be almost a source of religious inspiration to him. The war has brought a new emphasis to his work. Refugees displaced by the war from rural communities are a special concern; looking after the morale of the families of the bereaved is another.

Not every town or village in Nicaragua has a Catholic priest as committed as Enrique. Many have kept their distance from the revolution and continue to minister to their congregation in a traditional manner. There is no doubt that his identification with the process of change has made him into a potential target for the Contras. The army and the militias are usually informed when he intends to make a trip into the countryside, so that they can provide some protection. He had been told to avoid places like El Jocote.

There and in other nearby hamlets, fundamentalist sects had made inroads into what was previously an overwhelmingly Catholic population. (The proportion of Protestants in Nicaragua now stands at between 15 and 25 per cent of the population.)

Father Enrique agreed to let me accompany him on one of his journeys into the mountains. We left Condega at half past seven in the morning, with Father Enrique's pick-up truck full of people who wanted a lift. Parishioners in Canta Gallo had asked Father Enrique to hold a Mass in memory of two people who had died. Our destination was the co-operative of San Jeronimo – the place where Moisés Córdoba and Omar Cabezas had recruited _campesinos_ to the Frente. Only a year before, inhabitants had been driven from their homes by Contras who destroyed five villages and left over 900 homeless; some of the refugees were travelling with us in the truck. I had been there before with Mónica, the _Barricada_ reporter.

Spluttering and choking, the overloaded truck reached the top of the mountain. It reminded me of a Swiss or Austrian landscape, with steep hills covered with pine forest and a few wooden chalets. Through the mist and the pine trees we could see land cleared for new homes. A few structures had gone up, their white corrugated zinc roofs glistening in the half-light. There was no sign of any construction work going on – labour is in short supply. As we drove on, Pedro, one of the refugees, pointed to the places where the Contras had laid ambushes. We drove fast.

A man ran out of the cloud and motioned us towards a little shack emerging from swirls of white fog. It was new, its walls made of narrow tree branches tied together. The roof was incomplete. Someone had set up a table outside and pinned a piece of paper to the branches: 'To the memory of our beloved mama.' A wreath of dried flowers was pinned onto the middle. This was where the service was to be held.

Father Enrique was not used to rain and cold, so I lent him my plastic raincoat while we waited for a congregation. He chatted to the militia men who had been allocated to look after him. These were members of the co-operative – the rifles on their shoulders and magazine belts round their chests are normal dress in these parts. Most of their colleagues were off patrolling the surrounding forests.

The priest fished out a brass cross and a couple of biscuit tins from a string bag. Someone brought a jam jar full of water. They were placed on the table alongside a solitary vase of flowers. Enrique's assistant – a lay preacher who works as a chemist – placed a pile of newspapers on the table. _Tayacán_ is a religious magazine which uses cartoons to tell bible stories and gives news of the progress of the revolution. Though many _campesinos_ attended literacy classes, they get little practice, so the magazine is popular.

With rain now beating down on the group, the militia men fixed up a veranda for the congregation, using corrugated iron and tree trunks. Through the mist people were arriving from the settlement. They were all women, clutching babies in their arms, with toddlers clinging to their legs. Many of the children had colds and runny noses, and many were in rags – testimony to the speed with which the people had been forced out of their homes by the Contras. One or two had woollens which looked like second-hand cardigans donated by some charity. Most women wore thin dresses and plastic flip-flops – woefully inadequate for the mountain climate.

Enrique had abandoned my raincoat for his long white robes, his old jeans poking out underneath. His words were simple and direct: 'We are here today accompanied by the rain and the cold and the comrades round about defending us. . . .' The tunes of the peasant Mass were familiar to all present. The children sang out too. People began to cheer up. The congregation grew.

> Jesus died not in his bed, but was crucified for his people because the Roman imperialists decided to kill him for what he was doing. . . . Jesus is our liberator. He encourages us in these difficult moments. . . . We must work to unite our people and our communities so we can fight better. . . .

Children gazed wide-eyed at the priest as he took the round wafers from a biscuit tin and laid them on tongues. A volunteer read the lesson and the congregation waited patiently while he struggled with the words. Prayers were dedicated to those who had died defending their country, to the mothers of boys doing military service, to the comrades building houses and to those defending them. The service broke up with people smiling and chatting excitedly. Many wanted Enrique's opinion on their problems. Quite a few had turned up hoping for a lift in his truck down the mountain.

A second Mass was held further down the mountain in Darailí. It was in memory of a twenty-two-year-old who had shot himself in remorse after accidentally killing his best friend. Accidents are frequent in these communities where virtually every man or boy over thirteen is armed.

Little benches had been set up outside the shack but were abandoned in favour of the warm communal kitchen inside. In a corner wood burnt in a clay oven. More woman and children crammed into the space, their long dark hair swept into clasps at the back of their necks, crucifixes prominent, babies suckling at their breasts: this time some babies were to be christened with water from a jam jar. Enrique's white robe and blond features were in strong contrast to their dark skins and black hair. Two serious young lay preachers were present. They were invited to express their opinion on a biblical point. Their explanations were long and rambling.

But theoretical points seemed unimportant to the congregation. What mattered was the ceremony and the atmosphere. Enrique himself confesses that not many of the people really understand what he says. A plate of hot stew was placed into our hands before we left. On the way back down to Condega we passed one of the lay preachers walking the twelve miles home on foot.

At the crossroads on the Pan American Highway stood the same group of twenty-five people sheltering from the sun that we had passed on the way up. They had been there for six hours waiting for a bus. Enrique said he would go back and pick them up; he is one of the few people with a vehicle and access to petrol, he explained – just the slightest hint of despair in his voice.

Liberation theology

People like Father Enrique are the product of a revolution in the Church in Latin America that began in the 1960s. It produced a generation of priests and theologians without whose contribution the Somoza dynasty might well still be in power.

In Nicaragua Catholicism took root in its own specific way. The first Catholic missionaries to arrive in the continent came with the colonialists from Spain in the sixteenth century. Their purpose was to bring European values and religious beliefs to the indigenous peoples they considered 'uncivilized' – an inherent part of the colonization process. But the nature of the terrain made it impossible for their influence to penetrate fully into the most remote and isolated areas.

The urban-based Church hierarchies lived and worked amongst the rulers and colonialists, and later the small middle class of the towns. Here they became well entrenched and built the fine cathedrals and churches which still stand in Nicaragua's old cities: León, Granada and Managua.

The rural priests worked in a different atmosphere. Unlike other, more prosperous areas of Latin America, Nicaragua did not have a strong or wealthy indigenous ruling class, capable of financing the institutional church in the countryside. By comparison with Mexico or Argentina, the big landowners lived modestly. With the gradual transformation of Nicaragua into a large capital export farm for the USA, its owners tended to spend their time in the cities or abroad. The countryside remained sparsely-populated and poverty-stricken.

Even now there are only eighteen inhabitants per square kilometre.

Though the Nicaraguan peasant is profoundly religious, the expression of his faith is not very institutionally-orientated. Contact with the Catholic clergy is infrequent. Around Condega, even today, the small communities probably only see the priest twice a year. Because of this, Catholicism revolves around the celebration of Christian rituals, almost as a continuation of old indian rituals, based firmly in the agricultural seasons. In Condega people would leave to find seasonal work in October and return in December to buy clothes. Just after Christmas they would leave to cut coffee until the end of March. The traditional Holy Week celebrations would coincide with the end of the coffee harvest.

Catholicism in the countryside reproduced itself as part of the culture of the people, working through the family and small community, rather than through the ecclesiastical apparatus. The priests were aloof and remote figures, traditionally perceived as part of the authorities of the countryside.[3]

People like Don Antonio Centeno in Condega now feel ashamed of the respect they were taught to have towards the figure of the priest:

> The priests were robbers. They would charge people for Mass;
> they owned land, they could afford to keep a car, they were on
> good terms with the Guardia. Now that I have begun to
> understand the bible, I can see that our biggest enemy was those
> priests. Even though I am a Christian and believe in God, I can
> say that the Church was perverse because they kept the people
> fooled and made money out of the people's unhappiness.

Elsewhere in Latin America, however, poverty amongst the peasantry and urban masses began in the 1960s to awaken the attention of some Catholic priests and theologians. Many of them were recent arrivals from Europe. They were influenced by mass protests and liberation struggles in other parts of the world.

The result of this new awakening was the movement which has been called liberation theology. It was officially endorsed at the Latin American Catholic Bishops' Conference in Medellín, Columbia, in 1968. Medellín produced a blue-print of a socially-committed Church, and shattered the centuries-old alliance of Church, military and the rich elites. Announcing the conference, Pope Paul said 'we wish to personify the Christ of a poor and hungry people.'

The conference stressed two crucial elements; liberation (in the biblical sense of physical and spiritual salvation) and participation. Participation was to be encouraged by the formation of Christian grass-roots communities, which would bring together smaller groups of people with more similar backgrounds and aspirations than had been the case with the old heterogeneous parish. They would come from the poor people themselves, with lay preachers assuming many of the responsibilities of the priest for catechism classes. Community members would help each other out in life, sharing material, as well as spiritual resources.

In Nicaragua not all Catholics embraced the new philosophy with equal enthusiasm. The Church hierarchy lived comfortably alongside the Somoza dictatorship. In a moment of enthusiasm the Archbishop of Managua once even pronounced the first Somoza dictator 'head of the Church' after his assassination in 1956. The injustices, lack of liberty and constant repression imposed by his son, Anastasio Somoza Debayle, seldom came in for formal criticism. The attitude of the bishops was equivocal and respectful. Somoza's electoral frauds and massacres were never condemned as openly or plainly as were the actions of the FSLN. The massacre of FSLN members at Pancasán in 1967 was excused by the auxiliary Bishop of Managua on the grounds that 'they were communists'.[4]

But there were a growing number of exceptions to this situation. Missionaries responded to Medellín by attempting to help with education, medicine and social work – activities seldom tackled by Somoza's state. The Bishop of Estelí was also sympathetic to the new role of the Church. And his was the diocese that Father Wésther López joined in 1973 to take up the position as parish priest of Condega.

Father Wésther López

Father Wésther López was the man who started the Christian base groups at which the Centenos began to question the social relations in the town. He trained a whole layer of lay preachers who went out to encourage the _campesinos_. He denounced the activities of the National Guard from his pulpit. When the town of Estelí erupted in insurrection in 1978, he opened the doors of his presbytery to look after the wounded. During the 1979 Revolution he helped bring in food for those stranded, and at the end acted as a mediator to enable members of the National Guard to surrender their weapons and leave Nicaragua.

I found him in a nearby town, Pueblo Nuevo, where he had been parish priest since 1983. I was ushered into the presbytery by a serious, balding man in his forties, looking older than I had expected. He had a matter-of-fact manner, speaking quickly and eloquently. We began by talking about 1973, the year he took over the Condega parish.

> What influenced me more than anything were the events in the country. The situation of oppression, the dictatorship, the lack of freedom, the poverty. We were living in a situation of economic exploitation. The dictatorship exerted a huge force through the army, the National Guard, There was strong repression in the countryside. We couldn't hold any type of protest against the oppression or the exploitation of the regime because we would immediately be labelled as communists or supporters of subversion.
>
> In the diocese of Estelí our mission was to find the salvation and liberation of all aspects of man – economic, political, social, cultural and religious. We worked to raise consciousness and educate people, and to get them to commit themselves, with the lay preachers, to fight against the dicatorship.
>
> We used to hold weekly seminars and meetings. All types of people came, youth, women, men from the ages of seventeen to sixty. Christians were becoming conscious of the need for change, the need to fight for the transformation of the country.
>
> In Condega the local elite really had no education or theoretical training. There weren't really any bourgeois people there. I had practically nothing to do with the people who owned land and firms. They criticized my work constantly. They didn't like it and didn't agree.

As the work of lay preachers expanded into the rural areas during 1974 and 1975, often linked to the fledgling cells of the FSLN, Wésther López found himself drawn into the struggle against Somoza. His reputation for courage and commitment in Condega is almost legendary.

> Politically we were in a state of effervescence. People were beginning to be conscious. They worked clandestinely in their neighbourhood or in rural communities. You could feel the effects of this work with the peasants. It was waking them up and making them conscious that they had to fight against the dictatorship of Somoza.

Though he supported the work of the FSLN, Father Wésther López drew back from joining the organization.

> They asked me several times to join – even one of the commanders asked me. I told him No, I could develop my mission more freely in the Church, through the sermons, training courses, education groups. I didn't want a commitment to the Frente that would limit my pastoral work. I collaborated not directly with the Frente, but on the side of the people, working with the people so that they would fight.

Elsewhere other priests took a different stance. Father Fernando Cardenal, a Trappist priest and Vice-Rector of the University of Central America in Managua, did not hesitate to join the FSLN, as he subsequently wrote:

> I immediately thought of the parable of the Good Samaritan and it struck me as obvious that I couldn't be like that priest and Levite who passed by the sick man on the other side of the street. The Samaritans of Nicaragua were asking me to help them take care of our wounded people and in my Christian faith I found only one answer – to agree. I continued working with the students, giving the spiritual exercises, directing courses and keeping my position as Philosophy Professor in the Autonomous National University of Managua (UNAN), but all the while collaborating secretly with the FSLN in its struggle for national liberation.[5]

Fernando Cardenal went on to become Minister of Education in the Sandinista Government.

One of Wésther López's lay delegates in Condega was an eighteen-year-old student at the Institute who hoped to enter the priesthood, Ermen Rodriguez, now the mayor of Condega (see Chapter 15). At the time he trained other lay delegates for the work in the communities, whilst being constantly on the look-out for potential recruits to the Frente.

> We would start with a biblical text and conclude in the present. For example in the bible it says that Moses saved his people from slavery. 'Well comrades here we are, living just such an exodus. Already many people have started to go on this exodus. We are here, working, studying. Others are only half-eating, hungry. Others are being tortured in prison. The exodus has started. The people are enslaved. Someone has to come forth and

unite us and fight for the liberation of those who are oppressed –
that's you and I. In those days Moses came forth. Today there
is no Moses, but there is something. It is an organization which
started in the 1960s with the aim of liberating the people. It is
the FSLN.'

People would come to the grass-roots meetings and listen. They
saw more truth and objectivity in that, than what they heard
on the radio, the official voice of the Republic. So word got
around. This person brought another along. He got enthusiastic
and brought another. Little by little it grew until they would
organize to send people out to the mountains and organize and
take up arms,

In a community we, the lay delegates, would find out which
young person had the most leadership qualities and then we'd
invite him to a meeting. We never violated Christian principles.
I mean as Christians we started to talk and as Christians we had
an understanding with people and as Christians they threw
themselves into the struggle and were capable of dying in that
same struggle. As Christians they identified the cause of the
suffering and what was the best action for the poor to take.

The attitude of the Catholic hierarchy remained hostile to the
Sandinistas during much of this period. The turning point, however,
came with Somoza's state of siege, imposed in 1975. With thousands
of *campesinos* disappearing from the northern mountains, Father
Fernando Cardenal went to Washington in 1976 to report to Congress
on violations of human rights in Nicaragua. He outlined a series of
atrocities ranging from murder to torture, rape and arbitrary arrest.
He pointed to the existence of concentration camps set up by the
National Guard.[6] On several estimates the number who had died
was around three thousand.[7]

Cardenal's testimony was followed by a report from American
Capuchin priests based in Estelí and Bluefields. They had travelled
from village to village on foot and by donkey, and gave a list of
atrocities committed by the National Guard. These included beating,
extraction of teeth, electric shocks, rape of women, mutilation of
faces with knives, making a person swallow a button with a string
on it, while the accuser pulled on the string. *Campesinos'* homes had
been burnt down, infants and old people killed, and their land,
livestock and crops distributed among officers of the National
Guard.[8]

The Nicaraguan Church hierarchy could stay silent no longer. On

New Year's Day 1977 they issued a pastoral letter which was read from all pulpits in the country and then distributed in duplicated form to get past censorship of the press. It condemned the 'state of terror' in the countryside and called for the right to live and work, for the return of civil rights, due process of law for criminal and political offenders and freedom, justice and equality.[9]

Partly as a result of this, Somoza, who had enjoyed the backing of most US government departments both for his internal policies and his intervention in neighbouring states, began to incur criticism in the USA. President Carter had come into office, pledging to improve human rights. In September 1977, amid continuing reports of atrocities and murders, Somoza agreed to lift the state of emergency or risk losing military aid.

More importantly the Church hierarchy's statement, weak as it was, symbolized the growing disenchantment of the Nicaraguan middle class, and even sections of the business class, with Somoza. It was their defection, together with a bold plan of military action by a section of the FSLN, that was to put the last nails in the coffin of the Somoza dictatorship.

The view from Pueblo Nuevo

Unlike Father Enrique in Condega, Father Wésther López did not appear to be playing an active role in support of the Sandinistas in Pueblo Nuevo. (Pueblo Nuevo is a cattle-ranching area the other side of the Pan-American Highway from Condega, geographically and historically somewhat cut off from the mainstream of events.)

The day I arrived there on the back of a farmer's lorry (the only form of transport into the town) the Frente office was deserted apart from one secretary. There was little activity in the town. Father Wésther López confirmed that times were hard for enthusiastic Sandinistas.

> I have only been here for a while but I have noticed there's an attitude of rejection of the Frente and the Government here. The majority don't want to know.
>
> I think it's because people have not received what they were expecting. It's a crisis situation, the war, so much suffering, the problem of military service, the shortages, the price rises. People are just not participating.

He was unsure as to whether the rejection of the Frente was due to lack of proper leadership from the authorities, or whether it was a natural consequence of the war:

> People don't want war. They want to work in peace to produce their necessities. They don't want any more kidnappings, deaths, pain and poverty. They say they don't want them [the Frente] to keep taking our boys away to military service and bringing them back in a coffin. And they don't accept it when the Frente offers them flowers or a wreath or whatever.
>
> A lot of children are not being sent to school because people here don't have clothes. They are too expensive. They don't earn enough even to buy sugar. A lot of people are out of work. There are hardly any medicines in the health centre, a shortage of educational material. All of this creates non-conformity in the people. People are without hope, disillusioned.

The difficulties were pushing more people back towards the Church, where they sought a more traditional comfort in religion, said Father Wésther:

> People here attach themselves to the Church, pray for peace a lot, for reconciliation, for a definite solution to the problems. They want to live in peace, they want an end to the many years of war. I try to create a consciousness in people.
>
> The role of the Church is now no longer to find material solutions. We no longer have the problem because the Government is charged with dealing with it. So we dedicate ourselves to our other mission without being ignorant about people's material problems.
>
> On a spiritual level the Church is consolidating itself. People are occupying the Church as a space in their life to discover their own spiritual identity.

Behind Father Wésther's perceptions, I thought I detected a note of disillusion with the course the revolution was taking. He was clearly staying out of politics these days.

The split in the Church

There are at present really two camps in the Catholic Church in Nicaragua. On the one hand, the 'Church of the poor', with the vast mass of ordinary Nicaraguans and many priests. On the other, the Catholic hierarchy. Relations between the Catholic hierarchy and the Sandinista Government have become steadily worse during the last few years.

At the time of the insurrection, the Archbishop of Managua, Obando y Bravo, and the Bishops' Conference welcomed the new Government with a pastoral letter, saying:

> We are confident that our revolutionary process will be something original, creative, truly Nicaraguan and in no sense imitative. . . . What we seek is a process that will result in a society completely and truly Nicaraguan, one that is not capitalist, nor dependent, nor totalitarian.[10]

Four Sandinista priests took positions in the new Government. The Maryknoll, Father Miguel D'Escoto, became Minister of Foreign Affairs, the poet Father Ernesto Cardenal became Minister of Culture, Father Edgard Parrales became Minister of Social Welfare (he is now Ambassador to the Organization of American States). Father Fernando Cardenal became Minister of Education, and ran the literacy campaign.

Today the support of the Nicaraguan bishops has waned. This change began with the literacy campaign, which they condemned as political indoctrination. Later they expressed fears about atheism and totalitarian rule. They criticized the 'popular' Church and its Christian base groups. Their criticisms were reinforced by the Pope during his visit to Nicaragua in 1983. He stunned Nicaraguans by attacking the Sandinistas and refusing requests to bless the mothers of boys who had died in the war. There was a feeling of great disappointment. 'He was not briefed properly,' was the charitable reaction of Don Antonio in Condega.

It was the hierarchy's attitude towards the military conscription law, introduced in September 1983, that set them on a course of confrontation with the Government. Their subsequent refusal to condemn the Contras made matters worse.

In January 1985 minister-priests were told in a directive from Rome that holding political office was incompatible with their holy orders. Father Fernando Cardenal was expelled from the Jesuits. Thus began a round of worsening relations and retaliatory action by the Church hierarchy and the Government. 'I do not object to being identified with people who have taken up arms,' said the Archbishop Obando y Bravo, speaking to Spanish television on being appointed Cardinal to the Vatican in April 1985. In October of that year he called for reconciliation with the Contras. The Government subsequently closed down the Church's printing press.

In March 1986 the Vice-President of the Bishops' Conference, Bishop Pablo Vega, appeared at a seminar of the right-wing Heritage Foundation attended by leading Contras. Next he was appearing in Washington with Contra leaders trying to win Congressional approval for funding. The Government responded soon after by closing down the Catholic radio station, Radio Católica. In July 1986, after Vega met the military commander of the FDN, he was expelled from Nicaragua 'for political reasons' . . . 'until the war is over'. It followed the expulsion of the editor of Radio Católica and the magazine *Iglesia*, Father Bismarck Carballo, at the end of June. Arriving in Honduras, Vega talked of a 'complete denial of fundamental human rights' in Nicaragua, and compared the present situation with 'the lack of civic participation which happened under the Somoza regime'.

The Sandinistas defended their action on the grounds that the counter-revolution makes use of the Church hierarchy as a major part of its internal offensive. They argue that 'pluralism means that people can criticize, but not destabilize the revolutionary process'.[11]

Bishop Vega, and others like him, are openly hostile to the Government and prepared to call for its overthrow. The word communism is used frequently to describe the Government, but it is never defined or justified. In their vocabulary it is a somewhat loose phrase, signifying 'evil incarnate'. Their hostility focuses on the work of the 'Church of the Poor' and the Christian base groups. These were the very people who began the struggle against Somoza, inspired by liberation theology.

At the end of 1986 a new Church–state dialogue began, assisted by the arrival of a new papal nuncio from Rome, Paolo Giglio. There are some signs of reconciliation, since even Archbishop Obando y Bravo has changed his position, and has criticized US aid to the Contras.

11. Born again

The Reverend Santos Casco

The Reverend Santos Casco lives in some style. His large, modern house, which belongs to the Baptist Church of the Good Samaritan, is reached by a drive which takes callers across a sizeable piece of land. The house and church take up the whole of a block on the outskirts of Condega. Near the house there are trees. Entering up a flight of steps, I suddenly felt as if I was in another country. Like any middle-class suburban home in Britain or the USA, it has a hallway with proper flooring, a fitted kitchen with a working gas cooker, a library and comfortable wicker chairs for visitors. The space is unusual too. Most people you visit in Condega welcome you into a one- or two-roomed wooden shack where the whole family eats, sleeps and lives. Their children cannot disappear into playrooms, so they live on top of the adults at all times. There is no privacy.

I was not expecting to bump into the Reverend in the street – the members of his church had a reputation for refusing to participate in the mass organizations or in communal activities. One of the post office clerks belonged to the church. He often came to work wearing a baseball hat with the slogan 'Christ Saves'. His son had left the country to avoid doing military service.

The Reverend wasn't at home much either. He co-ordinates pastors in several neighbouring towns. Sometimes he goes to Honduras or even to the USA for seminars. The man he meets there most regularly is a US citizen from New Jersey, Robert Tyson, the founder of the Church of the Good Samaritan in Condega, and the man who built the house that Santos Casco lives in. Robert Tyson left the town in July of 1979 and never came back. I rarely got much further than the gate on the several occasions I tried to find the Reverend at home. An old man who behaved like a servant was deputed to tell me I was unlucky. He cheered up a bit when he heard I was British, and uttered a few words in English.

This seemed to have had some effect, because the next time I found the pastor at home. With the bible in his hands, he invited me into the house for an interview. He was a tall, well-built man.

When I dropped in on a service later that day I saw him in action, putting the fear of God into his small congregation with emotional appeals, admonishing gestures, dramatically-delivered warnings, raising his voice one minute, dropping it the next – and all to the accompaniment of a tension-building rhythm on an electric guitar. The man from the post office turned round in the next pew to acknowledge my presence, hopeful perhaps that the message on his hat had got through and that they were about to recruit a new member to the congregation.

But to be received into this Church – one of the plethora of small fundamentalist denominations (some would say sects) that have mushroomed in Nicaragua in the past few years – I would have had to change, repent and follow the bible. As a good Christian, according to this Church, I would have to recognize the contradiction between the Church and the revolution. I would have to break with the 'religious people who say they are Christians but who adapt themselves to adultery, fornication, swearing, alcohol, having three or four wives'.

The bible would tell me not to raise a hand to hit an aggressor. My Christian principles would oblige me to help those wanting to avoid military service. Indeed, as Reverend Santos Casco said, as we sat on wicker chairs in an alcove of his hallway, 'If men feared God, there would be no war in Nicaragua. I have taken Christ into my heart so I have no problem if the Contras arrive at my house.' As a member of the Good Samaritan Baptist Church I would believe that God had prophesied the war and that things will get worse. 'He who does not fall by the bullet will maybe die of hunger,' said the Reverend, who preferred talking in biblical terms: 'It was also prophesied that the Church will suffer,' and he added 'And we do feel psychologically under pressure. If Nicaragua is going towards communism,' he said, 'and maybe it is, it wouldn't be dangerous to me because I'm not going to be a communist.'

The growth of the fundamentalists

The rapid growth of churches such as Assemblies of God, Pentecostals, Jehovah's Witnesses, Baptists and others began in earnest in the 1960s and 1970s, funded and sponsored particularly from the USA. Since the early 1980s the number of churches has mushroomed again. There are now thought to be some half a million adherents, that is some 15–20 per cent of the population, organized in some eighty-five denominations. There are over two thousand pastors and fifteen hundred temples.[1]

The Protestant churches are divided in Nicaragua between those who broadly support the country's transformation and those who see in it the work of the devil. Many Protestants joined in the struggle against Somoza. After the 1972 earthquake, Protestant churches formed a Protestant Committee for Aid and Development (CEPAD) to respond to the desperate situation in Managua. Their disgust at Somoza's personal enrichment from earthquake funds reinforced a commitment to social change. CEPAD continues today as a Protestant relief and development agency and a council of churches, and is in the main supportive of Sandinista reforms. Forty-six of the eighty-five churches are members, including the Moravian church, the Assemblies of God and the mainstream Baptists, who are perhaps the most pro-revolution of all.

But the inherent conservatism of the fundamentalist message and its concentration on the afterlife set many of the Protestant missionaries at odds with the atmosphere of revolutionary Nicaragua. None of the hundred or so US missionaries who worked in Nicaragua before the revolution stayed on. In Condega the missionary Robert Tyson, who had built up a huge congregation of young people in the early 1970s for his Good Samaritan Baptist Church, lost many of them in 1978 and 1979. Santos Casco now has only forty members in his church, though 120 attend services, he says. Orlando Navaretto, Condega's magistrate, was an active lay pastor of the Baptists until the village began to organize to resist Somoza.

> We were involved in a hard struggle here clandestinely, but Tyson recommended that Christians should not get involved in these things. In his sermons he would denounce 'brothers who have got caught up in revolutionary things', and say they were committing a grave sin because 'God did not recommend this. God wants peace. God is love and God doesn't want intrigues between men. The war is a crime and those who go to the mountains assassinating members of the National Army are criminals.' These were the words Robert Tyson used.

The Good Samaritan Baptist Church is not the only conservative evangelical church in Condega. The Pentecostals have built a new church in a *barrio* near the river, and the Assemblies of God, the second-largest denomination in Nicaragua, have a hall not far from the central square. Outside in the rural areas, a number of sects are active, particularly around El Jocote, El Bramadero, Guayucalí and neighbouring hamlets.

Few of these churches belong to CEPAD. Many are part of a rival organization, the National Committee of Protestant Pastors of Nicaragua, CNPEN. It represents 500 to 700 pastors, many of whom make no bones about their hostility to the Sandinistas. When floods drove thousands out of their homes in Managua in 1982, some said it was 'the judgement of God' being wrought on the Sandinistas. They preach against participation in the mass organizations, calling the Sandinista Defence Committees, the CDS, 'the ears of big brother'.

Using US funds, the Assemblies of God – with 60,000 members, the biggest of the denominations and in fact part of CEPAD – set up an agricultural programme in the north. The pastors instructed their members not to sell their products to the Government at the fixed prices set. When sugar ration cards were introduced, some sects advised their members not to accept the cards, which were a sign of the 'apocalyptic beast'. The Assemblies of God in Nicaragua maintain close contact with their international headquarters in Springfield, Missouri. Like the Reverend Santos Casco, they refer constantly to the words of the bible. But it is the conservative, anti-communist ideology of middle America that colours their attitude to social change. Some pastors see the revolution as fulfilling the prophecy of 'the last days'. The Antichrist is represented by the 'atheistic communists' – by which they mean the Sandinistas.

Reverend Santos Casco told me there were very few Christians in Nicaragua. 'There are many religious people,' he said, 'but we are quite different from the religious people. We follow the bible. The bible comes from God.' The ideas of 'the vast majority of people in the revolution are atheist', he said. He said he was on good terms with the authorities and had freedom to preach and worship, but he was unhappy at being associated with the Contras. 'They say we are Contras because we don't adapt. Psychologically we are under pressure. From that I can see that there are people here against the Christians and that there is a contradiction between the Church and the revolution.'

Inevitably, much of the pressure he feels revolves around the touchy subject of military conscription. 'It's logical that we will help those youths who are being pressured to do military service,' he admitted. 'It is a Christian principle that I cannot take up arms. If someone has the same conviction as I, he cannot go to the army – it's in accordance with the bible.'

Several of the churches had attended a meeting in Estelí with

Comandante Pichardo to try to resolve the problem. It ended in stalemate. They were told there could be no exemptions to the draft. Some of the Pentecostal members were detained. The Baptists so far had been left alone.

Why the fundamentalist message should find a foothold in Nicaragua can be attributed to many causes. To the very poor and traditional peasant, cut off from any direct contact with political events, there must be something very reassuring about such a fixed vision of the world in which everything has been foretold, everything has been explained in the bible. In places where news of the Sandinistas' policies reaches the peasants through diffuse sources, rumour and gossip, there must be something very settling and safe in the conservatism of the 'born-again' faith.

Fear of change is reinforced by the propaganda and distortions – even direct lies – of the radio broadcasts funded by the CIA, which beam directly into their homes. In isolated places people have little direct knowledge with which to counteract such impressions. Another factor lies undoubtedly in the growing economic problems. After the food subsidies were cut, price rises in basic food products coincided with shortages of supply and rocketing prices for clothing, shoes and any imported goods – an alarming prospect for the small farmer on a monthly trip to the market. In places where the Sandinistas have political roots and a physical presence, there are constant efforts to explain the causes of the economic crisis. In more remote places, the explanations of Sandinista officials during their weekly visits would fall on deaf ears.

Reagan's evangelists

Undoubtedly, however, one of the primary reasons for the mushrooming of the fundamentalists in Nicaragua is the concerted effort being made in the USA to send preachers there. They are directly financed by the headquarters of their churches in the USA. The proceeds of a Sunday collection at a church in the Mid-West are equivalent to a small fortune in Nicaragua.

Under the Reagan administration there has been some careful nurturing of evangelical missions whose message coincides with the White House's own view of the world. The interest of the authorities in religion in Central America dates back to 1969, when the Rockefeller mission reported on the rise of liberation theology and suggested that support for some of the Protestant churches might undermine its influence.

In 1980 a conservative 'think-tank', the Council for Inter-American Security, produced what is known as the Santa Fé Document. Attacking liberation theology, it accuses 'Marxist-Leninist forces' of using the Church 'as a political weapon against private property and productive capitalism', by 'infiltrating the religious community with ideas that are less Christian than Communist'. US foreign policy, the document says, 'must begin to counter liberation theology as it is utilized in Latin America by "liberation theology clergy" '.[2]

In response, $500,000 was made available to neo-conservatives and evangelicals with links to the administration for the creation of an Institute for Religion and Democracy. Their publications were aimed at discrediting and blackening the name of progressive churches, including the World Council of Churches, who criticized US policy in Central America. Within US evangelical churches they moved to prevent progressive Christians in Latin America receiving funds. In line with the administration's view of the world, which looks at any independence struggles through the prism of an East–West conflict, the Institute set out to carry this through into religion.[3]

In 1983 the White House hosted a meeting of Latin American pastors to urge support for the administration's Central America policy. Kerry Ptacek, of the Institute for Religion and Democracy, was invited to give the keynote speech, and denounced the 'communist corruption of our churches, particularly in Nicaragua'.[4] In Nicaragua the US Government created a new post at its embassy: Secretary for Religious Affairs.

In 1985 and 1986 Conservative 'born-agains' were amongst those who lobbied Congress for funds for the Contras. Meanwhile, right-wing conservatives were adding their donations to those raised by US fundamentalist churches to finance the work of pastors on the ground. From Costa Rica the Institute of Basic Evangelism sends out monthly payments to 600 evangelical pastors. Reverend Santos Casco and his fellow pastors in the north receive monthly payments sent from Honduras. Orlando Navaretto said that in the 1970s every pastor received $150 a month, the lay deacons $40. 'All pastors of evangelical churches receive dollars. We know because of the cheques that come in. These churches would not exist were it not for the finance – to maintain vehicles, etc. And also the pastors benefit by receiving a tenth of everyone's income.'

The Government of Nicaragua has refused to give official recognition to churches which are controlled financially from the USA, and this applies to most of those in the CNPEN.

It is a fact that the communities around Condega where there are the most sects are also the places where there are the most Contras. It is hard for the Sandinistas not to draw their own conclusions. Ermen Rodriguez, of the *junta* in Condega, said that about six pastors in the area had actually joined the Contras – somewhat making a mockery of the pacifism preached. He could not give me names.

> At first these churches were just in the town and now they have spread throughout the rural communities. People say to me: 'But the pastor came and told us it's forbidden to take up arms, forbidden to defend the patria because if we defend it we are making communism.' So the people have no defence. In all our frontier communities they are doing this work, creating a social base for the Contras. And they generate a situation where people no longer want to come into Condega to consult people to resolve a problem, neither do they participate in the meetings when we go there to explain why there is a certain situation. This work is first of all done by the evangelicals and then reinforced by the arms of the Contras, and the next thing is we have to have a soldier to accompany us because it's too dangerous to go around by ourselves. And when they see the guns it's as if they are seeing the devil.

The FSLN political secretary in the region, Agustín Lara, concurred:

> It's not that all the groups are instruments. But we know that there are among these groups forms of clandestine organization which aim at creating a receptivity to the counter-revolutionary plans. It's difficult to pin it down to specific sects. Rather it's within the sect that there is this type of activity.

During the state of emergency, many pastors were asked to report for interviews with State Security, and others were arrested for short periods. But there is no attempt by the authorities to clamp down on the religious activities of the evangelicals. Freedom to profess religious faith is one of the tenets of the revolution. Any departure from it would bring upon the Sandinistas a hail of international condemnation.

For the Reverend Santos Casco, however, the charge of persecution had become central to his faith. 'It was prophesied in the bible that the Church will suffer,' he said. 'I am prepared.'

12. Uniting the people

The closure of *La Prensa*

Imagine Britain under threat of full-scale invasion. A foreign power is openly calling for the removal of the democratically elected government whose policies they oppose. To achieve this they have hired a mercenary force in Britain to destroy bridges and communications, sabotage food production, and mine ports.

The country is on a war footing. National service has had to be introduced and is unpopular. Casualty figures are high. Hundreds of thousands of people have died, most of them in the fighting between mercenaries and soldiers. Thousands of the dead are civilians, murdered in terrorist attacks by the mercenaries.

But the foreign power has an ally amongst the British press. The *Daily Bugle* is hostile to the British government and carries article after article attacking its policies and blaming it for the country's economic crisis. While the foreign power prepares to authorize a new round of funding for the mercenaries, the editor of the *Daily Bugle* arrives in its capital city to add his voice. He is given a column of a leading newspaper to set out his reasons for backing the mercenaries. The foreign power decides to give $100 million to the mercenaries. It means they can purchase the latest weaponry and step up their attacks on Britain.

Would you be surprised if subsequently the British government suspended publication of the *Daily Bugle*?

La Prensa, in the 1970s a long-standing opponent of the Somoza dictatorship, had in the 1980s become a mouthpiece for the right-wing opposition to the Sandinistas. It was the recipient of funds from US pro-Government sources and in 1986 lobbied US Congressmen to approve a grant of $100 million for the Contras.

In the run-up to the vote in Congress the Editor of *La Prensa*, Jaime Chamorro, wrote in the *Washington Post*:

> Those Nicaraguans who are fighting for democracy have the right to ask for help wherever they can get it. Those who argue that

to give aid to the Nicaraguan rebels would be a violation of the principle of a people's right to self-determination are mistaken [since] self-determination applies to peoples, not oppressive governments that do not legitimately represent the will of the people.[1]

When the Nicaraguan Government announced the closure of *La Prensa* on 27 June 1986, there were howls of condemnation and accusations of censorship from a wide section of liberal opinion outside Nicaragua. In Condega, however, people took a more sanguine view. When lives are being lost in war, a free press seems more like an expendable luxury than an article of faith.

The hypothetical British analogy may seem far-fetched. But to the Sandinistas the threat which Nicaragua faces from the USA is experienced in just those terms. By February 1987 a total of 19,553 Nicaraguans had died in the war. Over 12,000 of the dead were Contras, and some 5,000 'people's fighters'. On the basis of these figures, more than two thousand civilians had died. Together with the wounded and kidnapped, the total number of war casualties was over 37,500 – or 1.25 per cent of the country's population.[2]

The Government's response – a state of emergency, censorship and now the closure of *La Prensa* – is to many regrettable, but understandable. It is no more than any other government at war would have done in the same circumstances. There was opposition to the closure of *La Prensa* even within the Sandinista camp. Perhaps as a result, President Ortega offered to lift the suspension if the owners of *La Prensa* 'adjust their behavior within the legal institutional framework and break their links with those who run and finance the war of aggression against the Nicaraguan nation'. The offer was rejected.[3]

Henry Vargas and the older generation

People in Condega are not blind to the dangers of censorship. The man who perhaps knows most about it is Don Henry Vargas, who worked for *La Prensa* as a reporter when censorship was routinely practised by Somoza's regime. Despite the paper's firm opposition to Somoza in his last year, its owners' support for the Sandinistas in government was short-lived. When in 1980 the paper moved sharply to the right, Henry Vargas and the bulk of the reporters broke away to form a new daily newspaper, *Nuevo Diario*, in sympathy with the revolution. It is a job he still holds today.

It was impossible to avoid meeting Henry Vargas in Condega. I had first noticed him at the funerals taking photos with a tiny camera, and took him for an amateur. He was a thick-set man with a kindly face, and I judged him to be in his late fifties. From then on, whenever something was happening in the town, I would find Don Henry there before me.

His job takes him all over the north, reporting. One of his biggest problems is getting his hands on photographic material. In order to save newsprint his newspaper has had to cut down on the number of pages it prints. Unlike most press photographers, he has only one or two 'takes' of every photo that the paper might need, because of the shortage of film. He looked enviously at my fancy modern Minolta camera. Whenever I met him after that, I felt somewhat guilty about the abundance of film at my disposal.

I managed to catch him in one evening and he welcomed me enthusiastically to his brick house near the central square. He showed me his garage, which had been converted into an office. This was where he had stored medicines and supplies on behalf of the defence committees in 1978. He is in no sense a young radical, being one of the most respected 'elders' of the town. He doesn't say much, but he observes – and brooks no fools. He is not uncritical of the authorities, particularly local officials, whose decisions sometimes exasperate him. But then he is from a much older generation. He puts a lot down to inexperience and immaturity. He is sensitive to the mood in the town and quick to follow up complaints of corruption.

1977: *La Prensa* and the Twelve

Though Don Henry and *La Prensa* have now gone their separate ways, the story of their support for the opposition to Somoza in the late 1970s has many parallels. It illustrates a key factor that enabled the Sandinistas to secure Somoza's fall – the unity, behind the Sandinistas, of the middle class, sections of the business class and the mass of impoverished urban youth and working people in the *barrios*. *La Prensa* played a key role in cementing this alliance. At that time it was owned and edited by Pedro Joaquín Chamorro, a member of a leading Conservative Party family, and the man who led the 1967 demonstration opposing Somoza's presidency.

When he was _La Prensa_'s reporter in Condega, Don Henry worked closely with Father Wésther López as a lay delegate in the rural areas. It took the National Guard some time to suspect that this innocent-looking man was part of a growing network of ordinary people who could foresee an end to the dictatorship.

The autumn of 1977 was a crucial time in bringing about the alliance. The FSLN's work was much weakened by the effect of the state of emergency and the reprisals against the _campesinos_ around Condega (see Chapters 9 and 10). Luisa Centeno, for example, had lost contact with the organization. Her family was split up between those in exile in Mexico and those who had stayed. Her father, Don Antonio, remembers the atmosphere in the town: 'We didn't like the situation, but we could only be silent. Nothing else. We didn't get involved.'

Deaths had reduced the leading cadres of the Frente from twelve to six. The FSLN itself was divided into three tendencies. Those members, like Omar Cabezas, who continued to believe in 'prolonged popular war' and a slow build-up of peasant support in the mountains were now effectively isolated from developments in the towns and the new militancy of industrial workers.

In September 1977 pressure from the Catholic hierarchy and US President Carter forced Somoza to lift the state of emergency. There was an explosion of working-class protest in the _barrios_ of the major towns, given full coverage in _La Prensa_. The 'proletarian tendency' of the FSLN was active in the big towns. They saw the dispossessed and landless urban peasants as the new vanguard and placed a premium on the creation of a marxist–leninist-style party to lead an insurrection in the towns. Their programme went further than the other tendencies, demanding nationalization of basic industry and wide-reaching collectivization of the land.[4]

With the lifting of press censorship, _La Prensa_ published full details of the peasant massacres that had taken place during the emergency, giving considerable coverage to the growing opposition to Somoza within the business class. Chamorro himself became the leader of the middle-class opposition to the dictatorship.

Reporters like Don Henry began to be carefully watched. He showed me the barracks where the National Guard had their head-quarters. It was within a stone's throw of his house. 'When things got hot, I came under pressure from the Guardia and their spies who suggested it would be much better for me if I supported them.'

The turning-point came in October. On the twelfth the paper reported three daring armed FSLN attacks on National Guard targets in different parts of the country, one of them in nearby Ocotal. These attacks were the work of yet another faction in the FSLN, the Insurrectionals, and demonstrated that the Sandinistas were far from being eliminated.

As if in confirmation, the following week the paper published a statement by a group of twelve prominent Nicaraguan professionals living in exile: 'For more than a decade, the FSLN and the blood spilt by so many young people are the best testimony to the permanence and the presence of this struggle, carried out with an ever-greater degree of political maturity.' They added that there could be no solution to the crisis in the country without the full participation of the FSLN. The explosive declaration was signed by two lawyers, two businessmen, two priests (Fernando Cardenal and Miguel D'Escoto), an academic, a writer (Sergio Ramírez), an agronomist, an architect, a banker (Arturo Cruz) and a dentist. They became known as Los Doce, the Twelve. (Many of the group are now ministers in the Sandinista Government.)

The next day Chamorro's paper went even further. It reported the existence of fifty FSLN training camps, attributing the report to Humberto Ortega, an 'Insurrectional' FSLN leader (now Minister of Defence).

The Insurrectional Tendency, formed by Sandinistas in exile, was to prove the most decisive for the growth of the FSLN and its ability to unite whole sections of the Nicaraguan population around the FSLN banner. Noting the growth of the middle-class opposition to the Somoza dictatorship – from professionals, from Catholic activists, and even in business sectors – the Insurrectional Tendency argued for a tactical alliance with such sectors behind a strategy of insurrection. They were confident that the masses could be galvanized into insurrection by the example of decisive and successful military action from the vanguard. They aimed at mobilizing support from neighbouring countries: an important factor which increased their standing.

1978: Chamorro's death and the United People's Movement

Within three months Chamorro was murdered – gunned down on his way to work on 10 January 1978. Suspicion focused on Somoza. But the plan to break the opposition by eliminating its most respected representative back-fired. Chamorro's murder succeeded in uniting the opposition as never before.[5] Nicaragua exploded in an outburst of popular anger. Somoza businesses were burnt to the ground; banks, finance houses, factories went up in flames. Spontaneous strikes turned into a general strike. The Sandinistas launched more armed attacks in the south of the country. The indian _barrio_ of Monimbo in Masaya rose up in a sea of Sandinista flags, barricades and home-made bombs before being gunned down by the superior fire-power of the Guard. In León the _barrio_ of Subtiava followed suit.

In Condega the death of Chamorro and the activities of the Twelve became an important rallying point in the town. It brought the youth out onto the streets and it radicalized people like Henry Vargas, putting them into contact with FSLN cadres in the mountains for the first time.

> I went out to see the work of Omar Cabezas. We saw the doctrine he was giving and how it would benefit the peasants. We had clandestine documents of the Frente. We analysed them as lay preachers and realized it was our responsibility to start to work with the Frente. Our religion teaches us that man doesn't save himself by prayer but by action.
>
> We had already started to see the outrages suffered by the _campesinos_ around here. Somoza's local sheriffs (_jueces de mesta_) had their spies and would denounce people. _La Prensa_ was censored but we had to protest. Pedro Joaquín Chamorro was a martyr. We retreated to church and held a Mass to tell people what was happening.

By 1 June 1978 a mass organization was being formed by a wide spectrum of opposition organizations throughout Nicaragua. The United People's Movement (MPU), as it was called, was the brainchild of all the FSLN tendencies. Don Henry convened the first meeting in Condega:

> We held the first meeting at my house. The Barredas came from Estelí.[6] They were teachers and active Christians. Father

Wésther López was there. At the second meeting we were joined
by local traders and a photographer in the town. By the third
meeting the headmaster of the school here had joined us, some
farmers, and Don Antonio, the miller. At the fourth meeting
thirty people turned up. We started to be surveilled. By the time
the fifth meeting took place we had to hire the church hall and
we filled it.

The United People's Movement drew together political parties,
trade unions and youth groups, women's organizations, and workers'
committees. It demanded the unity of all anti-Somoza forces, a
government of democratic unity, democratic freedoms, the dis-
mantling of the National Guard, a non-aligned foreign policy, confiscation of Somoza's lands, trade union rights. These were basically
the demands of the FSLN, though spelt out in greater detail.

The importance of the MPU lay not just in formulating a united
opposition bloc at national level, but in the organizational structures
which it strove to promote within the population. Women, men and
children were drawn into the creation of civil defence committees,
the function of which was both political and defensive and to prepare
for the coming insurrection. In Condega people responded vigor-
ously. Don Henry's garage, where he now keeps his photographic
equipment, became one of a network of secret medicine stores,
containing all manner of emergency supplies for use in civil defence
against the Guardia. As he recalls:

> We set up four committees in four zones in the town, each divided
> into blocks. There would be one person in charge of each block.
> Every block and every street would have a medical store. We
> began collecting stretchers, injections, antibiotics. Our aim was
> to make people conscious of the stage things had reached and
> prepare for the armed confrontation that was coming.

The Centeno family, even the parents, threw themselves into the
work: 'We were enthusiastic because we didn't know what to do
ourselves. We knew we had no arms and no money. The support was
massive,' remembers Don Antonio. Luisa Centeno, by then married
with a child, had in 1977 begun working with an organization of
women: the Association of Women Confronting the National
Problem (AMPRONAC). Now the work of women and the civil
defence committees was merged into one.

> There was no formal membership. People just came to the
> meetings. We would visit at home those who didn't have time.

They could always contribute something. We started to collect food, medicines, water, to distribute them to cases who deserved it. We made stretchers for the wounded – which we still have now. Every zone had a representative and every block. It was so nice, it was a dream.

On 5 July 1978 the Twelve returned from exile to Nicaragua, defying threats from Somoza that he would imprison anyone involved in open opposition. Thousands of people were at the airport and in the streets of Managua to welcome them, one of the biggest demonstrations Nicaragua had ever known. Sergio Ramírez, now Vice-President of Nicaragua, described the scene.

When we left the plane the airport looked like it had been attacked by a foreign military power. There were soldiers everywhere, helicopters circling overhead, machine guns on the roof. But it was the first opportunity the people had to express themselves massively in favour of the Sandinista Front and there were more than 150,000 people in the tremendous mobilization that took place in Managua on that day.[7]

The impact of the return of the Twelve stretched further than Managua. They toured the towns and villages of Nicaragua spreading their message that Somoza had to go – the message of the Sandinistas. Miguel D'Escoto, the present Foreign Minister, came to Condega and spoke to the MPU in the church hall. The older citizens were particularly impressed. As Don Antonio said:

They explained the international situation to us and the social and economic problems in the country and told us we had to do something and get organized for the struggle. They told us what the aims were of the movement of the Twelve. They told us victory was near and that if we needed arms they would get them for us.

Dachsun Cattin and the youth

Meanwhile, amongst the youth of Nicaragua an unprecedented level of militancy had taken root. Demonstrations and protests burst onto the streets of major towns. FSLN slogans appeared on the walls. Tyres were burnt as symbolic barricades on street corners. It was the young who were to be in the front line of the urban insurrections

and formed the bulk of FSLN columns in 1978 and 1979. The
dramatic press photos of young people, scarves wrapped around
their mouths to avoid identification, manning barricades, have made
that image one of the revolution's most identifiable symbols.

Condega was no exception. A whole generation of young militants
in their early teens came onto the political stage in 1978, willing to
risk tear gas and even bullets to protest against the regime. Of
these thousand or so young people, few have remained in the town.
Dachsun Cattin, the CDS co-ordinator, is one of them.

> We took over the church and started to ring the church bells,
> calling people. Five hundred people turned up. That was the first
> time the National Guard used weapons against us. I used to speak
> to the people with a megaphone. People came and stood on the
> street corners and we would tell them about what was happening
> elsewhere. We'd tell them, 'Look, you don't have electric light,
> you don't have water. Don't you think you should have it?' And
> the people would shout 'Yes!' We got 400 people out on a march.

Several members of Don Antonio's family took part in the demonstrations, Don Antonio recalled:

> In those days there was a great upsurge. The youth would go out
> and occupy the churches and school. They would go into the
> streets and start demonstrations, burning tyres at street corners.
> The Guardia came out behind them and shot tear gas at them,
> firing bullets into the air. The youth would run away and come
> back down another street to taunt and shout at them and then
> run out of another street. It was a terrifying thing for parents.
> So we had to go into the streets ourselves and risk our lives
> because we knew that our children's lives were right in the middle.
> We weren't worried about ourselves. I used to go out ready to
> be killed rather than let them kill my children.
>   And we reached the stage when the whole village – thousands
> of people – went into the streets with stones, spades, pistols,
> petrol, with whatever, shouting slogans.

The youth of Condega gradually drew the older generation into
the street protests. Even the 'respectable citizens' like Henry Vargas
took part. He remembers dipping handkerchiefs in lemon juice to
dispel the effects of tear gas.

The penalties of being known to the National Guard seemed not
to deter young people. From the top of the hill which overlooks
Condega, Dachsun, a serious young man in his twenties, showed me

the roof of the old National Guard headquarters in the central square. He said: 'The National Guard got to know me. They threatened me when I was walking past the command post one day and shot at me. They said they knew that I was a communist. My family came and argued with them but they threatened them as well.' Dachsun had lost several friends in 1978. Pointing to the bridge over the dried-up river at the entrance to town, he explained: 'That was where two more friends of mine, Alejandro Ramos and Orlando Pineira, were shot. They came down on a mission to attack the National Guard,' he explained. 'They were badly armed.' Dachsun liked talking about those days. They were, after all, more exciting than the present with its shortages, its military draft and declining participation in CDS meetings.

August 1978: the war begins

It was left to the Sandinistas, and in particular the Insurrectional Tendency, to draw together the growing unrest across the country into a coherent plan of action against the regime.

In August 1978 a force of twenty-six of the FSLN's best fighters, dressed up as members of Somoza's crack force of Guardsmen, stormed the National Palace in Managua, taking the whole building hostage. Hundreds of hostages, including nearly fifty deputies and relatives of Somoza, were held against the release of eighty-five Sandinistas languishing in Somoza's jails. The action, the most daring yet of the FSLN, was designed to inspire a national insurrection.

Somoza capitulated, and fifty-eight Sandinistas who had not already been killed in prison were flown out on Panamanian and Venezuelan planes. The action was accompanied by the publication of a political document calling for a popular and democratic government, the removal of the Somoza state and the unification of Sandinista tendencies. Radio and television broadcast the statements as demanded by the guerillas. Thousands lined the streets as the freed prisoners were taken to the airport.

The National Palace action was the spark which finally set the whole of Nicaragua alight. A business strike was soon followed by a spontaneous uprising in Matagalpa to the east of Condega. Boys armed with a handful of weapons held the town for a week against 400 heavily-armed troops. The FSLN decided to take control of the

spontaneous actions spreading throughout the country and pro-
claimed the 'hour of the Sandinista popular insurrection'. By September 1978 the uprising had spread to all the regional capitals of
the country.

In Estelí, Condega's nearest large town, young people used sticks,
stones, bottles and knives to fight the National Guard. Their ranks
were swollen by guerilla columns which had come down from their
mountain hideouts to launch major assaults on military targets.
Some were boys from Condega. The Guard responded with aerial
bombing raids. Men, women and children built barricades. For
twelve days people held the town.

Condega became an important source of supplies and medical
attention for the wounded – Father Wésther López opened his doors
to provide a clandestine medical service. The Centeno family helped
ferry refugees made homeless by the bombing raids to accommodation in Condega. For the authorities, Condega was a strategic
crossroads and an important staging post for the truckloads of
Guardsmen moving south or north. It was tightly controlled, and
Guardsmen were instructed to be on the look-out for any attempts
to spread the insurrection.

But without heavy weapons the uprisings in Nicaragua's cities
stood little chance of success against the ferocity of Somoza's
response. Aerial bombardments, heavy artillery fire and brutal
repression broke the people's control of the streets, leaving six
thousand dead, throughout the country. Juan Aburto of Estelí
described the 'mopping up' operations carried out by the mobile
elite forces, the two-thousand-strong EEBI:

> In Estelí, after the racket of the machine guns and the thunder
> of the bombs and the buzzing of the planes, everything was
> suddenly calm but you could hear a noise in the distance. We
> heard the shouts of frightened boys and women crying. We heard
> the noise of doors being broken in and windows shattering.
> Afterwards, shots getting nearer all the time, shouts full of
> hatred and threats. You could hear people all around crying –
> loud wailing from little boys and from their mothers protecting
> them. People running here and there but they would keep running
> back from the street corner because they were surrounded. They
> would run into each other, desperately trying to escape. They
> vainly knocked on the doors of the neighbours asking them,
> begging them to be allowed in. And still the shots getting nearer
> all the time, doors being knocked down in other houses; first the

great thuds, the crude threats, the sound of walls crumbling and
the shouts of people whose hiding place had been discovered.

We couldn't find where to hide, we tried under the bed, in the
kitchen, in closets, huddled under the piles of wood on the patio.
But it was impossible. The noise came nearer and nearer. We
tried to pray but we kept mixing up Our Father and Hail Mary.
We'd try again; 'Hail Mary, mother of God, blessed be thy name.
Come here darling, hug me, don't cry, it will be over soon.' And
in the street the horrible confusion kept on. Trucks arrived, men
jumped out and we heard the sound of their weapons. Some went
one way, some went the other way, all searching, house by house.
They were now approaching our doorstep. We waited with our
hearts in our mouths. We couldn't swallow. We were sweating,
we held hands in our cold sweat. We hugged each other tightly
in little groups, all over the dark house in every nook and cranny.
We moved slowly so they wouldn't hear us, but they did.
Suddenly we heard the banging on our door. They were trying to
knock it down. First they made a hole, then a batten fell down,
then a plank of wood, then another as their rifle butts continued
to beat at the door.

We could see their bodies now, their horrible blackened faces
like demons dressed in green with helmets on, a pistol or whip
in their hands and still those sons of bitches were still trying to
break in. Once they had knocked the door down, some of them
rushed in, and others pointed their weapons at us from outside.
'All the boys over here.' They pointed their weapons first at the
boys separating them and wounding them right there. They
dragged them out by their hair from under the beds, from under
tables, from cupboards. First they kicked us hard. But they
couldn't drag the boys away from us, then they would push the
whole group down and they even laughed, the bastards. The
women tried to run away and the guards were left with shreds
of their dresses in their hands. And then they would just blow
their brains out.[8]

The young people took the brunt of the National Guard's reprisals.
Their response was to join the guerilla columns as they left the cities
to go back to the mountain camps of the Frente. After joining the
FSLN columns Dachsun was sent to Honduras for medical treatment
and was arrested by the Honduran police who worked closely with
the National Guard. He and others spent two months in jail and
he was only released after a publicity campaign denouncing the

authorities there. He was given asylum in Panama. Later he returned to fight with his friends in the northern guerilla columns during the final offensive of the Sandinistas in 1979.

Dachsun regretted that so few of his comrades were in Condega to tell their story. Many work in Managua with responsibilities in the revolution; others died in the insurrection – amongst them his cousin, Juanita Viscaya.

The death of Juanita Viscaya

Juanita Viscaya, had she been alive, would no doubt have been working in quite a senior position in the Revolution. She was from a better-off family and attended the secondary school in Condega during the 1970s. Her death at the age of sixteen at the hands of the National Guard gave Condega a martyr who is honoured in the new structures the revolution has thrown up. Every one of the co-operatives and state farms in the area is named after one of the young people who gave their lives for the revolution in a local battle.

Juanita's father, Ramón, became a local magistrate after the revolution and now runs a tailor's business just off the central square. I called round one afternoon. He makes denim caps and trousers and regulation army hats. The shutters of the front room remain open, and you can hear the electric sewing machine burring away.

The family were all involved in one way or another with the clandestine opposition to Somoza in Condega in the last years of the dictatorship. Along with Don Henry Vargas, the Centeno family and countless others, they were helping to build up defence committees in the town under the guidance of the United People's Movement.

Ramón took off his glasses and pointed to the fading picture of his youngest daughter – an attractive girl who looked older than her sixteen years – which had pride of place on the wall.

> She was more advanced than others of her age. She got involved in politics while she was at the institute. She used to go out burning tyres with the other youth and make speeches in the street. The whole family supported her. What we didn't know was that she had joined the Frente from the beginning.

Juanita, like Dachsun, was a member of the Revolutionary Students' Front (FER). They were close friends and he has fond memories of discussing the programme of the Frente with her and jointly reading about the history of Sandino and Carlos Fonseca, and the famous FSLN battles. Ramon was used to telling the story of his daughter, but there was no hint of impatience in his voice.

> It was during the insurrection in Estelí in September 1978. She was out with a column in a place called La Mesita between Condega and Estelí. We lost contact with her. Her job was to do support work near the Highway – ambushes, and so on. Apparently the messenger failed to get to tell the column that the withdrawal had been announced. The Guardia were mopping up.
>   We got worried because we hadn't heard a word from her and we knew that several people she was with had passed up through Condega on their way to the north. But her name was never mentioned.

After a week Ramón and his wife decided to seek information from others in the town who would know of Juanita's fate. Luisa Centeno, one of the most actively involved in building up the civil defence committees, was someone who might know. 'I saw Luisa coming down the street but whether she saw me I don't know. Anyway she turned down a side street. I called her back and said I wanted to know the truth. She said that as far as she knew all the comrades had left for the north.'

Luisa herself still remembers that day with anguish. She was part of the network of communication with the Frente and knew what had happened:

> I knew that she had died but I couldn't bring myself to tell the family. Several times I passed near their home, but didn't have the courage to go in. I was avoiding them.
>   When her father stopped me at first I said I thought Juanita had left for Somoto. Then I couldn't stand it and I broke down. I said they should look for her in La Mesita.

Ramón Viscaya went to La Mesita and eventually made the terrible discovery:

> I knew from Luisa's reaction that Juanita must be dead. I decided to go and look for her myself. I went twice and could find nothing. The third time I went with my wife. When we arrived the army was clearing it. We found a body but we couldn't identify it because it was headless. My wife recognized it as

Juanita because of her pants. It was getting dark already. There was no time for a funeral. The body was already decomposed. We travelled back with the army and buried her in the cemetery that night. We never found her head.

I did not like to ask what else the National Guard had done to Juanita's body. From the reports of their actions in the aftermath of the Estelí uprising I knew what they were capable of doing.

13.   The revolution on the land

Occupied

Condega does not forget its martyrs. The memory of Juanita has
been honoured by the decision to link her name with the process of
land reform that followed the victory of 1979.

Just south of the town, close to the Pan American Highway, lies
a piece of fertile agricultural land which can be reached on foot by
following the banks of the river. It belongs to the Juanita Viscaya co-
operative farm and is worked assiduously by a group of enthusiastic
campesinos who grow tobacco, maize and beans and keep cattle.

In 1980 there were twenty-five of them and most were unemployed
landworkers. They clubbed together shortly after the revolution to
look for land to cultivate and soon fixed their sights on this particular
plot. It was unploughed and unused – the property of a doctor who
worked privately in the slaughterhouse nearby. As I was told: 'He
didn't need it. He had fees from the slaughterhouse and the tannery
on the other side of the road.'

So at four in the morning one day in March the twenty-five men
arrived to take it over.

We began by clearing the land with our machetes. Two employees
of the doctor arrived a bit later and we appealed to them to join
us. Then the foreman's son arrived at 8 a.m. We told him we had
the support of the Rural Workers' Association, the ATC, to take
over the land. He hummed and hawed and went away again. At
twelve noon he came back. By that time we had most of the land
clear. We asked him to join the group and explained that we were
going to cultivate the land. He said 'No'.

The next day the foreman himself arrived. He asked who gave
us permission to work the land. 'No one,' I told him. 'And please
mind your horses' hooves over there. . . .' I said this so he would
get down to talk to us. We wanted to show him that we weren't
going to harm him. But he said he was going to see the boss. 'Go
on then, go and tell him we're waiting for him here,' I said.
'Because we are the people in charge here now. It's not your boss

or anyone else. We are the people who are going to work these lands, whether you like it or not.'

Daniel Flores, a founding member of the co-operative, which came into being that day, chuckled as he recalled its early days. I sat on logs under some trees late one afternoon talking with its fourteen remaining members. The trees threw long shadows across the tobacco field – a new crop they had only just started growing. They had spent the afternoon spraying the precious leaves with insecticide, carrying large canisters on their backs, and also their rifles which they rarely abandon. Daniel's colleagues nodded in agreement as he recounted the story. They, like him, were older men, the lines of poverty and hard work drawn across their handsome faces. They left the talking to Daniel, who was the most confident and loquacious. He enjoyed telling the story.

Until the revolution Daniel, who is now in his forties, was an agricultural labourer employed by wealthy landowners in the area. For three months of the year he and the majority of men living in Condega itself were allowed to rent a small plot on the estates to try and cultivate food. At other times they were unemployed, sometimes for the whole summer. 'My *compañera* lived in her parents' house and looked after our little boy. I looked after myself. Life was quite expensive and we lived in sheer poverty. Sometimes I ate, sometimes I didn't. That was how we started to see the huge need for land.'

The action of the twenty-five men was probably the only 'spontaneous' land seizure that took place in the Condega area after July 1979. It took even the newly-formed branch of the landworkers' union (the ATC) by surprise.

The doctor went up to the offices of the ATC to denounce us for taking his land. They called us in, and all twenty-five of us went. There were five in his group. So the ATC comrade told him, 'Look, doctor, you have five workers but they have jobs in the slaughterhouse. These twenty-five men are in need. They don't have anywhere to even sow a yard of maize or beans. You have your surgery, your shop, your fees from the tannery and the slaughterhouse. You should leave the land for these comrades.' Eventually he agreed to take up a contract for a year. One of our group whom we had elected president signed it.

Land reform under the Sandinistas

Land seizures are nothing new in Nicaraguan history. As early as 1881, indigenous indian communities in Matagalpa waged war against the destruction of their communal property. In the 1950s and 1960s there were several uprisings and land seizures against the encroaching cotton landlords, especially in the Pacific areas, León and Chinandega. In the 1970s such protests grew, assisted by the clandestine trade unions that were growing up and by students of the FSLN. All of these were put down brutally by the National Guard. Trade union leaders were assassinated and accused of being guerillas. The people replied with hunger-strikes and protests.[1]

In the Condega area, however, there were no such incidents. Mass resistance to land encroachment was difficult, given the isolation of so many of the *campesinos*, and the mountainous terrain. In the 1970s landworkers in other regions were forming committees of the ATC with clearly formulated demands. In the Condega area the ATC arrived only after the revolution.

By 1979 the FSLN slogan, 'land for whoever works it', had become a powerful rallying cry for the landless all over the country. During the insurrection of 1978 the FSLN encouraged spontaneous seizures of land as part of its strategy. Landworkers in some areas armed themselves to defend their gains, and at the end became offensive combat groups. Around Condega the promise of land won the guerillas much support and has never been forgotten.

Once the Sandinistas were in government, however, there was nothing inherently revolutionary about their approach to land reform. They called a halt to the movement of land seizures. Anxious not to encourage a loss of manpower for the vital agro-export crops, they concentrated their efforts on creating state enterprises out of the former estates of Somoza and his friends, which accounted for only 20 per cent of cultivable land. (Even today more than 60 per cent of the land is in private hands, and proper collective farms work only 7 per cent of the land.)[2]

The action of Daniel and his friends was backed by the ATC in Condega, and eventually received government endorsement. But there was little material support:

> We got some loans from the Government to buy insecticides and
> seed but it was hard. In the first three months we had to wait
> for the harvest. We had nothing to eat. Then we realized that we
> would have to stop the doctor taking the land off us again. He

used to come every day and tell us to get off. So we borrowed a
pump for irrigation and planted tomatoes and vegetables too.
Then we were able to say to him, 'How do you expect us to leave
the land now? It has cost us so much to work it. Look how we
have done. You're not going to take it away from us now and
leave us without work?' At that time the agrarian reform
programme of the Government was just starting up. And with
the vegetable garden the man saw the big force that we had.
Every day he and his wife would come and talk about how they
were going to sow the land. But we told him we would be
continuing the following year.

Meanwhile eight members of the group left because things were
so hard. All we had to eat was the maize we had grown. Finally
we had the agrarian reform people draw up the papers for us.
The doctor refused to sign and so did his wife. We told him to
take his cattle out of the fields. In 1982 we got the title deeds to
the land.

The doctor has left the country now. He is in Costa Rica.

In 1982 government policy began to shift, as the result of a
perceived drop in the support for the FSLN in the countryside. Real
wages had fallen, unemployment was growing, and the demand for
land had not been satisfied. Only 4 per cent of national arable land
had been redistributed, benefiting some eight thousand families.
Many peasants saw in the state farms just a continuation, under
better conditions, of the old employee–employer relationship (see
Chapter 16). Many large and medium-sized estates remained in
private hands. Most co-operatives were not given the technical and
financial support they needed.

The Sandinistas did a U-turn. From 1983 to 1985 30,000 *campesino*
families were given the titles to the land they already worked.
Between 1983 and 1984 over 22,000 families were given land previously run by the state to farm collectively in Sandinista farming
co-operatives. By the end of 1985 some 69,000 families had benefited
from land reform in some form.[3] By the end of 1986 this figure
had risen to 97,000 families and affected a total of 31 per cent of
agricultural land.[4] To achieve this the Government began to buy
land from private landowners on behalf of new co-operatives. I had
an opportunity to witness a group of *campesinos* parting company
with the landlord who had ruled them for years.

The *campesinos* get their land, the capitalists their cash

Just west of Estelí a track climbs high into the mountains leaving wide views of the town and the tobacco farms on the plain below. I rode in a convoy of jeeps bearing officials from the Ministry of Agriculture, the National Bank and the Frente. There was a general holiday atmosphere: it was a chance to get away from the office desk. I had been pressed into accompanying them on what was, they stressed, an important occasion.

The deal was the culmination of several months of haggling over the price of a large cattle ranch. The owner, with his eye on a restaurant in the town of Matagalpa, was not making huge concessions on the price. But, unlike the majority of large landowners, he was happy to sell to the state.

The jeeps made their way over the deep furrows left by rain in the dry mud, through gates and down into pine forests. There is not one single village or hamlet between Estelí and this isolated estate, Los Robellitos. Suddenly, ahead was a group of colourfully dressed women, men and children making their way along the track. They turned and waved us on excitedly. The women wore lipstick on their bright grins. These were the beneficiaries of the deal: from today the proud owners of land. Yesterday they did not even own their own houses. The track ended at the side of a field of mud, heavy rainfall having left nothing but large puddles across the entrance to the cluster of buildings which made up the farm.

The landowner's ranch was a modest white brick bungalow: landlords in Nicaragua bear little resemblance to the *latifundistas* and grand style of South American states. In fact the young landlord had not owned it for very long. He was delighted at the deal he had struck. 'I bought it for two million cordobas and sold it for six million. With devaluation that's about right,' he told me, as he walked about in smart leather cowboy boots and a new hat, sharing a drink with the farmworkers. He owned several other large estates and was in effect an absentee landlord, leaving the estate in the hands of a foreman.

The landworkers were arriving from all sides. Rum was flowing. A party in that area must have been an almost unheard-of event. Someone made the sensible suggestion that the rifles be removed before an accident happened, and they were stacked up round the back of the house. The landlord had donated an animal towards the festivities. I was pressed into accepting a strip of grilled cow, scarcely cooked. Women cut up hundreds of oranges to make juice, chatting and laughing together. A band was playing in the house.

People gathered on the veranda for the speeches: the peasants at one end, the government officials and the party spokesman at the other. Throats were cleared. 'This is the day the revolution fulfils its promise to you, and you now have to take up the challenge,' began the man from the Frente. The speeches were short. Everyone clapped and the band struck up again for what was sure to be a long night. Normally there would have been a presentation of land titles – but the officials had not had time to prepare them all.

For this particular landlord there was clearly no conflict between the interests of the revolution and his own. In fact he was the perfect spokesman for the mixed economy.

> The agrarian reform is good. Up to a certain point it's very capitalist because you can own the amount of land you want. You are free.
>
> The revolution leaves us landlords in peace. They give us bank loans. For me it's OK. I don't get involved in politics but there's nothing particularly good about capitalism. What we need is a bit of capitalism and a bit of socialism mixed up. That's the best way we can all live together.

These words were to be expected from someone who had just been made six million cordobas the richer, thanks to the Government. The *campesinos* were enthusiastic about the changes:

> This co-operative means that we are going to have a pump for our water and our salary will have some relation to the value of our produce. We have been living in a very repressed situation. In the past we had no organization and everything was for the big landowners.

I wondered how these new owners would make out in this remote mountain area. The Contras had already targeted the new co-operative. The night before they had arrived at the peasants' dwellings, threatened the women and shot at the men working in the field. 'They want us cut off from the revolution so we don't improve our lives,' said Serafím Bernardes Cruz, a twenty-year-old member. He, like most of the younger men, was already wearing green fatigues. His ammunition hung across his chest. His father wore his Sunday best, a brown shirt with orange spots and a large stetson. He nodded agreement.

There was a feeling that everyone was stepping into the unknown: men who had spent their lives taking orders, living in abject poverty

Mass funeral in Condega:
four victims of the Contra ambush were buried that day.

Urban youth were in the front line of the insurrections of 1978 and 1979 that finally toppled Somoza.

Daniel Ortega, a member of the revolutionary *junta*, later elected President, at the victory rally in 1979.

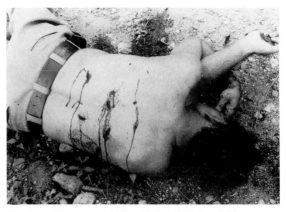

Condega, May 1979: the mutilated body of Juan Guillén, who – along with the headmaster Julio Castillo and both their wives – was the victim of a National Guard murder squad.

July 19th 1979. The scene in the centre of Managua after Somoza's downfall.

General Augusto César Sandino (standing, third from left) with Latin American nationalists. José de Paredes is on Sandino's right and Farabundo Martí is seated at the far right.

Don Leandro Córdoba, aged ninety-three.
In the 1930s he fed and ran messages for Sandino's guerillas.

Shortly before his fall, the strain shows on the face
of President Anastasio Somoza Debayle (far right), with his entourage.

Donatila and Antonio Centeno.

School students provided the bulk of volunteers in the 1980 Literacy Campaign. Today pupils in Condega celebrate its anniversary.

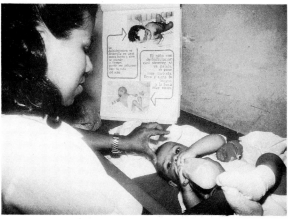

Volunteers have largely replaced
paid workers in the annual
coffee harvest. (Above) a Managuan
student nurse picks coffee on her
weekend off.

Luisa Centeno in the uniform she loves to wear.

Health education, also an activity of volunteers, takes
priority in Condega's new health centre, where the battle
against infant mortality focusses on the dangers of
dehydration.

Bertilda Villareyna (wearing a white apron) outside the home
she defended with her nephews. With them is her cousin's widow, Nicola,
who also lost a six-year-old son.

The village school at San Jerónimo,
destroyed by Contras in May 1984.

El Jocote: Roberto Pineda Rivas, who was forcibly recruited into the Contras,
with his mother María Luisa.

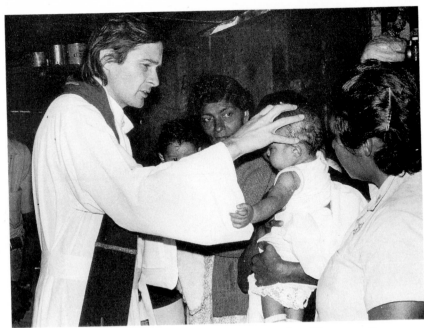

Father Enrique Oggier baptizes a new member of the Darailí co-operative.

(Above) Bishop Pablo Antonio Vega, later expelled from Nicaragua, speaks to journalists.

(Left) El Jocote: Moisés Córdoba, lay delegate and Sandinista, with his wife.

Condegans celebrate the Stations of the Cross.

Ampara Irías, CDS activist.

Julia Meza, Donatila's
daughter-in-law.

Miriam Centeno, who is in charge of education in
Condega.

AMNLAE day, Condega, 1983;
the mothers of heroes and martyrs give a clenched fist.
At the far right is Donatila, and next to her Juana Salinas.

The gallery of heroes and martyrs in Jalapa.

Workers from Condega marched to Ducualí to protest against the Contra attack on the depot there. They appealed for better defence in workplaces.

One of a fleet of lorries that was destroyed in the attack on the depot. Two hundred construction workers lost their jobs in the attack.

Members of the Juanita Viscaya co-operative tend their tobacco crop.

Daniel Flores.

At the San Jerónimo co-operative, members work and guard the coffee plantation in turn, rarely taking off their green drill.

Children of the San Jerónimo co-operative,
where one cold stream acts as bath and washtub.

were now to become the responsible managers and owners of land, making decisions in matters they had never needed to ponder before. The Contras would undoubtedly be back. Could the members cope with production and defence? The Ministry of Agriculture had promised that the rewards would be high if they could.

But the Ministry of Agriculture officials were apprehensive. As Dr Ernesto Pereira, director of the land-reform programme in the region, said:

> These people have no experience in cultivating good lands. They are going to have a tractor for the first time. So we have to train them. The peasants are not used to taking advice from a technician and not used to technology. At the beginning there's resistance to everything that's new. They don't believe, they don't understand, they don't know how it can be done. Then we have a problem finding a technician who will come and live here. We don't have the vehicles available to bring someone here every day from Estelí and back again. So that means finding the man who'll come here out of a commitment – it certainly won't be for the pay, which is not the best. We need people with consciousness and you don't find them in the street putting up their hands to volunteer. If we were at peace we could find such people. But they know that coming here is very dangerous.

The struggle of the co-operatives

The Government is hard-pressed to give co-operatives the attention they need. In 1983 it selected some 500 for special state attention to modernize their production methods. That still left three-quarters of the co-operatives cut off from any direct material aid.

The Juanita Viscaya co-operative by the river near Condega has had an uphill struggle to survive. Twenty-five men originally took over the land, but the co-operative now consists of fourteen; only seven of them are from the original group:

> For the first two or three years we weren't earning a salary. We lived on what we produced and nothing else. We had tremendous difficulties to survive. We couldn't buy clothes or shoes.
>
> Now things are changing. We have a proper salary from the tobacco project. Things are changing and we are going into

profit. I earn more in the co-operative than I did as a wage labourer. Now we know that the more we produce, the more we have.

Members of the co-operative spend every second night in the fields, on guard. It took me five visits to Daniel's little wooden shack in Condega to find him in and awake. We sat near the doorway where a shaft of moonlight provided the only light. As usual in Condega the electricity had failed. It matters little to Daniel. In the days that he sleeps at home he is usually in bed by 6 p.m. In addition to guard duty, co-operative members, being armed and politically conscious, are often asked to help the militia elsewhere.

We consider that if we sleep the enemy will harass us. You see we have quite a few things here: pumps, tobacco-sheds, cattle and all that. We can't neglect it for a single moment or the enemy will come. Then what happens is we are working OK and they [the militias] come and tell us they need so many comrades from the co-operative to go and fight the enemy. So we have to pack up and go. Nearly every day we used to be off on missions. It's got better recently because of military service. They are helping us quite a bit.

But in practice military conscription worked both ways. Although on the one hand it had helped ease the crisis in defence, on the other hand it had exacerbated the shortage of labour in the area. The absence of boys of seventeen and eighteen and the large number of reservists and militiamen mobilized had reduced the rural working population in the region by a third. In Condega it is quite easy to get a job and few are attracted by the hardships and risks of working with the Juanita Viscaya co-operative. As Daniel Flores said:

A lot of people don't want to be working in an organization. Secondly, they are afraid of co-operatives because they say we are soldiers of the co-operative. We have to be armed. They see that. And whenever there is any movement of the enemy we are there with our guns in our hands producing. When they call us, we go off. We are soldiers there. So a lot of people don't like co-operatives. They don't like to carry guns on their shoulders. They don't know what the war is and they don't want to sacrifice themselves too much.

A shortage of members was not the only problem. Another major obstacle to development was the low level of skills of men who until recently had no access to education and just took orders from a boss. Neither Daniel nor most of the members could read or write. They scarcely know how to write their names. On top of that came an unfamiliarity with co-operative methods:

> We lack administrative knowledge because we are illiterate. If anyone knows anything, we put him on the board which runs the co-operative.
>
> A lot of comrades are still not very clear about what a co-operative is. When you form a co-operative it is mutual. Everyone co-operates with organization, defence, production. We see that it's a very beautiful thing, because you work united, with social aims.
>
> But Nicaraguans are very hot tempered. What happens is that if someone doesn't like something, he goes, walks out. They get demoralized.

The farmers' union (UNAG) kept the men together and gave what advice it could. The day I visited the co-operative, Carlos, a young official of the farmers' union, came too. He spent nearly an hour with the men, urging them to send a representative to a training seminar, discussing the need for tools, grass for the animals and how the fence could be repaired.

When there are conflicts and arguments among the men, it is Carlos to whom they turn to settle the dispute – though he is less than half the age of most of them. The men looked unhappy while he explained why the Ministry of Agriculture was unable to supply them with new and essential tools, why there was no tractor available, why they have to go on using their broken machetes because there are no dollars to import new ones. It was a depressing account.

The problems of the Juanita Viscaya co-operative are in no sense unique. In some areas farming co-operatives have been hugely successful, in others they are regarded with suspicion. They were also unable to satisfy the increasing demand for land in individual plots. Pressure from below continues to shape Government policy, however. In 1985 an estimated 80,000 *campesino* families asked for land. The Government decided that its policy of trying to limit the proportion of individual small farmers to 50 per cent of cultivated land was back-firing. The demand for land could not be satisfied by the co-operatives and was leading to a disenchantment that was giving the Contras the upper hand in some country areas. Another

U-turn was made.[5] During 1986 the Government handed over at least half the available land to small individual farmers. A new law was enacted empowering the Government to take over lands that were lying fallow or to purchase estates over a certain size.

14.   A woman's place

The mothers of heroes and martyrs

It was early evening when I joined a group of women outside the CDS office and clambered onto an army transport truck. It rattled out of Condega's dusty streets onto the Highway and hurtled towards the military base two miles down the road. The twenty or so women wore carefully-ironed dresses, their hair was washed and shiny. One or two sported necklaces, another wore a pair of earrings. These women, the bereaved mothers of Nicaraguans who had died in combat, were to be amongst the most honoured guests of a graduation ceremony at the army base. They sat round the sides of the lorry gazing pensively at the mountains, their eyes screwing up against the low rays of the setting sun. Some smiled quiet, private smiles, or pursed their lips.

With them travelled all the female Sandinista officials in Condega. There was Eunice, and a charming woman called Rossita, one of the mainstays of the CDS and an activist from pre-revolutionary times; and Nidia, a serious, rather taciturn woman who worked for the women's organization AMNLAE. It is named after the first Sandinista woman to be killed, Luisa Amanda Espinoza. Nidia never seemed to finish making her house-calls on women to discuss their problems. Donatila Centeno was there, of course, and her daughter-in-law, Julia Meza, who lived next door with her family and who often came over for a chat.

The lorry turned into the base and stopped near the entrance. Military security applied from here and we walked the last two hundred yards on foot. Ahead, nearly two thousand young Nicaraguan conscripts in their late teens stood in ranks, chatting excitedly. Beyond them on a podium was a huge backcloth congratulating them on passing through their three months' military training and becoming part of the crack troops of the Sandinista People's Army – the irregular warfare battalions, the BLI. In the distance a hundred more descended the mountain in single file to join the battalion.

A legend of indestructibility inspires the BLI battalions. On their 'search and destroy missions' their units march for days into the most impenetrable terrain, surviving without food and carrying their wounded back to base. *Barricada* gives full coverage to their most daring exploits. It prints interviews with their heroes and with the demobilized, in which they talk of their political commitment and sacrifice.

The mothers of Condega took their place alongside another large group of women, relatives of the conscripts themselves. Some had travelled from as far as Managua to see their sons graduate – a rare opportunity to see a boy who might never return. On the platform there were military officers and FSLN officials, but pride of place was given to Donatila, the secretary of the Committee of Mothers of Heroes and Martyrs in Condega.

Donatila commands a lot of respect in Condega. With the help of AMNLAE she has brought together those who have lost sons in the war. The committee already has over a hundred members. It contacts bereaved mothers and widows, making sure that they claim their widows' pensions from the army. It works with the mothers of conscripts, keeping them in touch with their sons at the battle front through letters and visits. But one of its most important functions is political. It tries to boost the morale of the bereaved women, to prevent grief from turning to anger and resentment, to keep these women sympathetic to the revolution. The opinions of women, and especially 'mothers' are held to be crucial by the authorities. The mother is considered the linchpin of the Nicaraguan family, and she is in any case often the only parent: in almost half of Nicaraguan households women have the economic responsibility for feeding their children.

No mother watches her son leave for the army with anything but apprehension and fear. By being a 'mother of a hero of the revolution' her sacrifice is given public recognition. Many of the women at the military base that evening had only recently lost sons. Donatila herself still mourns the loss of her youngest, who died aged fifteen a week after joining the militias in 1983. Her eldest son, Toñito, the man who took Omar Cabezas into Canta Gallo, was killed while in exile in Mexico.

I stood separately from the group. Journalists, I was informed by a young lieutenant, could not attend the ceremony. By now the sun was disappearing behind the mountain which shelters the base, leaving the ground in semi-darkness and a sky illuminated in blue and red. The passing clouds were lit up in an eerie white. As the ceremony got underway, the voices of military officers, of FSLN spokesmen and of Donatila were carried off by the wind. On the crest of the mountain bush-fires blazed, forming strange geometric shapes of red flame which got stronger as the light faded. The soldiers stood to attention, their three months' training in 'revolutionary discipline, revolutionary morale and political education' on show to the spectators. Their slogans roared across the base and echoed against the mountain as if intended for the Contra camps in Honduras.

Juana Salinas

As we travelled back to Condega in the dark I noticed Juana Salinas, a thin, fifty-year-old woman with glasses, her face prematurely aged. She looked proud, positively happy and reinforced by the ceremony.

Since 1983 Juana and her family have had to live without the help of her eldest boy, Justo José. He died in combat that August. At his funeral she found the pain too much. 'I felt anger and pain. Anger against the Contras and pain because he died. But I couldn't cry. It was too much.' Yet Juana is a staunch Sandinista. At her son's funeral other women were astounded at her words. 'Son, I said, I will pick up the weapon and the flag which fell in your arms and I will follow you in your ideals. People thought I was mad.' For Juana the revolution has brought both recognition of her own sacrifice as a woman, and also a kind of security, neither of which are things that can be measured in material terms.

She lives in one of Condega's poorest *barrios*, Barrio Triumfo, down by the river. She has borne twelve children, but only seven survived infancy. Juana's little wooden shaçk, which I visited one evening, is virtually empty of furniture and possessions. In a corner of the room her disabled husband languishes on a bed: he has been bedridden for twenty years. Before, he worked on the land, breeding mules and cutting coffee. Until the revolution Juana had to work all the time to bring in some money to pay the rent and buy medicine for her husband: in the daytime she cut tobacco, evenings she cooked pork in a bar. 'I would leave home at 9 in the morning and return at 1 a.m. on the following day. For that I would get five cordobas. It was a struggle because my children didn't go to bed because they were afraid.' After 1979 some of her children began working and she was given a state pension.

It was getting dark outside, but Juana's house had no electricity or gas lamps. I asked what her family would be eating that night. Just beans and rice, she said.

> We don't have any sugar because one of my daughters is in Managua now and we don't get enough from the CDS. There are eight of us in the family, four adults and four children. With what I get we have to buy wood for the stove and everything. It's hard but we can just about manage.

From the point of view of diet it appeared that little had changed for Juana and her family. She found the price increases very hard too. 'A lot of people are unemployed. We don't know why the prices are going up but the Government must know why.' But none of the current hardships had erased her memory of the past:

> Before, you would be in bed and suddenly the Guard would arrive, shooting up, forcing the door down. Now we can sleep. I think about what the Contras are doing, but then I can get back to sleep. Yes, there are difficulties but we can tackle them in a different way.

1977: AMPRONAC is born

It was in 1977 that Juana's life began to change. That autumn, after the October offensive of the FSLN, some sixty women gathered in Managua to denounce violations of human rights. It began as a middle-class group; but soon, with the national strike organized to protest against the killing of Pedro Joaquín Chamorro, a wider group of women was drawn into its ranks. The Association of Women Confronting the National Problem (AMPRONAC) grew to reach eight thousand members across the country.

AMPRONAC was the brainchild of the Sandinistas, born out of a desire to mobilize ever wider sections of the Nicaraguan population against the dictatorship. In January 1978 women from AMPRONAC occupied the UN offices in Managua to protest against disappearances. Based on 'women's concerns', their demonstrations aroused world-wide publicity for the brutalities of the regime in a way which Somoza could hardly put down with the usual tear-gas and grenades. They were an entirely new type of opponent. The celebration of Mothers' Day, for example, was the occasion for an AMPRONAC demonstration under the slogan 'The best gift would be a free Nicaragua'.

The movement found support amongst the mothers of politicized students and children and provoked a radical and determined response amongst women who felt they had little to lose.

Luisa Centeno, one of AMPRONAC's organizers in Condega, came back into politics via this new women's organization. It brought her back in touch with the Frente after a two-year gap. Gradually she drew in other members of her family, including her mother Donatila. For the first time the house-bound woman had a field of activity in which to express opposition. 'Women were at the head here. They had a unique consciousness because they suffered. Women can sometimes be braver than men. I think women think more, they are more astute than men.'

Juana Salinas was one of the many women in Condega who had been drawn into AMPRONAC's work. She was influenced by her son Justo José, who was working as a messenger for the FSLN.

I was recruited by a young girl of sixteen called Marinita Perez who did the propaganda. It was totally clandestine. There were quite a few of us involved though not all of them had the courage to go out. We used to collect money and there were demonstrations. Later Marinita dropped out because she was afraid.

In Juana's house at night her son would take out his notes and messages before delivering them to the mountains. 'From the age of sixteen he was involved in political work in the struggle. No one knew what he was doing, not even my mother. My daughter asked me one day, "I think he's working with those Frente people." "No," I said. "It's just his friends." '

The women became mistresses of subterfuge. At the time the National Guard kept a look-out for gatherings of more than three or four people, which were considered subversive. People meeting could be charged with 'undermining public order'.

Across Nicaragua AMPRONAC's membership was becoming proletarian in character – a consequence of the rising militancy of people in the poor _barrios_. In the cities it organized protests against rising food prices and hunger marches, harnessing the energies of women around issues considered to be their domain. In April 1978, with its national membership at three thousand, AMPRONAC affiliated to the United People's Movement.

In Condega around 700 women were drawn into the organization.

The women threw themselves into the work of building defence committees in the town. They were the first widely-drawn movement to be organized and they taught the rest of the population how to get involved. It is no accident that there is a high proportion of women responsible for political work in Condega today.

As 1978 wore on the departure of men from the town to join the Frente left the women of Condega to take the initiatives in the struggle. Their experience became the basis for the building of defence committees in the neighbourhoods in which they were the most active participants. Meanwhile, all over Nicaragua younger women were joining the ranks of the guerillas themselves. At the time of Somoza's fall over 30 per cent of the armed guerilla fighters were women. In Condega Juana and other women formed a lifeline of support to the guerillas during the capture of the town.

Julia

Julia was another woman I met at the BLI rally. What I hadn't realized was how soon this was after the death of her son. He had been an active Sandinista studying agronomy and engineering when he was called up. He was sent to the Atlantic Coast, where he died six months later: he was one of seven to die from unattended wounds in a remote part of the bush.

I made a point of calling at Julia's house, which was not far from the Centenos'. The family had not been in Condega long. She was born in Limay in 1946 and married at the age of seventeen. Before the triumph, she said, the family were poor. But they were educated. Her family today live in a new brick house they built themselves. They have bought land too to grow maize and beans.

Julia was bitter about her son's death. I was not used to hearing people in Condega refer to the Sandinistas as 'they'.

> They say my son was defending his country but one doesn't always understand that. Some people in the towns have privileges and can avoid doing military service. Yet they say it's a law which you have to fulful. Military service should be on a voluntary basis. What we see is that it's only the boys doing military service who die, not the full-time soldiers.

Julia spoke slowly and sadly. She thought a lot about her answers. We sat in her darkened front room. A picture of the Pope hung above her – it had pride of place on the bare brick wall. As she talked she became more outspoken, revealing the source of some of her bitterness: 'They didn't want to take my son's body back on the helicopter. His cousin had to put a gun in the face of the pilot to force him to take it.' She was disdainful of the Government's claim that those unfit for combat are exempted from the draft. 'They take epileptics, deaf and dumb, flat-footed people. There was even a boy who went out with my son who was almost blind.'

I asked who she blamed for her son's death. Did she blame the Americans? There was a long pause. 'I don't know,' she said. What did she think of the Contras?, I asked. 'There are all different types of people with the Contras. I won't say they are just the Americans. Some used to be Sandinistas.'

Julia remembers her feelings when the revolution took place. 'We were afraid of the Guardia. Everyone was involved with the Sandinistas. We were happy because we were so afraid for our lives.' But it was above all her son, seventeen at the time of the triumph, who taught her about the Sandinistas. 'He had a lot of knowledge,' said Julia. 'I used to miss him when he went away but he explained he was fighting for the revolution. I was proud in a way.'

Julia felt in hindsight that the revolution had brought hardship after hardship. Eight relatives of hers had been massacred by the Contras in Limay. She didn't see any improvement in her living conditions. 'I'm not going to say that I'm happy about the situation. But I'm not going to turn against the revolution because my son has died.'

Ampara

Not all the women activists in Condega were born in the town. Ampara Irías, for example, was chased out of her village by the Contras because of her commitment. She was born in an extremely isolated district called Murra near the Honduran border. Today most of the subsistence farmers of Murra have been moved away from the area into resettlement camps.[1]

I had visited some of the resettled people of Murra in a camp near Jalapa. They had had little schooling and were very cut off from politics. That Ampara would have stood out in such a context was obvious. She is a self-educated woman, as poor as anyone else but bristling with intelligence. She was eager for me to come and talk to her about the revolution. She lives in a small wooden shack down by the river and works at the Juanita Viscaya co-operative. It was difficult to guess her age. She had ten children and five grandchildren.

Under Somoza, Ampara worked on the land growing maize, coffee and beans, while her husband worked up to fifteen days at a time for landlords. When they eventually got hold of a small plot, they could still barely make ends meet. Like so many others it was religion that brought her into contact with the revolution. The Church was 'where my political education came from', she said. In 1980 she joined AMNLAE, founded out of the cadres of AMPRONAC. She ran a sewing collective, worked in the CDS committee and taught adult education as a 'popular teacher'.

> The community where I lived was the poorest in Nicaragua. The women would suffer in the house and then go and wash twenty-four pieces of clothing for just six cordobas. One woman told me she used to faint from hunger. She could not even produce milk for her children. Through the CDS I managed to get her clothes and food.

In 1980 Ampara and her family started to be harassed. The Contras wanted her to stop organizing in the village. In 1981 there were real threats. 'Armed men came to the village and threatened to kill me. Between fifteen and twenty men left to join the Contras. What they said to the people was that under Somoza no one took your land away. They were people who wanted a leader.' Once a group of twelve Contras came to her house and Ampara had to leave quickly. Later the village was evacuated. Some of the evacuees went to Honduras, others stayed in Nicaragua. One of her daughters lost her husband, who was kidnapped by the Contras.

Like so many women I met in Nicaragua, Ampara had humility and honesty, yet also a commitment that defied belief. Ninety per cent of the participants of night-watch patrols are women. Women formed the bulk of volunteers in the literacy crusade and continue to dominate in adult education. Across Nicaragua women make up between a third and half of the popular militias. Condega's rural militias have over 200 women members.

Because so many men in Condega are absent on defence duties, women like Ampara have had to take much of the responsibility for CDS work in their *barrios* and have a particularly high profile in the political and community activities in the town.

Ampara was worried about the developments in the CDS in Condega. The drop in night-watch patrols, for example. They were down to only twenty-five people, she said. 'In the past we had 150 participants.' Most of those who had dropped out of night-watch duties were women. Ampara tended to blame a certain complacency, yet price increases and the draft were clearly major factors.

Ampara spoke of the difficulties she encountered, explaining the need for military conscription to some people in her neighbourhood. 'Some people blame me for the death of those who died. They lack consciousness. Mothers often misunderstand.' She was pleased to learn at a seminar in Estelí that the Government was going to revise some of the aspects of the military service law. There had also been a promise to improve supplies of food and basic goods into the town. All this would make her job as a CDS volunteer easier. Her own views were unshaken. 'In Somoza's time everything was convenient and cheap. The sugar price for example. But that didn't help because the rest of man's work was exploited. Life was much harder.'

She complained too about speculation. In the shops she had encountered hoarders who were trying to sell goods at inflated prices. On house-to-house calls some people had expressed reluctance to build shelters in their yards. 'We are in a dangerous situation. A lot of people say that God will save them. They don't believe that there will be war.'

Ampara also faced problems at work. It was a little ironic, I thought, that she should not be recognized as a full member of the Juanita Viscaya co-operative, though she spent the whole of her working day cutting and classifying the tobacco there. Indeed, there were no female members of the co-operative at all. When challenged, Daniel Flores looked a little sheepish:

> It's a difficult question. In Nicaragua women don't like working in the field and men are very macho. They get jealous. So the women bring us our meals at mid-day. They are first of all the wives of the comrades. Some of them have as many as ten children each, so they have to look after them at home. The women who work with us work for a wage.

Studies have shown that Ampara's problem has arisen in many co-operative farms.[2] Widows have problems, too, getting land titles transferred to their name. They were not issues that Ampara dwelt on, however. She had an unshaken faith in the revolution.

> The Nicaraguan situation today is beautiful. It is undergoing such a big change. We have co-operatives, health centres, roads, schools, people go abroad to study. The life of a co-operative is

a great thing. It's in the writings of Christianity as a natural thing, to be able to live and share things. It's really something for our children, this revolution. It will be great for them.

'We feel freer'

It is easy to forget, as a Westerner, how different things must have been in the past for women in a place like Condega. Eunice, the Frente secretary, feels that the revolution, in which women fought as equals alongside men in the guerilla camps, has established the 'real place' of the woman in society. 'Before, she was relegated to second place. She was like a slave. Women never had government jobs. Now they take part in all the tasks.' For the first time in this strongly Catholic, Latin American environment, their status as equals is legally unquestioned. Politically their role as activists in the revolution is as important as that of men. They are the people who could tell me most about the transformation of life since the revolution.

Donatila, who grew up on a coffee estate where she worked as a cook and bore twelve children, now travels to Managua to attend national meetings of mothers. She returns happy and full of enthusiasm. At the Frente office she goes along to argue the case with the army authorities for financial aid for a woman in need and for better communications with the front for the mothers of conscripts. On local platforms she is an inspiring speaker, encouraging women to stand firm in the face of difficulties, praising their courage. Before, she said, she could never have imagined playing such a role in the community.

For Donatila, the biggest change the revolution has brought is its commitment to progress.

Our young people have been to study in socialist countries. We are training teachers. We have more schools, health centres. Somoza was not interested in progress. In those days everything went to the USA and filled the pockets of the rich. Things were much harder then.

Julia Meza, Donatila's daughter-in-law, a housewife, talked of the changes she had experienced in the relationship with her husband.

I was very beholden to him because I never worked outside the house. I couldn't explain things to him like a professional woman would, but only like a housemaid. When I started doing some sewing to earn money, he stopped me. He said he was earning the money and I had to do what he said. We women were much more marginalized in those days. Women thought it was a sin to say no to their husbands.

I first met Casimira, a peasant woman of forty-two, at the funerals. She was burying her son, who had been killed in the ambush. Later she travelled into Condega from her village to meet me. She is a softly-spoken, humble person whose shy smile reveals a new kind of confidence. She recalled her childhood as one of a family of nine. Her father had a small plot of land and grew sugar cane. When he injured himself, her mother had to work to support the family.

She worked like a man to keep us. I started work myself from the age of eight. Later I went to school, but I can't really read and write properly, even now. At the age of sixteen I married and worked with my husband on the local coffee estate. We were very poor because he used to go off drinking. We women didn't have a value. We were like objects. We were really cut off in those days. Now we feel much freer.

Women in Nicaragua traditionally bore the brunt of the oppression that was rooted in the brutality of life under Somoza. Male supremacy in the home was absolute and reflected the authoritarian structures of the society. A woman was considered the possession of her husband, unable to travel or leave the home without his permission. She had to live where he said.

The attitude to women and childbearing was traditionally Catholic, and one which reinforced women's oppression, as Julia Meza explained.

Most women were married at sixteen. There were no contraceptives here, though people in the big towns knew about them. But only the rich could buy them. They would have only three or four children each. The poor had up to twelve and sometimes even twenty children. It was horrible.

Those women who worked on the land (25 per cent of the agricultural workforce) were not paid. Their wages went straight to their husbands. Many women who wanted to work were prevented from doing so. I met a group of peasant women tending tomatoes north of Condega. They told me how happy they had been since the revolution to be able to leave their houses and come into the fields. It had given them a huge sense of freedom.

Legally, women had few rights. If the husband abandoned a woman or beat her, failed to maintain her or her family or was unfaithful, she had no grounds for divorce. If she committed adultery, even once, the man had every right in law to divorce her.

Julia Meza told me about the prostitution that existed in Condega until 1979 – one of the inevitable consequences of the underprivileged position of women:

> Prostitution was rampant. It was horrible. It used to be a government business like a registered shop, called a *cantina*. People used to go and get drunk and then pay a woman and use one of the rooms behind. There were about five *cantinas* here in Condega. You used to see peasants who'd tie up their horses outside. It was embarrassing. The National Guard were involved in keeping some of those women. They even paid a tax to the state.

The revolutionary government set out to make fundamental changes. As early as 1969 the Sandinista programme had promised to 'abolish the odious discrimination women have suffered with respect to men' and to 'establish economic, political and cultural equality between women and men'. Ten years later the Statute of Rights of 1979 resolved that 'the state will overcome, with all the means at its disposal, the obstacles which prevent equality between Nicaraguans – without distinction between race, nationality, creed or sex'.

A range of new laws have been passed to set the legal framework: equal pay for equal work, the outlawing of female images in advertising, and the food law, which is aimed at making both parents legally responsible for child maintenance. New laws on family relations abolished the definition of the man as the sole head of the family, possessing absolute rights over children. Women can now claim maintenance payments from an absent father. Social security payments were introduced for widows, family protection rules enable women to claim payments from absent fathers, and a law of nurturing recognized domestic labour as useful labour.

The new women's association AMNLAE soon reached a membership of 85,000 in 700 local committees. Its programme aimed to promote women's political and ideological skills, to fight discrimination, and to enhance the value of domestic work. First and foremost, however, came the defence of the revolution. The women of Condega spoke proudly of the women's association. Not that it seemed to hold many meetings; rather, it was an expression of their approval of their *right* to organize as women and of their pride in their contribution to social change. Casimira explained:

> In the past it would have been impossible to talk to you like I am now. We have advanced a lot. We have our organization AMNLAE and hold our own meetings. Before, men were against that kind of thing. Now some men don't mind and even encourage you. These days you seldom hear of women being beaten up.

Julia, who in practice rarely had time to go to meetings, said:

> We feel freer since the revolution because we can go out to work. The law protects us and men are obliged to give us support. My husband is in favour of my getting involved. He says he will help so I can get to a meeting.

Machismo and the kitchen sink

It was through women like Donatila that I experienced some of the contradictions of life in Nicaragua. For, despite all these changes, here was a woman who spent virtually the whole of her day running a large-scale catering operation for her extended family. By 5 a.m. she was up and making tortillas for breakfast. I would hear her in the makeshift kitchen next to where I slept patting them into shape for the top of the clay oven, sending smoke wafting into the house. Throughout the day she prepared, served and cleared meals of rice, beans and maize – with meat if there was enough money – for children, grandchildren and visitors. When she wasn't cooking she was ironing, washing, or cleaning. And she saw this not so much as a chore, but as her contribution to the revolution which her children are carrying through.

It was not her life which was going to change under the revolution, she said once, but that of her children and children's children. It was hard not to draw the conclusion that in the home the position of Nicaraguan women has changed very little.

In the Centeno household it was the women who were expected

to cook and clean and whose day never ended. The attitude of men was a topic that Donatila loved to discuss, though rather sheepishly because it was not placed high on the agenda by the Sandinistas. AMNLAE promoted an image of women as caring mothers who had a duty to both the family and to the revolution. It has only recently begun to confront inequalities in the home, along with (tentatively) some of the more sensitive areas such as a woman's sexuality and a woman's right to choose. Donatila's attitude to domestic equality, as to machismo, was fatalistic. 'You'll never change men. They are always the same,' she said once, sitting with her feet up in a rare moment off in her arduous day.

The question of housework was not the only problem for women. I came across several instances of personal conflicts in the home between politically-active women and their husbands. Men were unused to wives whose political responsibilities kept them away from home for large parts of the day and evening. Many husbands were finding it hard to accept that they no longer had authority over their wives. Luisa talked of a colleague whose husband had walked out because she was never at home. 'He said she was going with other men, which was untrue. She was left to bring up her family on a pittance. We got some more conscious men to reason with her husband, asking him to prove she had another man. Eventually he returned home.'[3]

The old divorce laws have only recently been scrapped. With the adoption of the new Constitution in January 1987 marriage may be dissolved by mutual consent or by the will of one of the parties. Church marriages as well as 'stable unions' are recognized for the purpose of the state.[4]   However, the administrative apparatus for executing these new laws has still not been set up. And in any case in rural towns like Condega, it is still hard for women to contemplate divorce. The social stigma of being a divorcee is still too great.

Though blessed with a constant and loyal husband herself, Donatila never ceased to chide the male sex for its fickleness. She recalled with amusement an incident in Condega shortly before I arrived. A soldier was killed. Villagers attended his funeral – the usual expression of public mourning and anger at the Contras. The coffin was brought up to the front of the church for the man's family to stand round. There was not just one family in mourning, however, but five, all with between three and five children in tow. To the embarrassment of the army, all five women claimed a widow's pension.

Many women in Condega are bringing up large families by themselves. Some have never had husbands. Others had men who moved on. In the old days thousands of Nicaraguan landworkers had to travel across the country for work and would spend only three or four months in each place. Something like half the households in Nicaragua are run by women. Most of these single women are caught in a vicious circle of poverty and dependence which is being reinforced by the current economic shortages. Some have to spend hours collecting firewood for their clay ovens.

Sandinista policy on women, which elevates and demands respect for 'women's duties in the home', has failed to tackle head-on some of the basic factors that keep women prisoners of their conditions. The grip of tradition is strong, and, due to Church disapproval, contraception is rarely discussed openly, especially in the rural areas. If anything, the death of 50,000 in the insurrection stimulated public desire for women to produce as many children as possible. 'Women [are] as fertile in their wombs as they are in revolutionary consciousness,' said Interior Minister Tomás Borge in 1982.

On any typical day a succession of barefoot women would call at the Centenos' house, children clinging to their skirts, to ask if they could do some laundry. It was probably their only income. The Centenos, while not a wealthy family, had grown-up children in full-time paid jobs. They had moved up the social scale since the revolution. Sometimes Donatila paid a woman to help in the kitchen. At other times she would count up piles of dirty laundry on the veranda and wrap it in a large blanket which the women would carry away with them, perhaps to the river or to their own homes. For these women, bringing up large families by themselves, it is hard to find the energy to 'participate' in the revolution. AMNLAE has been slow in addressing its programmes to the problems of these women.

The war has had direct effects on the speed of emancipation. Condega boasts a new children's canteen which would provide one balanced meal for the children of working mothers, but in the time I spent there it remained shut. Any spare resources of the Ministry of Social Services were being diverted into refugee camps for displaced families further north. Day-care centres had been promised in all areas but progress was slow.

For many women the war has turned the clock back and re-imposed a certain isolation. Julia Meza's husband is away for months. 'We are alone a lot more now. It's frightening and we aren't used to it.' For Casimira, living in a new settlement in the mountains, going to meetings is almost impossible these days.

After the triumph mothers used to have regular meetings, but this is much harder to do now. We are very isolated now. We can't really be free under the circumstances. You might want to go to a meeting, but on the way you meet the Contras. We feel a real fear of the enemy.

AMNLAE was not a thriving organization in Condega while I was there. Nidia, the AMNLAE worker, performed the job of social worker and was identified in the eyes of many women with the pressure to send their sons to military service.

AMNLAE and women's needs

But there were pressures from below to change AMNLAE's agenda. In 1985 a report from the only women's hospital in Managua showed that ten women a day were arriving at the hospital with septic abortions. Self-induced abortions had become the principal cause of death amongst women of childbearing age.[5] It seemed that women were dealing unilaterally with the question of abortion. The report forced the issue of a woman's choice as to her fertility into the open. As in the past, however, those in favour of legalizing abortion found the Government slow to take on an issue which would give the Catholic Church hierarchy more grounds for complaint. AMNLAE itself discovered that working-class and *campesino* women were reluctant to discuss abortion publicly.

Pressure from women rural workers in the agricultural workers' union was one of the factors that pushed AMNLAE and the FSLN into more active consideration of women's domestic needs and rights and of its own role. Shouldn't AMNLAE articulate women's needs rather than merely encourage women into the activities of the revolution?

AMNLAE's Second National Assembly reported the results of 600 local meetings with 40,000 women from all social and economic classes. Women uniformly expressed the need for greater knowledge about and access to birth control. Women in the factory and clerical workers complained that their employers demanded sexual favours as a condition for them keeping their jobs or getting promoted. Wife-beating was reported as being most prevalent among the poor, but working and professional women also suffered from physical abuse. Women also criticized the FSLN itself, especially for the party's lack of initiative in raising its members' awareness of women's problems.[6]

By 1986 AMNLAE was reassessing its priorities, admitting that it 'had not successfully reflected the specific concerns of women'.[7] This was an admission of the failure of their previous agenda, which had been set by the FSLN, not by women themselves. It was a complaint that the FSLN was forced to take up, not least because of its own awareness of declining participation by women in the revolution in some areas and of the real domestic obstacles that limited the production levels of an increasingly female rural labour force.

In 1987 the FSLN published a new statement on women and the revolution. For the first time it specifically accepted the responsibility for 'education and consciousness-raising of *men and women* to oppose discrimination against women'. AMNLAE's role, it said, was to 'identify women's specific problems so that these can then be assumed as problems of the revolution'. 'We will promote, in the social and institutional spheres, stronger measures against irresponsible fatherhood and physical and moral abuse of women and children,' the statement ran. 'We will promote true solidarity within the couple with respect to domestic tasks and family responsibilities.'

Nonetheless, the FSLN explicitly rejected 'any group that proposes the emancipation of women through a struggle against men, as an activity exclusive to women. This position divides and distracts people from the tasks at hand,' it stated. And once again the Sandinistas re-affirmed their view of the primacy of the family – despite the fact that less than half Nicaraguan households have fathers. 'Women have been the pillar of the Nicaraguan family,' they said. 'We will fight so women can meet their maternal and family responsibilities under increasingly better conditions.'[8]

It is clear that the self-organization of women is still regarded by some in the FSLN leadership as a potential threat to the goals of the revolution, rather than as a means of involving women in its defence. Women make up 24 per cent of FSLN membership, yet there are as yet no women in its National Directorate. In 1985 less than 10 per cent of high-ranking public officials were women. Only twenty per cent of delegates to the National Assembly are women (a figure which is, however, much higher than the proportion of female members of the House of Commons in Britain).

AMNLAE has made a start in putting some of women's needs on the revolutionary agenda. It remains to be seen whether it can continue to set its own list of priorities in tandem with the country's defence needs.

15.   Ermen: ministering to the people

The *junta* goes to Santa Teresa

Ermen Rodriguez, of Condega's *junta* or municipal board, was not bringing much good news for the people of Santa Teresa. It took over two hours by road to reach this small community twenty kilometres west of the Condega. When it rains the journey takes even longer. The road becomes a morass of large puddles and red mud over which would-be visitors have to slither carefully, trying to avoid getting stuck. Santa Teresa was difficult to reach at the best of times. But the local bus had stopped running and the villagers were virtually cut off from Condega and the main road south. Villagers had come to the community meeting to get a response to their demands.

'The bus will start again soon', said Ermen, 'when the tyres come.' Hearts sank. The Condega municipality had been waiting for its complement of new tyres for weeks. Most of the vehicles were riding around with completely bald ones. Many were off the road completely. There would be a regional meeting tomorrow of the Ministry of Supplies, Ermen added. People seemed sceptical that Condega would be considered a top priority.

The villagers of Santa Teresa were crammed into the little school house. Outside it was dark and grey, and had rained recently. They were a community of peasant-farmers growing maize and beans on their own small plots of land. There were no proper co-operatives in this remote valley. But the farmers had grouped together into credit collectives to apply for technical and financial aid.

Two jeep-loads of officials had arrived in the village for the meeting. There was Carlos, a Frente organizer, Mauricio of the army recruitment board, Eric from the Ministry of Agriculture, Noel from the Ministry of Commerce, someone from the Education office, someone from the farmers' union, a woman from the AMNLAE office in Estelí and Ermen who, as head of the municipal *junta*, co-ordinates the work of various ministries. In his mid-thirties, he was probably one of the oldest of them all. He is a softly-spoken, serious, perhaps even slightly pompous man, an intellectual who speaks in

long sentences as if giving a lecture. While he was at school he had
hoped to become a priest. But along with the rest of his generation
at the secondary school in Condega in the early 1970s, he had been
drawn into the struggle against Somoza.

It was ironic, I mused, that some ten years after Ermen and other
students had occupied the church in protest at the mayor of Condega,
here he was as a kind of mayor or town clerk himself.

During the day his office in Condega, in a modern house near the
central square, is besieged by people coming to register marriages,
births, deaths and land transactions. Venancia of the local health
council also works there, making sure that old people, widows and
single mothers get their small social security payment. Ermen's job
as co-ordinator of the *junta* is basically administrative: answerable
to the regional government in Estelí he is responsible for executing
policies of the central government in housing, town planning, roads,
and other amenities.

Nicaragua has no tradition of local democracy, even of a nominal
kind. Under Somoza mayors were appointed with the say-so of the
president, and never forgot their allegiance to him. They received
kickbacks and bribes, and distributed licences according to where it
paid them most to do so. The revolution, which overthrew all of
that, confirmed the mass organizations as the vehicles for democratic
participation; the municipal boards are appointed, not elected.[1] The
guiding hand behind the mass organizations is the Frente – although
there are plenty of examples of pressure from the mass organizations
overturning a policy.

Ermen was the man who would put these demands to the relevant
ministries in Estelí arguing, cap in hand, for more money or better
supplies.

It was evidently a frustrating job, given the financial condition of
the country as a whole. In Condega, for example, Ermen had long
cherished a plan to secure new refuse trucks and to build a municipal
palace in the central square. He believed in formalities in the civic
field. But these were really just pipe dreams in the current climate.
What Condega needed most were 300 hundred new houses to accommodate its growing population, a new primary school, a recreation
ground and a new community centre, not to mention repairs to the
rubbish tip, better pollution controls, repairs to wells and water
towers, and a new municipal abattoir. Waste from the existing
abattoir and chemicals from the tannery had been flowing untreated
into the river and contaminating the crops which are irrigated from
its waters.

In the village of Santa Teresa the needs were even more pressing, but that didn't make it any easier to secure funds from the ministries. 'We are trying to form a transport collective', said Ermen in answer to the meeting of the villagers.

> Of course it's difficult with the shortage of spare parts. The problem with the roads is that all the construction teams in the area have been mobilized to build roads elsewhere. Perhaps the community here could repair some of the roads itself.... The *junta* could help in some aspects. Not with money but food perhaps for the people who volunteer....
>
> I feel really sorry about the situation. But you must remember that there are still communities that we cannot attend to at all. We have nearly twenty-nine people training in Cuba at the moment. When they come back they will be integrated into the communities and able to help.

It was a hard message. The villagers were not aggressive, but gently pressed their problems on the officials. They needed cement to build a new well. I agreed with them, having gone to a nearby house to ask for water and been offered a most unsavoury liquid which I thought best not to touch. But cement would depend on aid from Switzerland, Ermen said. They needed bank loans which had been promised ages ago. Why hadn't the man from the bank come back to see them, to explain the situation? They needed batteries for the radio – their only means of communication; milk – they had none in the zone; and new machetes – was there any chance of importing them? It was difficult for the children to get to school. What transport there was was very expensive. It was privately run and the man was overcharging ... could the state not make available a vehicle, even a lorry, so the community could run it themselves? And on top of it all the army was calling up their young men for military service.

'I have two sons in the army', said one man. 'There is one son left on whose labour I depend. I have ten children altogether. He has been called up now. He doesn't want to go, though he will go if it is necessary. But I can't pay back the bank loans without him.' A woman stood up to tell a similar story: 'My only son is doing his military service. But I can't manage without him. When he left he was trying to mend my house – the walls were falling in. I want help from you. The CDS isn't helping me.'

Carlos, a rather officious young man from the Frente, was not the most tactful of representatives.

A lot of people are raising personal problems. You are the members of the community board. A lot of these problems arise because people are not lending a hand in the communal work. You have to make people conscious of the economic and military measures we have to take. If the American trade blockade means we don't get petrol or diesel, we'll have to go back to the horse and cart.

There was silence. A man stood up at the back of the room, passing his stetson nervously through his hands as he strove to find the words:

The life of the *campesino* is the saddest of all. I lost four *manzanas* of coffee this year. Perhaps you're going to say that I don't understand or that I'm counter-revolutionary. No it's not that. I wouldn't be participating, going to meetings three days in a row, if I wasn't with the revolution. I'm glad that my son can go and contribute with the army. But the life of the *campesino* is lived with the machete. It is really hard work. It is not like an office job where you can at least eat. Sometimes the *campesino* doesn't eat all day for the amount of work he has to do. It is hard.

He wasn't complaining. Just pointing out a class difference between those on the top table and the people of Santa Teresa.

Mauricio of the army recruitment board was more sympathetic. His own *campesino* background showed in the way he talked:

All the youth you've talked of must go and explain these problems to the recruitment board. People whose fathers cannot work will not have to join up. Mothers must ask for economic help. There are other exemptions too but the board decides. We have to be clear that we are going to defend the freedom, our co-operatives, the mothers, Nicaragua. This is why we have patriotic military service. If US imperialism comes we won't be able to sow our crops. Do we want to work in peace or be molested by the counter-revolutionaries? Because the Frente will not allow the USA to put a step here.

October 1978

Ermen did not really seem to enjoy meeting the *campesinos* and having to face their questions. He explained after the meeting:

> A lot of people went to the mountains to help defeat the enemy
> but had no idea this would not change the economic structure
> of the country. Some of them are now against the revolution.
> There is a very low cultural level and a high degree of illiteracy.
> Some people thought they would get everything on a plate. But
> it wasn't like that. A lot of people are surprised and confused.

It was hard to wage a campaign against the Contras in remote areas who were telling *campesinos* that agrarian reform would deprive them of their land, he said. Ermen prided himself on his own *campesino* background. His parents had sacrificed income to send him to the secondary school, he explained, where he was one of the poorer boys.

I talked with him at length in the *junta* office in Condega on an evening when it was his turn to do guard duty there. He obviously liked to be asked about the old days and fancied himself somewhat as a local historian. When I asked him about his generation of students at the school he told me about a school magazine they used to publish in the early 1970s. To my amazement he produced a copy of the magazine there and then from the bottom drawer of his desk.

At the school he, along with others such as Amanda and Luisa Centeno, had been drawn into the Christian base groups and became an active lay delegate. Unlike the others, however, he had a theoretical and intellectual approach to liberation theology and the role of Christianity in Nicaragua. Where others speak in political terminology, Ermen speaks of ideas.

Ermen is one of many Condegans who remembers the year 1978 in detail. After the failed insurrection of September 1978 he returned to Condega from the seminary college, his plans to become a priest in ruins. He decided to do a teachers' training course in Estelí, but with the town in disarray even that was difficult. In Condega he began to help Father Wésther López with the teaching at evening classes in the church hall. But with the National Guard on the alert, night schools aroused suspicion.

> The National Guard hated us bringing so many people together
> in the church hall. There were around 150 – night after night.
> They used to harass us psychologically. They'd start shooting

near where we were holding our lessons and people would get frightened. So then people wouldn't come back to the lessons next time. We were fighting hard, but we couldn't teach.

The brutality of the National Guard was radicalizing the population as never before. The repression that followed the uprisings had driven most of the active youth out of Condega and into the mountain camps of the Frente. Condega was closely watched. But behind the scenes people were stepping up feverish clandestine activity of organization and politicization, despite the enormous risks. 'There was no problem in convincing people here. Ninety-five per cent were for insurrection', remembers Henry Vargas.

Ermen and hundreds more activists, worked to build up the civil defence committees – which later formed the basis for the CDS.

Through our contacts with Estelí we began to strengthen the committees. We could see how to organize, how we would have to look after the children, to distribute food, how to keep up the calories, which were the best foods to store – sugar or sweets; water. Also that we would have to protect one another. We couldn't go into the street but would have to communicate through the walls of our houses. We knocked doors into the walls and built hiding places. We also had financial quotas. We had to collect money to be sent to the mountains so the people there could buy things and keep up supplies.

Gradually all the major workplaces in Condega were drawn into the net of people's organizations; the abattoir on the Pan American Highway, the tannery, the electricity plant.

The church building itself had become an important sanctuary. Don Antonio particularly talks of this:

We used to go and pray in the church. That was a marvellous, beautiful thing. A great love felt by the whole village. A great trust. We felt a great unity. We weren't afraid there. If we were in the church, the Guardia couldn't gun us down. That's what we said. 'It's OK.'

Father Wésther López had come under close scrutiny:

Practically speaking I had no contact with the Guardia because I was afraid of them. Terrified. They kept up a constant vigilance of my sermons. I would denounce the injustices, the abuses, the repression, the lack of freedom, the poverty and call on our peoples to unite and fight. I would speak indirectly but people would understand me.

Somoza was being kept in power by the force of the Guardia, because they had the arms. It was a well-organized powerful force and the only way to fight it was with arms, to defeat and destroy the Guardia. No other way could be seen of looking for change.

Meanwhile, the lay delegates, and in particular Ermen and Don Henry, used every opportunity they could to alert populations to the preparations being made. The United People's Movement held meetings in nearby towns. At one such meeting in October, in Palacaguina, where the National Guard had strong links, they saw their opportunity to pounce. Ermen, Don Henry and Father Wésther López were arrested. Don Henry had been speaking:

I was addressing the meeting and I was talking about the things the community might need in their medical store. I mentioned sweets and the Guardia listening must have thought it a code word for arms. We were arrested outside the building and accused of being communists. They put us in a cell and started to insult us.

The response in Condega was immediate, as Luisa Centeno recalls:

We heard Padre Wésther had been arrested. Immediately the people took to the streets and demonstrated for his release. There were old people, children, everybody came out. The Guardia shot tear gas at us, but we stood our ground. They just had to release him.

Ermen and the others stayed in the Guard cell for only three hours. A large crowd had gathered outside the barracks demanding their release. The Guard started to shoot. In the end they thought better of it and released their prisoners.

There was similar anger over the arrest of Alcides Centeno, Luisa's older brother and a leading activist. A huge crowd came onto the streets threatening to kill the mayor and burn down the houses of prominent Somocistas, such as the judge. Don Antonio tried to calm the crowd. But the Guard were even more fearful of the consequences of removing their prisoner to Estelí. 'The priest and others followed the vehicles he was in. But they let him go. They knew it would end in something serious, in a big uprising of the people', said Don Antonio.

Death of a priest

During the fighting in Estelí, Father Wésther López's presbytery had been converted into a makeshift hospital. People would ferry the wounded up to Condega where a local doctor, sympathetic to the opposition, gave medical treatment. The defence committees being built in the town provided medicines and other supplies. One of the drivers who would bring people to the presbytery was a Jesuit priest, Francisco Espinoza, founder of the agricultural college near Estelí and a close collaborator with the Frente.

On the night of 18 October 1978, the same day as the Guard shot Dachsun's friends near the bridge, the Jesuit arrived in Condega with a pregnant woman and a fireman from Estelí. Ermen's night school had finished for the evening and the town was silent and dark. The car got no further than the crossroads in the central square. A hail of bullets from an M50 machine gun, fired from the National Guard headquarters, ripped into the vehicle, killing all three occupants instantly. Father Wésther López heard the shots:

> I heard the shooting but I had no idea who it was. No one could go into the streets for fear of being shot. We were shut into our houses. I was expecting the priest to come because he was bringing people wounded in Estelí. We had doctors and nurses from the village at the presbytery. He used to come everyday with women, men and children wounded by shotguns, bombardments or whatever. We used to treat them and give them food. Only that very same morning I had had breakfast with him [Francisco Espinoza] in the presbytery.

It wasn't until the next morning that Condegans could establish who had been killed. Henry Vargas, the reporter, was one of the first to find out:

> We all heard the machine guns but we couldn't go out. Two hours later the Guardia were in a local bar getting drunk. The next day we managed to find out that it was the priest they'd killed. The park keeper was watching them. He showed us where they buried the bodies. You could see the traces of blood on the road. The woman had aborted her baby on impact. We don't know who she was to this day. The Guardia helped themselves to the car and stripped down its radio.

Ermen and Don Henry are sure that the priest's frequent trips to

Honduras and Salvador before his death aroused the suspicions of the Guardia. They suspected him of ferrying not just the wounded, but also arms. They showed no mercy with suspected members of the Frente. The murder of the priest left the town in a state of shock. Somoza had imposed a new level of repression all over the country. Martial law and a state of siege were reintroduced. There was a news blackout while members of Somoza's mobile elite forces, the EEBI[2] 'mopped up'.

In the nights, fear gripped the town. Donatila often talks of the atmosphere in those days:

> You couldn't really trust anybody. Three per cent of the people in Condega were spies for the Guardia. They had denounced my family. Martial law and a six-o'clock curfew were imposed on the town. Going out was a crime. At six o'clock everyone was in their houses and the lights were off. We didn't even dare talk. We had to expect the worst. The Guardia would sometimes break people's doors down and rob them. No one could do anything.

The exodus begins

Thus began a gradual exodus of those who were able to leave the town. Donatila Centeno left and joined members of the family in exile in Mexico, where, with solidarity funds, the FSLN could provide for its supporters.

It was the shootings on the night of 18 October 1978 that finally convinced Don Antonio that his life was directly in danger. People had come to the conclusion that old Somoza wasn't in control, rather it was his son who ran the EEBI. Members of the EEBI crack troop were kept drugged and drunk and were capable of picking off any identifiable opposition activist.

On the same day as the shooting, Dachsun Cattin's two friends had tried to make their way to Condega to attack the Guard, but they had been detected and killed near the bridge. The National Guard had brought in reinforcements and were virtually occupying the town. Luisa Centeno moved to her husband's farm outside the town and continued her activities. She remembered the suspicion and hostility: 'People of thirteen and fourteen, even women, would be arrested just for wearing boots which looked like the ones the youth wore in the mountains.' Henry Vargas described the state of emergency:

By this time only police chiefs and their paid spies were in favour of Somoza. In practice there was a state of emergency for virtually a whole year. The Guardia had a special force against 'communists'. They used tear gas bombs against the students.

Throughout the country five or six people would disappear every day. By March 1979, a report on human rights carried out by Costa Rica established that 280 people were being murdered every month.[3]

But the Frente had the upper hand politically in the country. The same month as Father Francisco was killed, talks initiated by the USA between Los Doce and the business opposition to Somoza broke down. The USA announced plans for a provisional government in Nicaragua that would include Somoza's party and the National Guard. The FSLN was working nationally to win over the middle class and business classes and to undermine this move, whose objective was to dispose of Somoza while keeping his state apparatus intact.

By the end of January 1979 a number of the smaller parties had lined up with the Sandinistas to create a National Patriotic Front. This new broad alliance under Sandinista leadership called for national sovereignty, effective democracy, justice and social programmes. The three tendencies of the Sandinista Front were by now reunited formally. By early 1979, apart from some sections of the business community, few dissented from its leadership.

To succeed in the final push against the dictatorship, however, the FSLN still needed to isolate Somoza internationally, put the whole population on a war footing and weaken the National Guard.

16.   The people of Canto Gallo

Easter 1979: the boys move in

Around Condega the people with the longest links with the FSLN are the subsistence farmers and landworkers of the mountainous zone known as Canta Gallo. This is the area where in the mid-1970s people like Omar Cabezas built a base for the Frente (see Chapter 9). In 1979 it became the heart of the guerilla zone. It was to sustain the FSLN camps in this area that the population of Condega mobilized during 1978.

After the defeat of the September insurrection the camps were swollen with thousands of recruits from Estelí and Condega: young men and women in their teens who trained and prepared for a final offensive. The Condega–Canta Gallo axis was a crucial bond linking town and country, middle class and *campesino*, old and young, housewives and guerilla fighters, mothers and sons. It was the youth of these guerilla camps who captured all the towns of Las Segovias in the final offensive of May, June and July 1979. And it was the *campesinos* of Canta Gallo who kept them alive and protected them from a National Guard which had gone berserk.

The camps were run by people like Moisés Córdoba, who, since his return from jail in 1976, had lived as a guerilla in caves with his wife and children, along with seventy other families. His father Don Leandro found that he too was once again lending a helping hand.

I was in Los Planes. Imagine the day that Omar Cabezas came by, with about a hundred men. He came to the house and asked, did we have any food. He had just come down from the mountain, he explained. 'I haven't got much food, but you're welcome', I said. And my wife went off to find tortillas. They asked whether we had any tacks to mend shoes. They took us to the camp which they had in Canta Gallo. And thank God I had brought a hammer which I gave to them and they could patch up their shoes more or less.

The older *campesinos* in Canto Gallo would come into the town and gather all the information they could about the movement of the Guard to pass on to the guerillas. They carried messages in both directions and brought food and supplies back from the civil defence committees. Pilar Monsón, another old fighter of Sandino who had been tortured in 1976, kept an overall picture of the guerilla forces:

> There were five camps in the Bua area with between fifteen hundred and two thousand guerillas. Once a force of 500 Guardia attacked the camp but we fought them back. There were only twenty-five in the camp at the time. I knew the area and I got them out. Several Guardia died.

From such camps the FSLN was launching armed attacks against military convoys and economic targets such as coffee warehouses, sugar refining plants, etc., in an effort to damage the dictatorship's foreign currency earnings. On 21 February 1979, the forty-fifth anniversary of Sandino's assassination, National Guard posts were attacked in several towns simultaneously. A few days later an FSLN column took over the town of Yalí, to the east of Condega. Hit-and-run attacks increased in towns all over the north.

Another vital link in the clandestine communication chain was the priest of Condega and his lay delegates, such as Don Henry Vargas, the reporter.

> We were working directly with the Frente developing lay pastoral work even in towns like Somoto, Telpaneca. Somoza's National Radio kept saying that the communists were coming and would take away their cows, their wives etc. So there was constant political work needed. The boys from the camps would arrive on the doorsteps of the *campesinos* and would buy food they needed. So the *campesinos* became convinced that the Frente didn't wish them ill. And by 1979 there was a higher consciousness. People listened to the Frente radio station, Radio Sandino.

From the camps of Canta Gallo, 'los muchachos' entered Condega late on Saturday 7 April 1979. It was the day before Somoza chose to leave Nicaragua for an Easter break but also to drum up support for an application to the IMF for a $66 million loan. He had already imposed a 40 per cent devaluation of the cordoba, sending prices rocketing and causing an explosion of anger.

In Condega the people had been warned. Juana Salinas was told by her younger son:

> One of my sons said, 'Get under the mattress because we're expecting trouble.' 'What do you mean, trouble?' I asked. 'Later

you'll see', he said. We put out the lights and later we heard 'patria libre' shouted near here. 'Come forward so we don't shoot.' And the boys passed right by the house on their way in.

The priest Father Wésther López had also been forewarned:

> The boys took the village on the Saturday night. I knew they were coming. There was a wedding that day. But obviously it wasn't a joyful occasion, without the usual party. Some of the guests had their vehicles commandeered on their way back and had to walk home to their communities, including the bride herself. The boys needed the vehicles for the take-over.

At four a.m. on the Sunday morning – Palm Sunday – the guerilla column began their assault on the National Guard post. Four Guardia died. Black and red handkerchiefs masking their faces, the boys fought for four hours. The population of Condega acted as an important back-up to the guerillas, as Ermen Rodriguez remembers:

> People came out with food for the boys and took it up to their look-out posts. They brought cold drinks for each one. We knew they were coming and we were able to collect some things for them to take back with them which could be useful in their camp.

Father Wésther López also recalls that Sunday:

> Everyone was shut up in their houses, lying on the floor all Sunday. The boys left in the afternoon at about three and the Guardia took over again. We were terrified they would start killing. They arrived at people's houses to register but didn't take anyone away.

When the 'boys' withdrew from Condega they took with them nearly all the remaining youth between the ages of thirteen and twenty-two. They went on from Condega to Estelí, where in a repeat of the September insurrection they managed to hold the National Guard at bay for five days. Directed by Somoza's son Tachito, the Guard used Cessna aircraft to bomb the town and a thousand members of the Guard to break the Frente's grip. The column withdrew, urging people to join them to avoid the Guard's 'mopping up' operations. Over a thousand people died, killed by bombs or shot by the Guard.

Easter week, normally an occasion for national festivities throughout Nicaragua, was a muted affair in Condega in 1979. The colourful processions through the streets of Condega, the annual invasions of peasants from local communities in their best clothes, the packed church on Easter Sunday – none of this happened. As Wésther López said, 'No one came to the village and no one wanted to leave their houses. Just on the Friday we had a celebration inside the church. But very few people came.'

The high point of the week came when guerillas shot down one of the Cessna planes being used to bombard Estelí. They used anti-aircraft weapons that had recently arrived in the country, demonstrating a new fire-power of the Frente. The plane landed in the river and was later moved up to its spot on the top of the little hill overlooking Condega.

Meanwhile, more and more of Condega's youth were joining the Sandinista camps in Canta Gallo.

The San Jerónimo settlement

Today, the area of Canta Gallo is a flashpoint of the struggle; a crucial coffee-producing zone which has to be defended day and night from the Contras. The people have been driven out of their small communities and have retreated to settlements on the top of the mountains.

A few weeks after going there with Father Enrique, I travelled out to San Jerónimo again in the only vehicle which maintains communication with Condega on behalf of the co-operative. It makes a daily trip to collect supplies of petrol and food (vegetables and meat) and to ferry those needing medical attention or to run an errand in the town. By nightfall at six o'clock it is not safe to make a journey across the mountain. The road below is notorious for Contra ambushes. Not far from Canta Gallo are places like El Jocote, known for its Contra sympathies. As we swept by a crowded bus stop on the edge of Condega, the driver swore at the waiting men: 'Bloody Contras, the lot of them'.

The temporary shelters hastily thrown up around the crest of the mountain were gradually being made permanent with concrete bases and proper corrugated iron roofs. Inside, cardboard was stuck together to provide some privacy or to form rooms. The bedding was makeshift and crowded. The walls were the traditional thin tree branches – they provided little protection from the wind and rain so common at this height. The dirt floors were fine in the dry seasons, but in the tropical rains they become rivers of mud. The settlement had one temporary tap – in fact it was a hose pipe – bringing drinking water from a mountain stream. Washing clothes and bodies meant a trip to the river. There was no electricity. This is a remote area, and installing electricity or telephone lines is beyond the resources of the Government.

By the end of 1986 Nicaragua had over 200,000 displaced people, chased from their land by the Contras or, more recently, moved by the army away from the fighting around border zones. Where possible they are given land to work collectively. Virtually the whole of the country's welfare budget had been diverted to service and build their new settlements.

Further down the mountain is the wreckage of the old village. The little school building half destroyed; the concrete floors of what were houses strewn with the debris of fire and the odd personal belonging. The coffee-processing plant continues to be worked by well-armed men. The estate is one of the larger ones in a region which provides 15 per cent of Nicaragua's coffee crop. Getting the dollar-earning crop in safely is a high priority for the Government.

In the little shed that serves as an office, the management board – elected by the men – pores over the production plan, assisted by officials from the Ministry of Agriculture. On a Friday, members and their familes who have worked on the estate during the week come here to collect their pay. Next door is a medicine chest with a large store of contraceptive pills.

For the moment, two huts serve as a school for all the children. Other buildings in the central area are used for adult education and literacy classes. These are popular with all generations, though there is a chronic shortage of teaching materials. In a class I attended, two textbooks served a class of ten. The teacher was seventeen years old. Her pupils came after work in the afternoons, some with babies on their shoulders. 'We knew nothing before. We had no schooling. But it's not just learning to read. We want to know where we come from, where we are going, and what we are. So we learn about the history of the Frente and our struggle', explained one pupil, a man of twenty-six.

For single men there is a canteen in the centre providing beans and rice and tortillas all day long. This is also where the volunteers who come to pick coffee in the season eat.

Down near the river where the women do their washing, a group of older men has planted a vegetable garden. Some lost their own small plots of land in the Contra attack. 'We are happy because we are united. We don't rent land now, we have our own', said a fifty-year-old man.

The co-operative has the air more of an army camp than a farm. Twice a day the men gather for drill; their movements are co-ordinated with those of the regular army post nearby. As I took out my camera to capture the moment, firm hands were laid on my arm. Photographs were not allowed of military establishments, I was reminded. Production and defence were equally important, but defence always came first, a co-operative member explained.

At least a quarter of the seventy members of the co-operative are patrolling and guarding the estate at any one time, unavailable for farming. At night the men do patrol shifts in two-hour stints. If Contra activity is reported nearby, all the men become part of a defending army, leaving bed and family to descend to the woods with rifles and ammunition. Some men never bother to take off their green uniforms, even to go to bed. The night I stayed, there was an alert at 10 p.m. My host, a Chilean exile who keeps the co-operative's medicine chest, left his game of pelmanism by candlelight and put on his green combat jacket and rounds of ammunition with the familiarity of a daily routine. 'Don't bother to wait up', he said. A large group of Contras had been spotted by a patrol making their way across a nearby river.

From the neighbouring shacks, the sounds of rustling and preparation could be hear. By 10 p.m. most people have been asleep for several hours. There is no electricity and not everyone has candles; they are expensive and hard to find in Condega.

As I settled into a sleeping bag, wondering whether to be frightened, I could hear men gathering outside, clicking their rifles into the firing position, then driving off in the dark in the truck. It was raining and the wind drove the rain against the wooden shacks. Next door a woman was crying softly. Someone knocked at her door – another woman – and went in to comfort her. I thought about the tension these people must suffer every time this happens. Will all the men come back or will some get killed, right there, just down the mountain? Will there be a big battle? What will I do if the Contras get up as far as where we are now? I looked round the hut for something to defend myself with, then remembered that I wouldn't know what to do with it if I found anything. I would just have to talk my way out of the situation, I thought, before dismissing such a silly idea. There is no talking in Contra attacks. If you are not killed right away, you are raped first, then killed.

My host returned at two in the morning. No shots had been fired. The Contras were just passing through, and no one wanted a battle. Fully dressed, he lay down on his bed to catch a few hours sleep before morning.

'We still had a boss'

In Canta Gallo the war had distorted the process of agrarian reform that had taken place since 1979, and made it difficult to judge its progress. Many of the reforms themselves took place not because of a government plan, but because of pressure from below. The estate of San Jerónimo, for example, was not originally intended by the Government to be worked co-operatively. It was pressure from the _campesinos_ that pushed the Government into handing over ownership of the land.

In Canta Gallo the _campesinos_ had high hopes of change. People like Julio Calderon, now president of the co-operative in San Jerónimo, were longstanding Frente supporters. Julio had helped make weapons for the guerillas in the camps and took part in battles in the zone against collaborators of the Guard.

> I used to see what went on around me. It happened to my father. The poor peasant, the small producer, would borrow money from the bank. When his crop was ready the medium-sized producer would come along and offer to buy it. They would offer a low price but often the peasant would accept, say, because his wife was ill and they needed the money. Then they would get into trouble with the bank. The bank would take the land off him. The medium-sized producer, who had sold the crop at a profit, would then offer to buy the land back off the bank. That was how they grew to become the boss – by expropriating the poor.
>
> The Frente made the peasants aware who they were and who their landlords were. They made things clear, what the value of the peasants was. Nobody else talked like that.

The day after the triumph, on 20 July 1979 the coffee estates of San Jerónimo and Darailí in Canta Gallo were nationalized and became an 'Area of People's Property', to be run under state control. To their disappointment, the 500 or so landless _campesinos_ in the area found themselves still working as employees – but this time employees of the state. They benefited from immediate improvements in their wages, from the right to organization, and equal pay for men and women. But in the absence of real participation in management decisions, the faceless bureaucrats from Managua who had replaced the faceless absentee landlords did little to convince the peasants that their lives had been transformed. Julio, who had taught himself to read, began to articulate the discontent.

> The state enterprise started building dormitories and put in electric light. We had proper bunks and health care. Conditions changed a little. But we still had a boss. The proceeds of the coffee went to the people, not the landlords, yet the administrators were from the towns. We had our agricultural workers' union, but it was administered from the region. The peasants were asking, how come the revolution was supposed to be for us, but we have nothing? The Frente told us we must first learn to read. That meant we read the books and could see what the Frente had promised. People were saying that the Frente must be lying because they hadn't given us the land yet.

Julio, now aged thirty, began reading Sandino in his spare time. He and others were critical of bureaucracy and waste and the lifestyles of the managers. The newly formed farmers' union, the National Union of Farmers and Livestock Producers (UNAG), and the local FSLN leaders supported his suggestion that a co-operative be formed. 'I told the Frente office what was happening on the estate. I said: "Haven't we won the revolution to be able to defend the interests of workers?"'

At this time, in 1983, the Government was beginning to rethink some of its agricultural policies. Fear of losing the vital agro-export labour force had dominated its plan to keep the former estates of Somoza as state-run farms. But real wages had fallen due to inflation and peasant discontent was growing. On some state farms, where during Somoza's era workers received land to plant a subsistence crop, the managers had stopped this practice, which they saw as a backward and paternalistic form of exploitation. The peasants sometimes felt they were worse-off.

Throughout the country peasants began to press their demand for land, mindful of the promise of Carlos Fonseca: 'In Nicaragua no peasant will be without land nor land without men working it.' In response, the Ministry of Agriculture began to encourage the formation of new production co-operatives. Five hundred co-operatives across the country were chosen to receive special state attention for technical assistance. By the end of 1984, 33,000 families had joined production co-operatives, representing 22 per cent of the total number of peasant families in the country. More recently, the Government has concentrated on handing over land to individual landless families, rather than collectively.[1]

In Canta Gallo, not all the *campesinos* were keen on the idea of a co-operative, as Julio found out:

> I had formed a committee to show that we meant business. But when the state agreed to a co-operative being formed, the peasants started to get frightened that we wouldn't be able to manage it. A delegation came to take a vote. But three times we failed to get a majority to agree. The delegation left and told me to get back to them when I had made the peasants conscious.
>
> The peasants couldn't understand how it could be possible for the members of the co-operative to live if they weren't all sowing their own piece of land. They said they would die of hunger. So I took a blackboard and drew three circles and explained how the work would be divided between those who looked after the cattle, those who looked after the coffee, and those growing the food. Everyone will get a salary and buy their food from a store. When we held the next meeting everyone agreed.

Since getting their land in July 1983, the families of Canta Gallo have had little peace. Military exigencies dominate the co-operative's day-to-day priorities. They are a long way from implementing the words of Interior Minister Tomás Borge, who in presenting the title deeds said that co-operatives were 'not just for production but for a new education and the transformation of a generation of people'. 'There is permanent tension,' says Julio. 'We have lost members who expected higher profits. But this is impossible because of the war.' The co-operative needs $100,000 worth of new equipment. It needs more members too, but until there are houses to accommodate more people, the vicious circle will continue.

'We have no peace'

Many of the women and children in the settlement show the signs of the trauma of their existence. In May 1984 they saw their homes in Los Planes and Buenavista being set alight behind them as they ran to escape the Contras. 'They left us with nothing', said Corinna

Savala, who punctuated her remarks with peals of laughter. 'We had a nice house in Los Planes, and furniture. Now everything has changed. We couldn't take anything with us. The men don't rest. My husband comes in at five or six in the morning then leaves after breakfast to begin work, We have to be suspicious all the time.'

Corinna was a CDS volunteer in the co-operative. But few of the mass organizations functioned actively after the destruction of the communities. Most of the decisions in the settlement are being taken by the co-operative board. Even the women's organization AMNLAE had ceased to function. 'We don't want to divide people,' said Julio. 'There were conflicts between the AMNLAE and CDS groups here, and their national bodies', he added without explaining. Another man said the women's organization had been disbanded because of the danger the settlement would be taken over by the international feminist movement.

Many of the refugees fled for safety to Condega on the day of the attack. Some, like Angela Somorra from Los Planes, are still there.

> The Contras surrounded the community at breakfast time. They burnt the houses and our stores of maize. We had only forty militia men but there were over a thousand Contras. They left us with what we were standing in. We started walking – about 380 people. My grandmother had a fever. She was ninety-five. My son carried an eighty-year-old. By 3 p.m. we had arrived in La Laguna. All the families came to Condega. They put us up in the school, in the church hall.

In Condega the population stayed up all night arranging accommodation and food for the refugees. The school, the church hall, the CDS building, all became temporary homes. Two of the families, of which Angela and her four children, a sick grandmother and grandfather are one, have slept on the flagstones of the CDS building ever since the attack. They depend on donated food. But Angela's companion Roberto has not lost morale.

> Our communities were well organized. We had men and women in the militia. People there joined the Sandinistas before the triumph. In those days the Government didn't want to improve your life. They didn't want us to learn to read. We had neither hospitals nor schools. Today the enemy wants to push us back to the same thing. We're not going to let them, even if it costs us our lives.

For the families who have returned to the new settlement in San Jerónimo, there is a confidence in the complex defence arrangements. Antonia Talavera lives with six children in a house built of corrogated iron near the crest of the hill.

> I am much happier where I am. It's much more fun. We know we've got medicines if we need them. We're sharing things. Sometimes I look after young children. We can go to adult education classes. I was left with absolutely nothing after they burnt down my house. Not even a spare dress. But we feel safer up here with the defence system.

Like all the men, Pedro Bravia, fifty-three and with ten children, wears his green uniform all the time and is never without his rifle when working or walking about.

> People suffered the massacres of the Guardia in this area. At the time of the insurrection there were big battles here with up to a thousand Guards. We took the land and went on working.
>
> We see a future, despite the situation we are in at the moment of war, limitations of money, etc. We don't see ourselves as going back. This co-operative is our own work. But we have to be ready to sleep in water to defend it. The Americans are a strong force. But if they want to win they would have to destroy all Nicaraguans and bring in their own people.

It is not just the co-operatives themselves which the Contras have targeted, but also individual Sandinista activists in Canta Gallo. In July 1984, Angel María, a young farmworker in the neighbouring estate of Darailí, left early to look after cattle together with a well-known FSLN member, Lauriano Flores. He described what happened:

> Suddenly thirty Contras grabbed us. We were a way from the houses and we weren't armed. There were six of us working together but the Contras divided us up. I managed to escape in the evening. I walked back to the community and arrived there about 2.30 a.m. The next day we found Lauriano's body. They had tied his hands and tortured him. There were knife marks all over his body. They cut him into pieces and cut off his genitals.

Lauriano Flores had been a Sandinista since the arrival of Omar Cabezas in Canta Gallo, some ten years before. He was thirty-two years old and had been an authority in the community. Dachsun Cattin and other members of the CDS had to put together his body for the funeral. His skin had been peeled off. His body by then was in a state of decomposition. It was an experience that they will not forget.

Flores' friend Angel María moved to Condega with his family. To stay in Daraili would be dangerous for someone who is known to have escaped from the Contras. They live in a tiny shack divided into three compartments by brown paper walls. They have few possessions. The focus of their shack is a collection of brightly-coloured posters of Che Guevara and the founder of the FSLN, Carlos Fonseca. Angel María's wife and sister seem almost resigned to the cycle of the evacuations they have lived through. They have simply come to accept it.

17. The legacy of Julio César Castillo

A new education

Every weekday in Condega over fifteen hundred children and teen-agers dressed in blue and white uniforms make their way down one of the roads leading off the central square to the junior school. The school operates in shifts to cope with the huge expansion in demand that followed the revolution. There are only nineteen classrooms, and three of those are for children of nursery age. At nights the adults take over, many of them taking basic school lessons for the first time.

The school does not just lack space. Amanda, the headmistress, asked me to imagine teaching without blackboard, chalk, exercise books and often even textbooks. Pencils are strictly rationed. For the poorer families, buying pencils for a whole family of children is often beyond their meagre resources. From 1985 parents have had to buy the textbooks too.

The school is named after its headmaster in the 1970s, Julio César Castillo. If he had survived the events of 1979 to see the transformation in education that followed the revolution, he might well have been amazed. Castillo was one of the early members of the United People's Movement (the MPU) in Condega. From at least 1978 he and his family worked secretly with the Frente, looking forward to the fall of the Somoza regime and a government com-mitted to education.

Amongst young and old alike in Condega there is a tremendous enthusiasm for education. It began with the famous literacy crusade, in which over eighty thousand young volunteers were sent away for three months to teach people to read and write. The crusade was one of Nicaragua's straightforward successes. When the Government took over, less than half the people over the age of ten could read or write. After the crusade only one in seven or eight had not received some basic literacy skills.

Miriam, Luisa Centeno's older sister, who runs the education office in Condega, played me a tape-recording of the final ceremony in which *campesino* women talked of the new world that had opened up for them. Every March, schools hold a ceremony in the town to mark the start of the crusade.[1]

Where there were thirty-five schools in Condega's rural areas, there are now over sixty. Education has brought the *campesinos* in touch with the rest of the country, made them feel they are part of a nation, and is giving their children the opportunity to better themselves and break the cycle of dependence on the land. But literacy levels amongst adults in rural areas are still not high, despite adult education centres in the countryside. Most of the teachers in these popular education collectives are barely out of school themselves; and there is a dire shortage of books and reading materials.

Education has become one of the targets of the Contras. To destroy the support the Sandinistas have in the countryside, they have blatantly set out to destroy the new schools and to liquidate the teachers. Figures published at the end of 1984 showed that over 170 teachers had been murdered by the Contras, and 180 kidnapped. Over 800 adult education centres had been forced to close. Some 247 adult pupils had lost their lives. Twenty-four rural schools had been totally destroyed, and construction work in another thirty had had to cease. Altogether, 360 rural schools had been forced to close.[2]

In the Canto Gallo area of Condega the Contra attack of May 1984 left four schools burnt to the ground. Schooling had to continue in peope's homes. In communities around El Jocote, where the Contras had a certain base, teaching had virtually ceased as a result of threats to teachers and anti-education sentiments encouraged in the population. 'It's a very difficult period', admitted Miriam. 'The Contras say the Sandinistas are brainwashing people. Parents say they don't want to send their children to school. The children themselves are worried there will be reprisals if they go. We are doing our best to resolve the situation. But we can't send teachers out under these conditions.'

The first teacher to be killed in Condega was the headmaster of the junior school, Julio César Castillo. On 3 May 1979 he, his wife, his sister-in-law and her husband were murdered in one of the most brutal, cold-blooded massacres Condega has ever experienced.

1979: the May massacre

The May massacre has entered deep into the consciousness of the town's inhabitants. Every year since then, citizens have commemorated the day in ceremonies, meetings and church services. At the time, the massacre represented the last straw for the population of the town – a warning that no one, absolutely no one, was safe from the indiscriminate killings perpetrated by the National Guard as the regime tottered towards its defeat. Stories of National Guard atrocities had been commonplace ever since the insurrection of September 1978. There were over 600 political prisoners in National Guard jails.

From January 1979 Somoza had sent in his airforce to make air strikes and bombing raids in the mountains around Estelí and Condega, where heavy fighting was going on between the FSLN and Guard troops. The Human Rights Commission charged that the planes bombed not guerilla positions but civilian populations. Soldiers on the ground, they said, were raping women and murdering children and the elderly. They called 'on all democratic nationals of the world and especially on the Organization of American States to take immediate measures to prevent the continuing genocide'.

In April the Commission said that at least 500 people, mainly youths, had disappeared in the first three months of 1979, mostly killed. The National Guard lost fifty. Reporters who went into Estelí after the partial uprising at Easter found the city heavy with the smell of burning flesh, and buzzards circling overhead. The bodies of two youths aged about fifteen lay in a street filled with rubble, their throats slit, their hands tied behind their backs. Residents reported that the Guard killed around a thousand people in Estelí that week.[3]

It was the same as September, dragging people out of their beds at 4 a.m. and shooting them after the Frente had moved out. We were the only city that went through three separate uprisings and three waves of National Guard barbarity. April meant that there was no one at all left in Estelí who didn't support the Frente.[4]

Up until that point Condega had been let off relatively lightly from the repression going on in nearby towns like Estelí. Although the people were organized and conscious, the actions of the guerillas in Condega had been token. Condega was more important as a crossroads and means of communication for both the National Guard and the guerillas than as an important strategic site in itself. While the National Guard concentrated its efforts on squashing the uprising in Estelí, they did not have the men or the will to engage on other less important fronts as well.

The events of 3 May 1979 changed all that. The death squad arrived in town at one in the morning. They went first to the house of a worker in the slaughterhouse, Victor Palma, a collaborator of the Frente. He was shot dead on the corner of the street. Next they moved to the house of the headmaster, Julio Castillo. Neighbours heard the shots and found the children of the two families, and the two dead women, Castillo's wife and sister-in-law. But it was at least two days before people could trace what had happened to Castillo and his brother-in-law, Juan Guillén.

La Prensa reported the attack later that day under the heading 'Dreadful extermination of two families':

> This morning the whole population of Condega was overwhelmed by the dimensions of the tragedy. . . . Patrols, said to be drunk, invaded the houses, breaking down the doors and opening fire on the women and children who were still in bed. The heads of the families have disappeared. The massacre caused deep terror amongst the town's inhabitants. According to telephone information they did not emerge from their shelters until mid-day because of the atrocities.[5]

The reporter Henry Vargas, who was a friend of Castillo, is still visibly moved by the memory of what happened:

> He was killed by one bullet in his neck, the other in the testicles. They cut his wife's throat. They went on to the house of Juan Guillén. They killed his wife and a niece aged ten years, and took Guillén to Santa Rosa about twelve miles away. His body was riddled with bullets and wounded with sticks that they used. He had been completely tortured.

The priest, Father Wésther López, remembers the reaction of the town:

> They had told me in Condega that there was a list of people that the Guardia were going to assassinate. And they were already doing this in Estelí where they had assassinated honest people, businessmen etc., in their own houses. So when the assassinations happened here they not only surprised us but filled us with indignation. They were atrocious murders – people assassinated

without the right to defend themselves.

The massacre precipitated a stampede to leave Condega, which left the priest in an exposed position. He too had to lie low.

> The day after, people started leaving the town – leaving the place deserted, their houses shut up. There was nothing. Everyone left. There was a list. People said, 'It was them today, tomorrow it will be us. So let's go.' Many went to the rural communities and I went out to visit them to celebrate Mass and to encourage them. Afterwards I went to sleep at Somoto. I didn't stay in Condega either, as I was afraid. In fact I never slept in the presbytery again until after the triumph. If I stayed in Condega, I stayed with relatives.

Luisa was one of the few members of the Centeno family who had remained in the area after October 1978.

> I was living on the farm. A cousin arrived in a car and told me I would have to get out of the country. I left straight away in his car. I just left everything as it was. The National Guard stopped the car. I was with my boy. But a peasant who lived near me told them I was nothing to do with the Frente, though he knew I was. By 5 May I was out of the country. But the National Guard went to our house and ransacked everything.

Ermen Rodriguez had moved to a nearby community.

> Most people left Condega and went to Honduras. Others went to relatives in the countryside. The town was deserted. I wasn't living in the town but in a nearby community. The Guardia didn't really know what my role was because they would just see me in the church. But the priest told me I couldn't stay there. He had to go to sleep in Somoto, and he told me we would have to leave the country. I stayed, but moved to another community further away.

By the second week of May, Condega was deserted, the vast majority of its population having fled north in fear. Some people living in the poorest areas of the town had no choice but to stay. Juana Salinas, nursing a crippled husband, remembers:

> We had nothing to eat. But we weren't hungry. There was no water, no light, nothing in our house, so we went to shelter in another house. We were waiting for something to happen at night. My husband said to me, 'One of these days the boys are

going to come.' So I was alone and I began to collect pork fat, maize, beans, which I put in bags in a corner of the room. The village was deserted. Only a few people stayed in this *barrio*, Barrio Triumfo.

Honduras, and especially the small town of San Marco near the border with Nicaragua, became host to thousands of Nicaraguan refugees in that month, many from Condega. Luisa and others looked after comrades, found safe houses for the guerillas, and organized people to go and fight. Wésther López, still in Nicaragua, continued to act as a supply line: 'Caritas [the charity] sent me to Esteli, and we were able to distribute food to people once a week. From this food they used to send some to the boys in the mountains. I would take the food, celebrate Mass and go back to Somoto.'

Rough justice

There was an interesting corollary to the Castillo massacre affair. Just after the anniversary of the massacre at Condega, the Centenos held a party. Luisa and her family had recently moved to a nearby house they had managed to purchase, and the party was held in their backyard. The guest of honour was a rather shy man in his early thirties called Rubén. He arrived half-way through, wearing a brightly coloured shirt. It was nearly six years since he had been in Condega. There were tears and an emotional welcome, as if it were the return of the prodigal son. 'It's the best day in my life', said Rubén, through the tears.

The cases of Rubén Lira and his friend, Luis Manuel Silva, convicted in 1980 for complicity in the massacre at Condega, were not known to me until then. Luisa, who, along with Henry Vargas and the priest, Wésther López, had led the campaign for his release, did not talk much about the shortcomings of the revolution, one of which this certainly was.

It was a remarkable story however, and one which is to the credit of the supporters of the revolution in Condega and the local CDS officials, not to mention the priest and the Bishop of Estelí. Ultimately it is also to the credit of the Government, for correcting an unjust conviction. After the revolution, Rubén and his friend were 'denounced' by neighbours of the murdered family for having tipped off the National Guard and participated in the massacre of the

Castillo and Guillén families. Having been accused, they joined the ranks of some 7,500 others, mainly members and associates of the National Guard, who had been taken prisoner after the triumph. (In fact the prisoners represented only half of the members of the Guard, which had expanded from 7,500 to 15,000 after the September insurrection. Thousands had escaped imprisonment by fleeing to Honduras in the last few weeks of the war.)

The revolution had confounded its detractors by issuing strict penalties for vengeance killings and individual retribution against members of the Guard. Cases of residents taking their revenge on and killing members of the Guard (there were a hundred such incidents) were limited to the month of July 1979 and were quickly brought to a halt.[6] There were no mass executions. Abuses of power by the army and the police were severely disciplined. By March 1980 some fifteen hundred members of the Sandinista police had been dismissed for such abuses, particularly involving confiscation of property of 'known Somocistas' – a term which was being arbitrarily interpreted.[7] Interior Minister Tomás Borge insisted that the revolution must continue to prove its legitimacy by demonstrating its moral superiority over Somocismo. 'Implacable in combat, generous in victory', he said, quoting Carlos Fonseca.

The Government already had in place a new judicial system with a Supreme Court and Courts of Appeals, and had abolished the death penalty and enacted a series of basic statutes that guaranteed the right to a fair trial. But Rubén's and Luis's cases were heard by one of the nine special tribunals set up outside the normal court system to try to expedite the trials of the six thousand charged with having committed crimes under the authority of the previous government. The tribunals were created in response to public demand for justice (over 50,000 peope had died in the year of insurrection and nearly every family in Nicaragua had lost relatives), and to prevent the criticism, especially from abroad, that would be incurred by long periods without trial of those accused. The fledgling judicial system was unlikely to be able to handle the cases with sufficient speed.

The special tribunals used the existing criminal code, and could impose maximum penalties of thirty years' imprisonment. The three members of each tribunal were appointed by the Government. One member had to be a lawyer or law student near graduation, the others lay people of 'good moral standing'. There was no right of appeal to a higher judicial authority.[8]

Rubén and Luis were among the 4,331 convicted before the tribunals were dissolved in February 1981. In Condega, CDS activists reacted wth horror and disbelief. Both men had been active in the underground opposition to Somoza. Rubén had helped make grenades. Neither was a saint, but where was the evidence for murder? It appeared there was none.

Luisa explained how the convictions came about. 'What happened is that Rubén may have been guilty of stealing from the Gonzales' house after they were killed. Some possessions were found in his house. So the family denounced him. The evidence was circumstantial.' But there was not a shred of evidence of any implication in the murder. It did not seem that the boys were capable of such an outrageous crime, and where was the motive? Henry Vargas and others talked of a settling of scores. Father Wésther López launched his own investigation.

At the time, the rules of evidence used in the tribunals were coming in for criticism – in particular from the Commission on Human Rights of the Organization of American States, and Amnesty Internatonal. Reviewing case files at the tribunal offices, the Commission found 'many proofs that did not refer to the facts, but instead were value judgments about the individuals or the facts under investigation'.

In 1981 the Commission condemned the tribunals and their special expedited procedures. They submitted the accused 'to the legal judgment of people, some of whom were not lawyers, to the judicial decision of people who were not judges, to the verdict of political enemies and to the judgment of people more inclined to be severe than fair because of their victory'.[9]

Rubén himself explained what had happened at his trial.

> There was a prosecutor, a secretary and a president. They had no experience. They read all the accusations and then asked what I pleaded. I had a lawyer but I had no opportunity to state my case and bring evidence. If the system had been fair I would have been acquitted because everything that was said about me was false.

In October 1981 the Government responded to its critics and passed a Law of Pardon, authorizing the Government's own human rights commission to review the convictions and send their review to the Council of State, which had the power to pardon, commute or reduce sentences. The Commission was flooded with petitions relating to two thousand prisoners. The Bishop of Estelí put his name to the petition from Condega. Father Wésther López's letter said: 'According to the investigation and conclusions that I have reached with those responsible I can assure you that [they] did not participate in the said massacre and their conviction is unjust.' Luisa and Henry Vargas organized statements from individuals and organizations.

In December 1983, 300 prisoners were amnestied, but Rubén and Luis were not among them. There was despondency in Condega, but Luisa immediately began to organize yet another petition to the Commission. Her brother Alcides, political secretary of the Frente in Jalapa, gave a personal reference: 'I have known them since my childhood and observed good conduct and honesty ... I join the petition of the mass organizations, the town and their friends that they be set at liberty by our revolutionary Government.'

In 1984 the Commission completed its review of 250 cases. Pardons were granted in eighty-nine of these, and sentences reduced in four others. In May 1985, 116 prisoners were released under the amnesty granted to Contras. In early 1987 there were about 1,700 prisoners left from the original 4,300.[10] I was never able to establish what happened to Luis, Ruben's friend.

The day Rubén was freed, his mother came straight round to the Centenos' house, hardly able to speak for emotion. At the party she could hardly let go of him. Rubén was jubilant, as was Luisa. 'It was not the FSLN that put me in prison, but the people who denounced me,' said Rubén, in an astoundingly generous statement from someone who had just spent five years in jail for a crime he did not commit. 'All the people in Condega agreed that I should be free.' What was even more unexpected was to hear an ex-prisoner describe prison life in such glowing terms. Rubén had gone through his schooling in prison, and continued to be an ardent supporter of the revolution.

> They respect prisoners now. You just can't compare the old
> system with what goes on now. Before you had to earn your food
> by washing the floor. There were constant violations of your
> rights. Now there are different kinds of training available in
> prison – sewing, nursery gardening, carpentry, shoe-making and
> mechanics. I learnt bricklaying myself.

I had always found it rather difficult to believe those who talked of a holiday-camp atmosphere in Nicaragua's prisons. Rubén's words made it easier. In early 1987 the Americas Watch reported that Nicaragua had 8,562 prisoners, of whom just over four thousand were common criminals, around two thousand were former National Guards, 400 former military, and nearly two thousand were Contras and collaborators of the Contras (of whom 792 were convicted and

1,050 awaiting trial). Sixty per cent of the prison population work, mostly in agriculture, construction or services, and are paid at 30 per cent below the minimum wage (much better than in the UK or the US). Day-long family visits, sports and even conjugal visits are available for everyone, and workers are entitled to more frequent such privileges. Even weekend visits home are allowed. 'Prison conditions in the penitentiary system have continued to improve in the period covered by this report, and they compare favourably with many prisons visited by members of the Americas Watch teams in other parts of Latin America', was the verdict of Americas Watch in 1987.

Nothing is so precious as liberty, and Rubén and Condega celebrated that night.

18.   The politics of defence

The attack on Ducualí

I was out of Condega when the Contras attacked the construction depot in Ducualí, just four miles north of Condega. When I arrived back the day after, I found the whole town in a state of excitement and nerves. Donatila Centeno broke the news to me.

> The church bell started ringing. It was about midnight. Next thing we heard Rossita banging on our door telling us that the Contras were just up the road in Ducuali. My husband and all the men went up to the FSLN office to wait for news. But by the time they got there it was too late. The army had arrived in Ducualí and the Contras had gone. But I didn't sleep much that night.

The attack shook Condega. It was only six months since the Contras had destroyed the grain storage silos near Palacagüina, further up the Highway. The area's food supplies for the winter months had been set on fire and laid open to the rain and wind. The wreckage, a tangled mass of steel and corrugated iron, is a memorial to the vulnerability of Nicaragua's economic life; without better communications, more soldiers and quicker responses, there was little that people could do to contain terrorist attacks perpetrated by the Contras. And it is the economy which is proving most vulnerable in Nicaragua's war of survival.

The Ducualí attack brought a vigorous response from Condegans. Everyone with a weapon had rushed to the defence of the town, fearing (groundlessly in fact) that the Contras would come on to Condega itself. But it was too late to do anything about Ducualí. It was a hit-and-run attack. What telephone lines existed were cut right from the start. There was no means of alerting the army base just six miles away. As the Contras left, taking four vehicles, they ambushed a government truck and kidnapped the passengers.

I went out to survey the damage. The depot was a regional centre for road construction workers with a brand new fleet of East-German-built lorries used to carry cement and tar. Half of the fleet was destroyed. Burnt-out tins of food and medicines lay around the remains of four buildings. Typewriters seemed to have been singled out for a special bashing-up. Perhaps worst of all was the charred shell of the bus that carried the workers to the sites.

For the Contras it was a well-chosen target, and efficiently carried out. It was pretty obvious that there would not be much road-building in the region for a while after this. Inside the one office left standing, the harassed managers were trying to pull together the enterprise, counting the losses. Outside the gates a group of disconsolate-looking workers gathered, waiting for news about their jobs. The depot had employed 380. It looked as if up to 200 would be laid off. Without transport there was no way of getting to the parts of the region that so desperately needed roads.

I was reminded of a CIA-sponsored Contra pamphlet I had been shown with the title: *'Freedom Fighter's Manual: practical guide to liberate Nicaragua from oppression and the paralysing misery of the military industrial complex of the traitor Marxists – without the use of special tools and at minimum risk to the fighter'*. With cartoon illustrations it lists a range of sabotaging acts designed to undermine the economic infrastructure of the 'Moscow-financed terrorists'. These include disseminating rumours, leaving taps running, dropping typewriters, making false alarm calls and threatening calls to one's boss, causing electric shocks, cutting telephone wires, blocking toilets, destroying street lighting, laying nails on the street, puncturing tyres, sabotaging engines or army trucks, blocking roads, pulling down electricity cables, making molotov cocktails, and committing acts of arson.

The pamphlet is a cartoon version of the notorious CIA manual *Psychological Operations in Guerrilla Warfare* (see Chapter 7), aimed at those with a low literacy level. In the Ducualí attack it looked as if several of the sabotaging instructions had been followed at once. But it was certainly no individual act, no home-spun affair; it was an efficiently directed guerilla operation.

A chink in the armour?

'Revolutionary vigilance' is the system of self-defence run by the CDS which is specifically aimed at protecting towns, villages and economic targets from such attacks. In Condega it involves a nightly armed patrol which begins just after dark. I accompanied Ramón

Viscaya, father of the martyr Juanita, together with other volunteers on the early shift one night. The eldest of the volunteers was Don Francisco Aráuz, now in his seventies, who used to sell wood in the street for a living.

The streets were deserted and quiet. Not all Condegans have electric light, and in the poorer *barrios* near the river people go to bed at sundown. In every *barrio* we stopped at a volunteer's house to check in with women who take part in the night watch from their homes. Usually they were already in their night clothes. Ramón Viscaya carefully filled in his report, which detailed any unusual movements reported by the volunteers.

No one was expecting trouble that night, so there was time to stop for refreshment at one or two shops and listen to the local gossip. At every place of work – the tannery, the furniture co-operatives, the town administration, the water storage tanks and the generator – we checked in with others guarding their place of employment. It seemed that virtually everyone working in the town was on the rota for guard duty. Cigarettes were exchanged and people chatted. Most people knew each other. On the bridge on the Highway there was a permanent patrol and down by the river a contingent of the army had set up a machine gun. At midnight, after some five hours, we gave way to another team.

The purpose of 'revolutionary vigilance', or revolutionary night-watch duty, is not just to deter Contra activities, but to act as a kind of citizens' police force to protect the revolution from sabotage by counter-revolutionaries, from 'isolated or organized delinquency', drug addiction and prostitution.[1] As 'policemen' these people were a far cry from my picture of a Central American force.

The Sandinistas at Condega are particularly proud of having 'cleaned up' the town. 'Before, if you hung out a piece of clothing in your patio, it had gone by dawn. These days you can see all the patios full of clothes and nothing goes missing because no one is in the streets', said Orlando Navaretto, who took over the magistrate's job from Ramón. Under Somoza there were seven brothels, all run by members of the National Guard. 'People would arrive and get drunk. They would then be robbed of their money, their watches and everything. It was the Guard who did it', the magistrate Orlando Navaretto told me.

For Ramon and the other volunteers the main question in Condega is not now crime, but the real threat of a Contra attack. And although the town is prepared for attack – people have been encouraged to build air-raid shelters in their back yards, emergency brigades exist in each *barrio* for first aid, for evacuating children and for organizing supplies for the civilian population – CDS activists were worried about a decline in participation in night patrols. It was not just happening in Condega, but was a national trend. During 1985 the numbers taking part in patrols declined by 44 per cent across the country.[2]

This seemed to be part of a wider probem. In Condega, as many CDS activists admitted, there was no longer boundless enthusiasm in the neighbourhood for CDS meetings and communal tasks. People were getting tired of hearing about shortages and difficulties and were beginning to withdraw into their families. At one meeting which I went to with Donatila (in the Centenos' *barrio*) no one else turned up. It had been called to discuss a campaign to persuade more people to build air-raid shelters. The activists said the people were complacent.

A national debate was raging within the FSLN and the CDS on the question of popular participation. Interior Minister Tomás Borge, a member of the Sandinista leadership, blamed the propaganda of the Church hierarchy and the Contras, together with ideological weakness and lack of experience in the Sandinista leadership:

> The enemy's ideological organization is better than ours from a structural and technical point of view. We have to be involved in everything: fighting the war, resolving economic problems, the battle at international level. We have few cadres for the ideological conflict and they aren't the best.[3]

Others, such as the FSLN's political secretary in Region One, Agustín Lara, took another line:

> In the euphoria immediately after the triumph, where there had never before been the possibility of having a meeting, after years of tremendous repression people held meetings all the time, for anything, on any excuse. This has to change. There has been an abuse of the form of meetings and of people's patience. Often meetings were called that were without content. So people get fed up and don't go.

In Condega the CDS had new and difficult tasks. Military conscription had given them a new responsibility which was making them unpopular. The austerity measures were beginning to bite, sending prices up by over 300 per cent in some cases. Activists were constantly having to explain the reason for the shortages and price increases. When people complained, there was little they could say except 'it is necessary'.

How far would those who were not activists still see the CDS as a vehicle with which to lobby the authorities with their demands? I wondered. Though the mass organizations had guided and even brought about direct shifts in Sandinista policy over the years, it seemed their ability to do so in wartime in places like Condega was limited. There the strengthening of the CDS into a grass-roots movement will have to await the day when the revolution is left alone to get on with its job.

Meanwhile the Contras continue their mission of destruction.

Economic hardships and the trade unions

Three days after the attack on Ducualí, the workers of Condega decided to hold their May Day rally at the burnt-out plant itself. Trade unionists from the slaughterhouse, the tannery and the state tobacco farms joined students and children to march the five miles up the Pan American Highway. Among the debris of the depot, they joined a large group of workers who stood, grim-faced, listening to the speeches, the news of their job losses gradually sinking in.

The speakers from the mass organizations condemned the USA and vowed a greater commitment to the defence of workplaces, but, privately, recriminations flew. Some five or six people had been taken in for questioning in connection with the attack. Why hadn't the people of Ducualí living nearby got weapons? Had the depot been infiltrated? What were the depot's guards doing that night? Had they been collaborating or bribed? Who had neglected to do the political work in the community? There was anger, a search for scapegoats, and the realization that this attack had taken place only four miles away from Condega. 'Let them just try and come to Condega! We'll deal with them!' was the reaction of most.

The rally was a sober occasion and there was little of the cheering and defiant slogans I had come to associate with Nicaraguan rallies at the time. People worried not just about the vulnerability of economic targets to acts of sabotage, but also about the constant undermining of the economy by the costs of the war and other forms of US-imposed attrition.

A US trade embargo on Nicaragua was beginning to take effect. For the 330 employees of Condega's slaughterhouse, in particular, this was bad news. Ninety per cent of its output was exported and traditionally most of that went to the USA. Output had already been hit with the removal of cattle to Honduras by wealthier farmers. The embargo was the culmination of several years of financial and commercial aggression against Nicaragua. (For example, the USA had demanded laboratory tests on meat imports which they knew the Nicaraguans could not fulfil.) The $135 million worth of goods exported to the USA in 1984 would have to find new markets. Meat exports to the USA were then worth $18.4 million. Across the country as a whole, exports in 1986 were valued at less than $250 million, down by 20 per cent on the previous year and half the exports of 1981.[4] One of the most damaging effects of the embargo was that it denied Nicaragua spare parts for productive machinery. In a country which had previously been almost totally dependent on the USA, this was hard medicine. Ninety per cent of veterinary products came from the USA, as did 70 per cent of private-sector machinery.

Unemployment was already running at over 22 per cent, and inflation had started to rocket. In 1985 it was over 200 per cent. By the middle of 1986 it stood at around 1,000 per cent. But for government employees dependent on salaries, wages had increased by only a third of the rate of price increases on basic foods.[5]

For an outsider steeped in British trade-union attitudes, it was somewhat surprising to see trade unionists complain so little about the economic medicine the Government had prescribed in answer to the crisis. The Government had called for increased efficiency and voluntary work. Workers at the slaughterhouse told me that they were consulted on most management decisions by the administration. If they were dissatisfied they went to their union, or the Ministry of Agriculture. Strikes had been outlawed since the state of emergency was re-imposed in October 1985. 'The law says that the state has to look after the interests of the workers', said Teodoro Ruíz, the propaganda and political secretary of the slaughterhouse union. 'There is no contradiction between management and the union here.'

I was introduced to the production manager, a man who had been employed there for twenty-four years and who now worked closely with the union, agreeing production targets and working conditions. The union referred to him for information about production. They saw their role as looking after the interests of the workers, and maintaining 'vigilance' – that is, organizing the defence of the plant.

Teodoro and his friends took me round the factory, pointing out proudly how things had improved since the revolution. 'We used to have to buy our own food and even our own tools before. The boss dictated everything. The doctor only came once a week. Now we have a canteen with subsidized food and our own subsidized shop. They give us clothing and tools.' The factory was not in production that day, but in every room there was an adult education lesson going on for groups of employees. Here in Condega, at least, the Sandinistas appeared to have successfully harnessed workers' energies away from what, in any other society, would have been a class struggle, and into the struggle for national survival. The revolution has recognized the value of workers and given them unprecedented rights. And these are things that are, for the moment, more important than the questions of wages and living standards.

But despite the goodwill of the workers and their sense of patriotism, I could not help wondering how long the Government would be able to silence discontent about wages by invoking the magic slogan 'defence of the revolution' in mitigation of unpopular economic policies.

Captain Ferrei

The man responsible for the military defence of the Condega area is Captain Ferrei, Commander of the 33rd Brigade. I first met him as he drove through the Canta Gallo area in a jeep, checking on the militia posts on the way. He stopped at Santa Rosa, where members of two co-operative farms were holding a meeting to consider a request from the co-operative in neighbouring Dailí for help with the coffee harvest. As I stuck out somewhat amongst the men in green fatigues, he came over to ask who I was and what I was doing in the area.

The meeting had been interesting. The *campesinos* sat round on the grass in the school grounds fingering their rifles pensively. Many wore crucifixes prominently round their necks. Augusto, the man from the Agrarian Reform Office, made his plea for help with the harvest: 'Coffee is one of the most important sources of foreign exchange which pays for our health centres, our schools, and defence.' He was assisted by Victor from the Dailí co-operative itself. After successive Contra attacks they had trouble both in defending and keeping up the output. 'The Guardia destroyed our living quarters, our tractor and our truck. We have difficulties with production. The coffee is drying and getting mature.'

The men from Santa Rosa listened. They knew the circumstances. In the past most of them would have gone coffee-picking every year as a matter of survival. Now they had their own land they were in the luxurious position of being able to choose. It was a sense of democracy they enjoyed testing. Various problems and objections were raised at first. The most serious one was their own safety. 'We can't send everyone. We can't leave our own houses undefended to find the enemy in them when we return', said one man. Victor explained that Darailí had a new system of patrols worked out, which gave a circular defence of the coffee. 'We never cut in the same place. But obviously there can never be an absolute guarantee.' The mood of the meeting became more positive.

Then the question of transport arose. 'To be frank, we have no transport', said Victor. This was something of a bombshell. It meant that the coffee-pickers would have to stay in Darailí rather than return every evening. Amazingly, the men took this in their stride, especially after hearing that the wage rates had been put up. 'We can't deny them support because we know they are in the same battle as we are to keep up defence and production', said one. The others nodded gravely. It was decided. Five men would go for nine or ten days from the production co-operative. The president of the credit co-operative said they would decide the next day at their meeting.

From the Frente Sur to the People's Army

Captain Ferrei agreed to give Victor and me a lift to Darailí. Military men don't talk much, and he was no exception. He was clearly middle-class, and had an air of authority. His hair was greying at the temples. He was not from the Condega area, and this showed. Like several of the senior officers of the Sandinista People's Army, he had begun his political career in the Frente Sur.

Of all the battle fronts of the FSLN in the war of liberation, the Frente Sur, which began with 600 guerillas but which grew to 1,200, fought the most conventional type of war. In the flat scrub of southern Nicaragua they pinned down the best of Somoza's troops in almost regular trench warfare during June and July 1979, while in the rest of the country towns and villages were being liberated. Amongst the Frente Sur fighters was Amanda Centeno, Luisa's elder sister, who returned from exile at the end of 1978. The Frente Sur suffered huge casualties in Somoza's machine-gun and rocket attacks on their positions.

By the end of the war there were over fifteen thousand people under arms in Nicaragua. Of those, only two thousand could be considered in any way a regular army, and only three thousand of the rest were properly trained guerilla forces. More than ten thousand of the fighters were irregular militias and spontaneous combatants in the urban areas.[6] Immediately after the triumph, the militias were disarmed and demobilized – an attempt to assert discipline in a chaotic situation. The idea then was to set up a relatively small professional army and complement it with a popular militia based in factories, farms, towns and villages.

The Sandinista People's Army, which began with 8,500 members, set out to be a politicized national army whose purpose was to defend the gains of the revolution. The political education its soldiers receive ranks as high as military training. It had a seat on the Council of State (which preceded the National Assembly), and its cadres, a third of whom were illiterate and whose average age was between twenty and twenty-two, were amongst the first to be taught to read in the literacy crusade. 'In the People's Army we want every comrade to be able to read and write, so that he or she can understand all our country's problems and understand that the army is not a separate distinct institution isolated from the struggles of the masses', said Carlos Carrión. The theme of the EPS as 'the people in arms' is a constant one.

I was once given a lift to Managua with some regular soldiers in their early twenties. I was asked the usual questions: are you picking coffee with a brigade?; whose house are you staying in?; what do you think of the revolution?; what do the British think of it? I soon found myself having an intense theoretical discussion for the whole of the two-and-a-half-hour journey. Most of it revolved around the character of the Nicaraguan state – a country in transition, they said: it had a mixed economy and the people had power but it could not yet begin to call itself socialist ... this would only come after the defeat of imperialist aggression, they said.

No one in the army can opt out of the daily political briefings and discussions of theory. This was the strength of the army, that it understood its role – unlike the mercenaries in the Contras, the soldiers explained. The reward for my interest in their views was a lift right to the door.

Captain Ferrei did not strike me as a particularly political man, more of a professional. Military ranks were introduced into the army in 1980 and the chain of command is as vertical in military matters as in any other army. He talked with pride of the battles in the Frente Sur, but was more than guarded when talking of the politics or the situation in Condega. Getting information out of him was like getting blood out of a stone. His office was in Estelí but I never managed to get past his assistants in my efforts to track him down there. What I rather naively imagined to be a quite simple request – for a map of the Condega area – obviously rang alarm bells amongst the eager beavers of military intelligence, and I found myself being virtually interrogated for ten minutes. In a country as open as Nicaragua, it was sometimes easy to forget that a military emergency existed.

The second time I caught a lift with Captain Ferrei's convoy was on my way out of Canta Gallo one evening. His was the last vehicle to make the descent down the mountain and I was relieved to be offered the ride. There is no way one can make a journey down after dark: it is too dangerous. We stopped as before at some of the militia posts. The Sandinista People's Militias work under the command of the army, and close communication is essential in such zones of conflict. Villagers were not shy to offer refreshments, and at one hamlet I was invited into a home for supper with the Captain and his escort. The entire family sat round and watched us devour a steaming hot plate of rice, potatoes and beans in sauce.

Outside it was already dark and the militia was patrolling the hamlet. There had been Contra kidnappings only recently, and a member of the militia had lost his life. Under a brightly starlit sky the *campesinos* talked of what it was like to live and die in these little hamlets, constantly on the alert.

At La Laguna there was an interesting encounter between the Captain and the mother of a boy in the village militia. I recognized her as one of the mothers who had lost a son in the ambush. His brother had been detained after committing a disciplinary offence in the militias. On spotting the Captain, the mother rushed over to plead for his release. The Captain explained in great detail why it had been necessary to detain her son, but she continued to gesticulate and shout and plead. The conversation went on for some forty minutes, with neither side giving in. The Captain, the only man with the power to release him, needed to enforce rules which could mean the difference between life and death. The mother needed her son to help protect her home. In the end she gave up. They parted on good terms and she looked a bit happier for having had her say. It was not in many countries that people would have had such access to a commanding officer.

Patriotic military service

It was in late 1983 that the Government decided to introduce the draft. The weaknesses in Nicaragua's defence were glaring. Contra attacks on small communities in the north were growing. The whole country had to go onto a war footing to deal with the emergency. The Sandinista People's Army, formed in the tradition of guerilla forces and backed up by volunteer reservists and rural militias, needed a large injection of manpower. In September 1983 the Government introduced a compulsory military service law enabling them to call up men between the ages of seventeen and twenty-five. In practice only boys of seventeen and eighteen have been called up, in an attempt to minimize disruption to the economy. And, indeed, the striking thing about the Sandinista army is its youth. Since its formation it has grown from 8,500 to more than 62,000 soldiers.[7] A further 150,000 belong to reserve battalions and spend part of the year mobilized.

The call-up of the country's youth in a time of war, when casualties were rising, was one of the Government's first difficult measures. The Opposition was quick to pick on people's fears in an attempt to try to divide the population from the Government. The Catholic hierarchy led an active campaign of opposition to the draft, accusing the Government of 'totalitarianism and militarism'. Protestant fundamentalist sects that had mushroomed all over Nicaragua since the revolution added their voice, arguing that handling weapons was against the will of God.

There was no doubt that many of the urban middle class in Nicaragua were sending their sons abroad to avoid the draft. I remember meeting a woman in León who described herself as a Sandinista and who had looked after young fighters in the insurrection. 'I sent my son away,' she said. 'It costs me $17 a day to keep him in Costa Rica, but I'm not going to have him sent to his death. He is too young.' Her mother ran an import-export business and had access to US dollars. Few Nicaraguans would have access to such resources.

For many youths in the rural areas of Condega, patriotic military service was just an extention of their work in the militias. Up to a third of the labour force in Region One is mobilized at any one time, some as regular soldiers, others in the reserves and many in the militias. *Campesino* families like Bertilda's have no hesitation in sending their sons to military service. 'The majority of *campesinos* go willingly to the army. And we are the ones who suffer the attacks most, and we used to be the ones who were attacked most during the Somoza regime. We were the most exploited in different ways and it is we who are really defending the country.' 'It is the sons of the middle class who make trouble,' said Bertilda's cousin, 'but even they, when they get to the army, are shown the reality. And no one can fool one of those boys after they have done their SMP' (Servicio Militar Patriótico).

On the roads north of Estelí, a large proportion of the vehicles belongs to the army. Large green passenger lorries rumble at top speed over the potholes on the Highway with cargoes of young soldiers in green, clutching their AK rifles, adorned with red and black scarves. Those returning from battle are usually singing or cheering. Others might have fallen asleep with exhaustion, perhaps their first opportunity for days. I was often given lifts with soldiers, the smell of battle on their fatigues, sometimes blood-stained, usually muddy and in need of a wash. One or two might be cleaning their rifles, a meticulous process in which colleagues are consulted to examine a detail or try out a cartridge. Bullets roll around on the floor, apparently not valued highly. Morale is high. There is pride in their faces. They enjoy showing a foreigner what they are doing for Nicaragua.

At the small barracks in the centre of Condega I spoke to six conscripts during their three-month training period. Two were school students aged eighteen, one was a worker from the slaughterhouse, aged nineteen. Another, aged twenty-four, worked for a tobacco-processing factory and another, aged nineteen, on his father's farm. Another nineteen-year-old had been in the reserves since 1980. The group posed excitedly for photos, thrusting out their chests and displaying their rifles. The most loquacious amongst them were the two students.

Fabrizio, the son of the manager of the local state firm, compared doing military service with his experiences in the National Literacy Crusade: 'The crusade was the best experience of my life. I was only thirteen but I was teaching people of forty to read. I still visit them sometimes.' It was hard, he admitted, to leave home. 'But my parents take a good attitude. They are aware of the situation in the country.'

Marlon was quieter. He wore a large crucifix. 'It's my companion when we're fighting in the mountains', he explained. He had been involved in a fierce battle in the nearby hamlet of Guayucalí, along with forty others. 'We've been suffering from constant attacks. Now that 40 per cent of our resources go to defence, people are complaining. It was easier before because people could see the advances the revolution had made.'

Arturo, aged eighteen, was a member of the Sandinista Youth, and hoped to go to university. 'Nicaragua has a good future but we have to create it. We have decided to defend Nicaragua to the ultimate. We are not giving in. The main thing is to keep up morale so we don't retreat.' The boys were grateful to be stationed in Condega. 'This town is very active. People here understand.'

In Condega the draft is handled by a young man of twenty-five called Mauricio, whom I first met in Santa Teresa. It is a tricky job. Military conscription has had a profound effect on a country in which the volunteer spirit is the life and soul of the revolution. Over 300,000 people had joined the militias after their formation in February 1980, volunteering their services to defend farms, factories and _barrios_. Conscription, with its legal connotations, was different. It was full-time, it was compulsory, and it was dangerous. In 1986 alone over a thousand soldiers died and 1,798 were wounded.[8]

Mauricio is a quiet, sensitive, mild-mannered man with a twinkle in his eye. He operates out of three rooms, almost devoid of furniture, in the centre of Condega. The front office serves as a point of contact for relatives seeking news of their sons. Some of the women I found queueing there had come from rural communities to collect an army pension for bereaved mothers.

Parents of conscripts often put up some of the strongest opposition to the draft. Mauricio blamed this on the fact that Nicaragua had no tradition of conscription (under Somoza the only people trusted in the army were those who were completely dependent on his handouts), and on the high casualties in the war. 'The problem is that when the first draft began in 1984 it coincided with the Contras' new task forces, and a number of deaths occurred. Now the internal enemy is manipulating, using the feelings of mothers to make them think their sons will die.'

Neither Mauricio nor the Frente secretary in Condega, Eunice, wanted to reveal too much about the numbers evading the draft in Condega. There were just under a thousand youths eligible for conscription that year. But in 1984 a third of those eligible had dropped out. Most had lain low or left the country. In 1985 there seemed to be a steady exodus of boys of recruitment age, some of it organized for profit. Three boys from Condega were discovered on a private bus on its way to Honduras, full of evaders.

The Government's response was to toughen up enforcement of the law against what they saw as an enemy attempt to undermine Nicaragua's defence. One night the cinema in Condega was raided by the police and some sixteen evaders detected. Any lengthy bus journey across Nicaragua is interrupted by several police checks of the passengers, in which all young men have their papers carefully scrutinized for their age and eligibility. In Santa Teresa, where I attended a village meeting, a group of boys was subsequently rounded up and taken to be registered. The Pentecostal pastor said there were six boys from a hamlet near El Jocote in detention for refusing to be drafted.

There were exceptions to the Government's toughness, though these were not widely publicized. If anything, they showed a flexibility born of political expediency. There is no conscientious objection in Nicaragua, but the Sandinistas are anxious not to give their detractors grounds for accusations of religious persecution. In the Condega area the Baptist pastor, the Reverend Santos Casco, said God had intervened, because some of their youth had resisted the draft and had been left alone. On the Atlantic Coast there had been even more flexibility.

In Nicaragua itself the toll of wounded and dead continues to mount. By early 1987 there were 18,000 casualties on the Sandinista side (out of a total of 37,500 on both sides). Some eight thousand Sandinista soldiers and civilians had died.[9] There are hundreds of crippled young men in need of rehabilitation. Priority is being given to demobilized conscripts for retraining and education and help with adjustment to civilian life. The army has hardened their support for the revolution, but an important question is whether the revolution can give them the support they now need.

The decision to introduce the draft has, however, been a military success. There is no doubt that the boys of the BLI have been extremely successful in tackling the Contras. By the end of 1985 they had pushed most large concentrations of Contras out of Nueva Segovia. In 1986 the Sandinista army engaged the Contras in battle on three thousand occasions. The Contras lost four thousand men in 1986 alone, and have lost over twelve thousand since the war began.[10]

At the end of 1986 the Sandinistas were talking of a 'strategic defeat of the Contras'.[11] According to President Ortega, Contra forces had been reduced from an estimated twelve thousand at the end of

1986, despite the injections of funds from the United States. They had failed to capture a single inch of Nicaraguan territory. Their failure to secure a firm base of local support amongst the *campesinos* had forced them to retreat into an expeditionary force employing irregular combat methods. In early 1987 the Contra leaders said they would concentrate on mounting guerilla attacks on strategic and economic targets.

The approval in 1986 of $100 million of US aid for the Contras meant that the toll of dead and wounded continued to rise. In 1987, amid continuing revelations in the 'Contragate' affair, it was clear that the future of the Contras lay in the hands of the US Congress, the only body with the power to refuse President Reagan's persistent requests for more funds.

19. Free Condega

By the third week of May 1979 the Frente was ready to launch a three-pronged assault; a general strike, mass insurrection and military action. International opposition to Somoza had been growing. There were protests from Democrats in the USA over the IMF's decision to grant a loan of $66 million to the ailing regime. Mexico broke off diplomatic relations with Nicaragua, because of its 'horrendous acts of genocide', urging other Latin American countries to follow suit.

By now the Sandinistas' alliance with the Nicaraguan middle class was cemented under their leadership. Since February, the opposition parties had been working with the United People's Movement and Los Doce in a National Patriotic Front (the FPN) and had agreed on a programme calling for the overthrow of the dictatorship. The effects of the IMF deal dug a deeper rift between the business class and Somoza, and silenced voices within the FPN wanting a deal with Somoza. The Frente knew it could rely on help from employers when it called for a new general strike.

It was the United People's Movement, and through them the Frente, that had the leadership of the country. In every *barrio* and village the civil defence committees were ready. The guerillas were poised for assaults on major towns.

Condega was virtually deserted, most of the inhabitants having fled after the massacre of 3 May. Only the poorest and the sick remained. Juana Salinas, for example, with her sick husband. Father Wésther López would visit Condega in the daytime and make his rounds in the rural communities. Nobody was working. A charity, Caritas, sent food supplies which the priest distributed once a week. Henry Vargas, the reporter, had left Condega to stay with a relative. He brought medicines to the boys in the camps who were keeping the peasantry informed and doing military training. Not many people in Condega were therefore present to witness the capture of the town. But Don Henry had collected together an account from the fighters and published it a year afterwards in the paper *Nuevo Diario*. He stores these precious records in the garage next to his house – a kind of archive of local history. I owe these details to him.

The call for national insurrection and a general strike came on 31 May. In the guerilla camps of Canta Gallo and Cuba the boys, amongst them Dachsun Cattin, were told: 'We are going out to fight in the cities, highways and whoever we meet. We already have plans to follow. There's to be no holding back, even from death, because it's the final insurrection.' The squadrons left the guerilla camps near Condega to take part in the capture of nearby towns. The 'Northern Front', of which they were part, fought in León, El Sauce, Ocotal, Somoto and Estelí.

By 4 June 1979 the university town of León had fallen and the strike begun. By 8 June the FSLN controlled twenty-five towns and villages in the north. On 9 June the assault on Estelí began simultaneously with the Managua insurrection.

The capture of Condega took careful planning. The commander, Emilio Monzón, started out with a squadron of thirty-six. They ambushed the National Guard at El Bramadero, a small community near El Jocote, and captured their weapons. Knowing Condega was a base for the Guardia, other guerillas staged diversionary attacks in Yalí, Concordia and San Rafael del Norte. On 12 June eighty-five guerillas under Monzón's command surrounded Condega silently at 9 p.m., closing the exit routes.

The Guard was on its own in the town. No one brought them food or showed support. The evacuation of the town had left the field open for its capture with minimal casualties. However, the Guard had been tipped off and had sent for reinforcements. When these arrived in three lorries, the drivers failed to give the password and guards stationed near the water towers started to fire at them, taking them for Sandinistas. Both sides suffered losses. The reinforcements withdrew in confusion, leaving their dead.

At midnight the guerillas attacked the barracks in the central park and the command post on the hill. Their total arsenal was thirty-eight pistols, twenty-two rifles, two garands and thirty shot-guns, grenades and one Mauser. Ranged against them were the M50 and M30 machine guns of the National Guard. The boys gained ground from the beginning. When another lorry of Guard reinforcements arrived from Somoto at dawn it was ambushed and all the passengers were killed. The driver was taken prisoner.

Juana Salinas and other women kept the boys going for three days and three nights:

When the boys came into town that night, we began cooking the beans and making the tortillas and gave them to the boys as they went past. The Guardia came up to the command post and we had to make sure they didn't see the boys. I sent for a girl to make the tortillas and we sent them to the command no. 6 who was in charge and to command no. 1, and to the ambush. The girl took them up there on foot.

My sister was making the tortillas. There were three of us in the house. Others brought them ready-cooked from other houses and brought chickens and hens too. They brought a lot of things from Pirie where I had relatives with hens.

On the third day the weakness of the Guardia was apparent. Planes were flying above Condega, but were only shooting from very high, anxious to avoid being shot down like their predecessor in April. One plane which dared come lower was shot down and landed near the petrol station at Ducualí. Another was shot down near Estelí.

The Sandinistas began to shout to the Guardia that they would respect life. On the morning of 14 June the Guardia fled to the mountains, leaving their weapons, their uniforms and their boots. 'They didn't have the courage to die fighting,' wrote Henry Vargas. 'They left like dogs with their tails between their legs.' The bodies of the Guard who died were found in the water tower and in the command post. They were burnt to avoid an epidemic.

The Sandinistas suffered thirty-nine deaths in the capture of Condega. Their commander, Emilio Monzón, claimed victory. The town was left in control of mainly female fighters while the guerillas went off to Estelí. The priest's house became an important centre in this period.

I was in the presbytery. They brought ammunition and supplies to store there in one car. And then in another car they would take them to the front where the fighting was. I didn't go myself. I knew I was never going to take a weapon myself. But I knew that the only way to finish with the dictatorship was with arms.

At the end of June Father Wésther López left for Honduras, for his own safety. Here he continued to work for the revolution. His car was used to transport arms from Tegucigalpa and Choluteca to the border.

US citizens were already being evacuated from Nicaragua. Two days later a Provisional Government of National Unity was named in Costa Rica. Fierce fighting continued in Managua, Estelí, in all major towns and in the south. Thousands more were flocking to join the ranks of the fighters, many to fight with sticks and stones.

The USA had seriously misjudged the ability of the Sandinistas to launch another insurrection. Its strength took them by surprise. After the September 1978 offensive, the Carter administration had been working on a plan to ditch the isolated dictator and give support to a 'government of national unity' – Somozism without Somoza.

By mid-June 1979, with these plans in ruins, the National Security Council was arguing that only military intervention could prevent a Sandinista victory. But domestic support for such an option collapsed after the murder, on camera, by the National Guard of an ABC television reporter, Bill Stewart. Somoza was personally directing bombing raids on Managua against *barrrios* and the factories of opposition businessmen. On 21 June the US Secretary of State, Vance, asked the Organization of American States to send in a 'peacekeeping force'. It was rejected out of hand. Instead they called for Somoza's resignation and the recognition of the FSLN *junta*.

In the last week of June Somoza ordered 250- and 500-pound bombs to be dropped on Managua. They failed to destroy his target. Some six thousand Sandinista combatants simply withdrew on foot to Masaya. One by one, the important towns of Nicaragua were falling and Somoza's international isolation was becoming more complete. By the middle of July, with the final push on Managua beginning, the Americans were powerless and Somoza had his back to the wall. Huge groups of National Guard were deserting and leaving the country.

The last important military installation outside Managua – the barracks at Estelí – fell on 16 July. The following day Somoza resigned. An attempt to keep the National Guard fighting failed within twenty-four hours. On 19 July the last of the National Guard surrendered. Wésther López monitored their departure from the north.

The Frente looked for me in Honduras to ask me to act as a mediator with the National Guard on the frontier. I mediated with the colonel from Somoto who was surrendering weapons in exchange for free passage. I had to ensure that they would respect the life of those who surrendered their weapons.

As the Provisional Government of National Unity, so named in April, began to function, Sandinistas advanced into Managua, which had already been liberated by the people. Hundreds of thousands of celebrating people converged into Revolution Square. In Honduras the refugees from Condega celebrated 'as you can't imagine how', says Luisa. Father Wésther López said Mass in local churches: 'There were people there from all over the north of Nicaragua. There was a huge joy when Somoza left. People went into the streets and gave parties. There was a great hope after so much suffering, so many dead, so much destruction.'

Condega had been spared the heavy bombardments, though many had lost their lives in the fighting elsewhere. Gradually Condegans started streaming back from Honduras into the town. Everyone has their story and memory of the return. Some, such as Don Antonio Centeno, in Honduras with the younger children, thought it would be a return to the fighting:

> We were happy Somoza had gone but we believed the US would intervene. So we said we'd come back. We were all ready to come and fight.
> There was a crisis because there were no tortillas, no fowl, not even a mango in the village. There were no lights. Nothing. In Estelí there was grief and affliction because it was devastated; razed to the ground. There were no shops, nothing. But we were happy.

Luisa, like all the others who had actively involved themselves in the fight against Somoza, threw herself into organizing Sandinista Defence Committees, which would tackle the rebuilding of life in the town. 'There was nothing but misery and debts here. The bank had left long lists of debtors. We worked without pay. You had to work for the revolution without looking backwards.'

Father Wésther López returned from Honduras on 21 July. 'In the months afterwards there was so much joy and hope. I spent nearly all the time at Mass thanking God for this and that, commemorating the deaths of so many people – relatives of people in the town. Families wanted to remember those who had died.' Subsequently he worked closely with the mass organizations and the town *junta*. He was closely consulted on the choice of a co-ordinator, The decision was made in the church hall. Don Henry Vargas was asked to join the *junta* but declined, preferring to continue as a reporter.

What stands out for Wésther López, in retrospect, is how high expectations were in those days:

> People were confused. They thought it was a free-for-all, that

they would have lots of presents – houses, land, everything. That
there would be no need. Like a paradise on earth. This was the
mentality. The Frente would give us everything we need –
education, health, houses. We won't have to pay for anything.

The aid that poured into Nicaragua after the revolution did
nothing to dispel this impression. Even the Baptist missionary,
Robert Tyson, did his bit, sending a bus full of medicines and cots
for the CDS. 'We were expecting him to come. We had organized a
reception to thank him from the CDS. But he never came,' said
Orlando Navaretto.

For some, of course, the revolution meant they suffered material
loss – the four wealthy citizens of the town whose homes were
confiscated, for example. And the Guardia informer who lived near
the Centenos was killed. But, for the majority, the euphoria of the
return and the spirit with which thousands set to work to clean up
the streets, to build the health centre, to organize the literacy
campaign, will not be forgotten. Its memory sustains them in their
bleaker moments today.

20.   A heart of hard sticks

Several things particularly impressed me in Condega. One was an incredible optimism in the air, the feeling that people were making changes to their lives, that life was progressing, things were improving or going to improve. Past injustice was being rectified or would be rectified when the war was over. For instance, the brand-new health centre on the Highway (built, like most new buildings in Nicaragua, with the help of aid from the West) is a source of pride and enthusiasm for the people of Condega – despite the fact that it is desperately short of drugs, and has no ambulance. No one complains about the shortage of equipment: they feel privileged to be seen by a doctor in the first place. The health centre's existence has altered the value of life for people in the town.

Some would find this optimism idealistic, and it may be so; but I think it is one of the reasons why so many young foreign people are attracted by the Nicaraguan revolution: it represents hope, whereas at home they may face unemployment and political cynicism.

Connected with this optimism was the feeling that everyone's job was socially useful, was part of the process of change. In Condega someone like Daniel of the Juanita Viscaya co-operative – a simple peasant farmer who can barely read – is valued as highly for his contribution to the country as the political co-ordinator who sits in an office. Yes, there is bureaucracy and there are class differences – perhaps inevitably. Nevertheless, the advancement someone makes in their job is not seen in terms of personal gain, but in terms of its contribution to society as a whole. The ethos of private profit has been overtaken by that of national unity and national pride.

The low consumption levels of pre-revolutionary days have given people a particular strength which outsiders steeped in consumer values find difficult to relate to. In Condega all the shops are inside houses. There are no display windows. Where a product is in stock, there is probably only one brand available. Surprisingly, as someone used to being bombarded with colours and brand choice, I found this very restful. When I returned home I felt the heavy marketing of consumer products as an intrusion on my privacy. The shortages of goods considered luxuries, such as toilet rolls, really only bothered the Nicaraguan middle class. The majority of people in and around Condega could rarely afford them until the revolution. They did not particularly miss them now.

The example of the toilet paper shortage raises the important question of what the US administration thinks it is going to achieve by its blockade of trade, its cutting of loans and aid payments, and its destruction of economic and structural targets within Nicaragua.

Low-intensity warfare is the term used to describe US strategy in Nicaragua. In Condega people survive this on a day-to-day basis. The images I took away with me when I left – of the battered ruined grain storage silos at Palacagüina; the charred remains of the road-building depot in Ducualí, its twenty-two brand-new lorries lined up limply in a row, their cabs and engines in ruins; the shell of what had been a brand-new electricity generator at Ocotal; the coffee-drying and processing plant at Darailí and San Jerónimo reduced to concrete floors; the ruins of a little school building on the hillside, the sign on its door 'escuela' still visible – were symbols of a crass attempt to wreck the economy of a small and poor country.

The thinking behind the strategy, of course, is that if the USA pounds away at the social and economic fabric of Nicaragua, the Sandinista Government will be unable to meet people's material needs and will therefore lose support. _Ergo_ its defensive capacity will be weaker. _Ergo_ more favourable conditions will be established for either internal subversion or a military invasion.

The hatred of the Sandinista Revolution amongst US neo-conservatives is pathological. It blinds them to the fundamental truth of how the revolution came into being and what it represents. Few US administrators are heard to complain of the sufferings of the Nicaraguan peasants in Somoza's days. President Reagan's words of concern to help the people of Nicaragua win their rights are blatantly hypocritical. Reagan, who describes Nicaragua as a 'cancer which has to be excised', does this in the name of 'those who are demanding the rights to determine their own government'. He has described the Sandinistas as 'a communist organization', basing this on his belief that Sandino was a communist. 'They ousted all their other allies in the revolution and then they established a totalitarian communist regime.'[1]

Elliot Abrams, Assistant Secretary of State for Inter-American Affairs, and a leading young neo-conservative, puts Nicaragua squarely in the East–West context: 'the Soviets are attempting to create a new Cuba. They will push as far as they can go. Nicaragua itself is not the problem.... The threat is Soviet intervention in this part of the world.[2]

The issue of Soviet trade links with Nicaragua is almost a self-fufilling prophecy. Trade, and particularly imports from the Soviet bloc, has increased almost in direct proportion to the decline in trade with the USA.[3] That this represents a friendly disposition on the part of the East towards Nicaragua is without doubt; but no more so than Mexico, which supplied oil, or European countries which made up the gap after the USA banned Nicaraguan imports.

The Nicaraguan Government pursues a strictly non-aligned policy and is pledged to diversify economic and financial dependency equally among four main groups: the USA, western Europe and Japan, eastern Europe and the Third World. At the Harare summit of non-aligned heads of state in September 1986 President Ortega spoke of Nicaragua as 'the strategic reserve of non-alignment in an area that US military power considers its strategic reserve'. He called for constructive dialogue with the US Government and stressed that Nicaragua wants to have 'normal relations' with them.[4]

When Mexico, under pressure from the USA, cut off oil supplies to Nicaragua in June 1985, citing Nicaragua's bad debts as a reason, President Ortega travelled to Moscow to ask the Soviets to step into the breach. To make such a widely publicized move at a time when Reagan was approaching Congress for more funds for the Contras was criticized by many as the height of stupidity (Congress approved the money). To Nicaragua, however, which feels it has nothing to hide in its relations with Moscow, it was – as well as being a last resort – a statement of its independence, a sign of David's will to survive despite the odds Goliath places against him.

Nicaragua, though continually branded as a communist state, has, with over 60 per cent of the land in private hands, a larger private sector than many West European countries. Its adaptation to a war economy has forced it to regard the mixed economy as the only way left open. State investment has had to be reduced, prices paid to private farmers have had to be increased, and dollar incentives for producers introduced. More than a quarter of gross domestic product is thought to be the result of an informal economy. In 1982 alone some 30,000 workers went into business or became middlemen.[5]

The USA has put the screws on Nicaragua ever since Reagan's inauguration. Since 1983 it has vetoed loans to Nicaragua through the Inter-American Development Bank and the World Bank. In 1984 Nicaragua was the only Latin American country not to receive money from the IADB. The result of the embargo and the policy of isolation has been a massive increase in Nicaragua's foreign debt from nearly $2 billion in 1980 to nearly $5 billion in 1985. Half the debt is due to the war. Direct damage caused by the Contras in 1986 was around $1,215 million. Total economic losses in 1986 were $2,821 million.[6] Other consequences have been a 44 per cent fall in consumption per person since 1977, a 52 per cent drop in the average real wage, and a rise in unemployment from 13 to 23 per cent.[7]

I once hitched a lift to Condega from a wealthy private farmer driving from Estelí to Ocotal. As his white air-conditioned limousine purred over the pot-holes of the Pan American Highway, his small son sat in the front seat in a pair of American-made shorts with socks and tennis shoes to match, sucking a sweet. After several weeks in Condega, I now felt I was in a time warp. After extracting assurances that I was not working for the Interior Ministry ('some foreigners are here for that reason, you know'), he began to rail at the 'communists' in power and the impossible position farmers were in because of the price of fertilizers and insecticides. But wasn't this a product of the international blockade of Nicaragua?, I asked. (Nearly all fertilizers and insecticides come from the USA.) He shuffled in his seat uncomfortably, unwilling to be caught out by that one. 'Well yes,' he admitted, 'If this blockade goes on we'll be ruined.' But he was convinced that if the Sandinistas could be defeated, his problems would go away. This rather begs the question: is it not the USA, rather than the Sandinistas, that wants to ruin the private farmers? The more private farmers the USA can turn against the Government, the more credibility is given to its claims that the Sandinistas are communists.

What the people of Condega showed me does not qualify me to pass judgement about the feelings of *all* Nicaraguans. The purpose of staying there was not to conduct a kind of opinion poll – a measurement of popular satisfaction or dissatisfaction with the Government – in the way that countless foreign correspondents do after talking to a taxi driver or standing in a food queue in Managua. Condega is too individual and its circumstances too specific for that. What the people could give me was an insight into the *character* of the Sandinista Revolution – a view of the motivation, the strength of feeling and the social basis of the dramatic events of the past fifteen years.

That the USA and the Contras do cause disruption and suffering in Condega goes without saying. What shows the depth of the revolution above all has been the response of the ordinary people to these hardships. In and around Condega the armed forces, the territorial militias and the reservists are all ordinary Nicaraguans, and more often than not peasants.

US policies and the Contras' activities weaken the Sandinistas' ability to respond to the needs of isolated rural communities. But that in itself does not bring about a loss of support for the Government: rather, a polarization of opinion. The indifference of some isolated rural peasants towards the revolution often turns to support in the wake of a Contra atrocity. The conscription of their sons, though resisted by many, brings a new generation into contact with the revolution and its aims.

Some people remain indifferent to the revolution. And some are manipulated into a position of hostility towards the Government – perhaps even serving a spell with the Contras. But the enormous losses sustained by the Contras have made this a risky venture. To join the Contras these days means virtually living outside Nicaragua, with little prospect of a triumphant return.

In Condega the biggest fear is of direct US intervention. One doesn't forget easily, sitting in Condega, that the USA has eleven military bases just over the border in Honduras. There are three such bases within a radius of about seventy miles. In the 'Big Pine III' exercise between February and May 1985 three thousand US and five thousand Honduran troops practised counter-insurgency 'defence' from an imaginary Nicaraguan attack. In Operation 'Universal Trek' that April, seven thousand US troops made amphibious landings. Throughout the rest of 1985 and 1986, the USA was building roads, staging heavy artillery practice, training its troops in counter-insurgency and practising 'command and control' in Honduras. Over $85 million has been invested in military installations in Honduras.[8]

It is a fear that underlies the energy with which young people join the health brigades, the coffee-picking teams, the literacy classes. It is a fear that makes Luisa uneasy about being away from home. In a way there is no point in discussing it. It goes without saying that if the USA pitted its military strength against Nicaragua, there would be a bloodbath. But thousands of Sandinistas would take to the mountains and continue to resist. It would undoubtedly be another Vietnam.

I talked to Agustín Lara, the regional FSLN secretary, about the US hope that, through its war of attrition, Nicaraguans will tire of the economic problems and become disenchanted with the revolution. His reply was:

The revolution is not just a material conquest bringing land and jobs. It's more than that. It contains a deep sense of national unity, of unity of race. It's more than just a simple sum of economic and social interests. There's a nationalist tradition here, an anti-colonialist, anti-imperialist tradition.

The _campesinos_ have these deep feelings too. They are the social class of the country which has most suffered the effects of the counter-revolutionary war, the most economic losses, loss of life, loss of houses, crops, etc.

I think the failure to understand this leads the North American rulers to persist with their plans. They don't realize that the struggle reproduces energies and cohesion in the people who have a national identity, a popular identity, a class identity.

Nicaragua is not a country which has only been struggling for a handful of years. It is a country of indians. They have never had peace. From the time the Spanish entered this country we've been at war. War against the Spanish, war against the Yankees who intervened twice, war against the Somoza regime supported by the Yankees. There were fifty thousand deaths in that war. And the war continues.

In Condega I heard many people say this. But it was Bertilda who, for me, expressed it most poignantly:

It is we, the peasants, who are really defending the country. We are the ones who were attacked the most during Somoza, because we were the most exploited in different forms and we are attacked the most today.

I was going to go to the USA to explain the reality, what we were living through ourselves in our own flesh and blood. They would have to believe our words. No one can put me up to that, nor take it away from me. We were going to say it, in our own simple way, we were going to tell the truth as to what is happening to our people. It is not just. He who finances it has to stop this injustice because it's hard. Nicaragua doesn't want war. It wants peace so we can be free and work freely.

We sent him [Reagan] a letter. But if he doesn't understand what was said in that letter, then he doesn't want to understand. Or he has a heart of hard sticks.

Notes

References are to the bibliography

1.   The post office
   1.   Instructions from the Civil Defence Staff, Condega-Palacagüina.

2.   Condega
   1.   The phrase 'the Triumph' is commonly used to denote the Sandinista victory of 19 July 1979.

4.   The silhouette of Sandino
For more detail about Sandino see in particular Crawley, Selser and Ramírez.

   1.   Editorial Vanguardia, *El FSLN: Antecedentes y Estructura orgánica*, Managua, 1986.
   2.   David Raddell, 'The Indian Slave Trade and Population of Nicaragua During the Sixteenth Century', in *The Native Population of the Americas in 1492*, ed. William M. Deneven, Wisconsin, 1976; and Stanislawski.
   3.   *Monografía de Estelí*, Esteli, 1967
   4.   Quoted in Crawley, p. 57.
   5.   Quoted in Selser, p. 93.
   6.   Quoted in Ramírez, p. xli.

5.   Don Antonio and the question of land
For more details of the Somoza dynasty see Diederich, Crawley and Black.

   1.   Diederich, p. 37.
   2.   See Crawley, p. 99.
   3.   Krehm, p. 166.
   4.   Leonardo Argüello was Somoza's nominee for President in 1974 when, constitutionally, Somoza himself was no longer entitled to stand for office. Argüello was declared the winner in the election, despite the fact that 75 per cent of the votes went to his Conservative opponent. When Argüello moved to isolate his sponsor, reorganizing the National Guard and then ordering Somoza's expulsion for resisting the changes, Somoza mounted a coup. With military control back in his hands he had Congress declare Argüello mentally incompetent and send him into exile. Somoza became President again and rewrote the Constitution.
   5.   A *manzana* is 1.68 acres.
   6.   Interview with Filemón Muñóz.

7. *Monografía de Estelí.*
8. Figures from the Casa de Gobierno, Estelí.
9. Ibid.

6. Luisa

I am indebted to Hermione Harris for permission to quote from her 1984 interview with Luisa Centeno and for background information on Amanda.

1. For more details on the role of the CDS and other mass organizations see Hermione Harris, 'Nicaragua: Two Years of Revolution', in *Race and Class*, summer 1981; and Gary Ruchwarger, 'The Sandinista Mass Organizations and the Revolutionary Process', in Harris and Vilas.
2. This and the previous five quotations are from the Harris interview.
3. Hermione Harris, interview with Amanda Centeno, 1984.
4. Ibid.

7. Families in the Contras' firing line

For further information about the Contras see Dickey and *The Tower Commission Report*, New York, 1987.

1. 'Que se rinda tu madre': famous words of the Sandinista fighter Julio Buitrago to the National Guard, who had him surrounded; meaning approximately 'go fuck your mother'.
2. *Barricada Internacional*, 4 April 1985.
3. Testimony to the House Intelligence Committee, November 1984.
4. Witness for Peace, *What We Have Seen and Heard*, March 1985.
5. Americas Watch Committee, *Human Rights in Nicaragua 1985–1986*, New York, 1986.
6. For these and further details see NACLA, 'The Pentagon's Proteges: US Training Programmes for Foreign Military Personnel', in *Latin America and Empire Report*, vol. X, no. 1, January 1976; and Pearce.
7. NACLA, 'The CIA's War', republished in *Barricada Internacional*, 23 October 1986.
8. Testimony of Edgar Chamorro before the International Court of Justice, 1986.
9. Report of the Arms Control and Foreign Policy Caucus, Washington, 1985.
10. International Court of Justice, Nicaragua v. USA, Netherlands, June 1986.

8. El Jocote: the enemy in our midst

1. The National Union of Farmers and Livestock Producers (UNAG) was formed in 1981. It organizes most of the small and medium-sized peasant farmers, including members of farming co-operatives.
2. Ministerio del Interior, *DGSE: La Guerra no Declarada*. For more information about the DGSE see the 1987 report of the Americas Watch Committee.

3. *Central America Report*, 7 November 1986.
4. For more information about the state of emergency see *Envío*, September 1986; Americas Watch Report, 1985–86; and Amnesty International, *Nicaragua 1986*.
5. Americas Watch Reports, 1985–86 and 1986.
6. Ibid., 1985–86.
7. Ibid., 1986.

9. Moisés Córdoba: *campesino* of the Frente

1. Diederich, p. 115.
2. There are very few descriptions of life in rural Nicaragua under Somoza, but a useful chapter is included in Collins et al.
3. Translated by the author from the Spanish edition of Omar Cabezas' autobiography, which was published in English as *Fire from the Mountain*.
4. Ibid.
5. Ibid.

10. A tale of two priests

Liberation theology is covered in detail in Berryman, Gutiérrez and Lernoux. For further reading on the question of religion see Luis Serra, 'Ideology, Religion and the Class Struggle in the Nicaraguan Revolution', in Harris and Vilas; and *Nicaragua, Church and Revolution*, a pamphlet published by the Catholic Institute for International Relations (CIIR), London.

1. Statement on religion issued by the National Directorate of the FSLN, October 1980.
2. For more details see César Jeréz, *The Church and the Nicaraguan Revolution*, CIIR Justice Paper no. 5, London, 1984.
3. This question is discussed in 'La Crisis del Catolicismo Nicaraguense', interview with Francois Houtart in *Amanecer*, January–February 1985 (magazine of the Centro Ecuménico Antonio Valdivieso, Managua).
4. 'The Catholic Church and Nicaraguan Revolution: a Chronology', in *Envío*, no. 30, December 1983.
5. Fernando Cardenal, 'Letter to My Friends', in *Amanacer*, January–February 1985.
6. Testimony to the House Subcommittee on Foreign Affairs, 8 June 1976.
7. Black, p. 89.
8. Diederich, p. 124.
9. Statement of the Nicaraguan Episcopal Conference, 1 January 1977.
10. 'Compromiso Cristiano para una Nueva Nicaragua', pastoral letter of the Nicaraguan Episcopal Conference, 17 November 1979.
11. Comandante Bayardo Arce, National Directorate, FSLN.

11. Born again

For further reading see Ana Maria Excurra, 'La Ofensiva Neoconservadora. Las Iglesias de USA y la lucha ideológica hacia America Latina', IEPALA, Madrid, 1982; and Debora Huntington, 'The Salvation Brokers: Conservative Evangelicals in Central America', in NACLA Report, January 1984.

1. _Envío_, December 1986.
2. _The Santa Fé Document. A New Inter-American Policy for the 80s_, Council for Inter-American Security, Washington 1980.
3. Cayetano De Lella Allevato, 'El Rol del Instituto Sobre Religión y Democracia en la Ofensiva Neoconservadora', a paper given at a symposium on religion and politics, University of California, San Diego, October 1983.

    Also published by the Institute for Religion and Democracy are: _Religion and Politics; is there a problem in your denomination?_, and K. Ptacek, _Nicaragua: a Revolution Against the Church?_
4. Debora Huntington, 'The Salvation Brokers'.

12. Uniting the people

1 _Washington Post_, 3 April 1986.
2. The figures in this paragraph are taken from a speech by Daniel Ortega, 15 February 1987, and from _Barricada Internacional_, 25 December 1986.
3. A full account of the circumstances behind the closure of _La Prensa_ appears in _Envío_, August 1986.
4. For more detailed information on the three tendencies in the FSLN see Black.
5. In January 1987 eighty people who had been found guilty of the murder of Pedro Joaquín Chamorro had their sentences confirmed. _Central America Report_, 29 January 1987.
6. Felipe and Mary Barreda, christian activists, were kidnapped and assassinated by Contras in 1983. Their story is told by Teófilo Cabestrero in _No los separó la muerte_, Managua 1984.
7. Quoted in Arias, p. 158.
8. Ibid., p. 166.

13. The revolution on the land

For further reading about land reform see Collins et al., and E. Baumeister, 'The Structure of Nicaraguan Agriculture and the Sandinista Agrarian Reform', in Harris and Vilas.

1. _Pensamiento Propio_, no. 33, May–June 1986.
2. _Pensamiento Propio_, no. 30, January–February 1986.
3. 'The Nicaraguan Peasantry gives New Direction to Agrarian Reform', in _Envío_, no. 51, September 1985.

4. *Boletín Informativo ANN*, no. 48, 22 November 1986, and *Discurso DOS* for 25th aniversario and for the end of 1986.
5. *Envío*, no. 51.

14.   A woman's place

For further reading about women in Nicaragua see Deighton et al; Maxime Molineux, 'Activismo sin Emancipación', in *Pensamiento Propio*, July 1985, and Randall.

1. Resettlement camps are discussed in *Pensamiento Propio*, no. 22, April 1985, and 'Peasant Resettlements: Protection or Pacification?', in *Envío*, no. 48, June 1985.
2. The slow pace of women's entry into full membership of co-operatives is surveyed in *La Mujer en Las Cooperativas Agropecuarias en Nicaragua*, ed. by CIERA (Centro de Investigaciones y Estudios de la Reforma Agraria, Managua, 1983.
3. Hermione Harris, unpublished interview with Luisa Centeno, 1984.
4. Nicaraguan Constitution, Chapter four: Family Rights, Article 22.
5. *Somos AMNLAE*, no. 27, 1985.
6. *Barricada Internacional*, 9 October 1986; and 'Women's Association Addresses Machismo in Nicaragua', Central American Historical Institute, update no. 77, 29 October 1985.
7. *Barricada Internacional*, no. 240, 26 March 1987.
8. Ibid.

15.   Ermen: ministering to the people

1. Under the new Constitution ratified in January 1987, elections will be held for municipal representatives.
2. Escuela de Entrenamiento Básico de Infantería (Basic Infantry Training School).
3. *Report on Human Rights in Nicaragua*, Centro Victor Sanabria, San José, Costa Rica, March 1979.

16.   The people of Canta Gallo

1. See chapter 13 and *Envío*, no. 51, September 1985, for a detailed report of the pressures governing the Sandinista agrarian reforms. Also *Pensamiento Propio*, nos. 30 and 33.

17.   The legacy of Julio César Castillo

1. The best and most detailed account of the literacy crusade in English is Hirshon.
2. *Barricada Internacional*, 4 April 1985, p. 6.
3. The aforementioned details and others are to be found in Diederich.
4. See Black, p. 150.
5. *La Prensa*, 3 May 1979.
6. See Amnesty International Annual Report, London, 1980.

7. *Barricada*, 7 and 8 March 1980.
8. For a detailed report on the special tribunals see *Nicaragua: Revolutionary Justice. A report on Human Rights*, by the Lawyers' Committee for International Human Rights, New York, April 1985.
9. Inter-American Commission on Human Rights, 1981 OAS Report.
10. Americas Watch Committee, *Human Rights in Nicaragua 1986*, New York, 1987.

18. The politics of defence
1. CDS, *Los CDS Somos: Poder Popular*, p. 3.
2. Luisa Maizal, 'Consideraciones Sobre un Modelo', in *Pensamiento Propio*, June–July 1985.
3. Interview with Tomás Borge, ibid.
4. *Envío*, September 1986.
5. Ibid.
6. Black, p. 224.
7. *Central America Report*, 25 July 1986.
8. *Barricada Internacional*, 25 December 1986.
9. Speech by President Ortega, 15 February 1987.
10. *Barricada Internacional*, 25 December 1986, and *Envío*, no. 66, December 1986.
11. *Central America Report*, 7 November 1986.

19. Free Condega
Details of the countdown to victory are from Black.

20. A heart of hard sticks
1. *Time Magazine*, 31 March 1986.
2. *The Times*, 25 June 1986.
3. In 1977, 29 per cent of imports came from the USA. By 1984 it was only 16 per cent, whereas 25 per cent of imports came from COMECON countries (UN Economic Commission on Latin America, based on figures from the Ministry of External Trade). *Pensamiento Propio*, no. 37, November–December 1986.
4. Quoted in *Envío*, no. 63, September 1986.
5. Carlos Vilas quoted in *Central America Report*, 29 August 1986.
6. *Boletín Informativo ANN*, no. 44, 17 November 1986.
7. *Central America Report*, 29 August 1986.
8. 'The National Guard in Central America. Organising Guide.' National Guard Clearing House/St Louis Pledge of Resistance.

Select bibliography

Books

Much of the detail about the overthrow of Somoza comes from George Black's *Triumph of the People*, which remains the most comprehensive account of the events of the 1970s.

Other invaluable sources are:

Arias, Pilar, *Nicaragua; Revolución. Relatos de Combatientes del Frente Sandinista*, Mexico, 1980.

Berryman, Philip, *The Religious Roots of Rebellion. Christians in the Central American Revolution*, London, 1984.

Black, George, *Triumph of the People: The Sandinista Revolution in Nicaragua*, London, 1981.

Borge, Tomás; Fonseca, Carlos; Ortega, Daniel; Ortega, Humberto; and Wheelock, Jaime, *Sandinistas Speak*, New York, 1982.

Cabezas, Omar, *La Montaña es algo más que una immensa estepa verde*, Managua, 1983. Published in English as *Fire From the Mountain*, London, 1985.

Collins, J., Lappe, F., and Allen, N., *What Difference Can a Revolution Make?*, San Francisco, 1982.

Crawley, Eduardo, *Dictators Never Die; A Portrait of Nicaragua and the Somozas*, London, 1979.

Deighton, Jane; Horsley, Rossana; Stewart, Sarah; and Cain, Cathy, *Sweet Ramparts*, London, 1983.

Dickey, Christopher, *With the Contras; A Reporter in the Wilds of Nicaragua*, New York, 1986.

Diederich, Bernard, *Somoza and the Legacy of US Involvement in Central America*, London, 1982.

Gonzalez, Mike, *Nicaragua: Revolution Under Siege*, London, 1985.

Gutiérrez, Gustavo, *A Theology of Liberation*, London, 1973.

Gutiérrez, Gustavo, *The Power of the Poor in History*, London, 1983.

Harris, Richard and Vilas, Carlos M. (eds), *Nicaragua: A Revolution Under Siege*, London, 1985.

Hirshon, Sheryl, *And Also Teach Them to Read*, Connecticut, 1983.

Krehm, William, *Democracia y Tiranías en el Caribe*, Mexico, 1951.

Lernoux, Penny, *Cry of the People*, New York, 1980.

Nicaragua: The Sandinista People's Revolution, speeches by Sandinista leaders, New York, 1985.

Pearce, Jenny, *Under the Eagle; US Intervention in Central America and the Caribbean*, London, 1981.

Ramírez, Sergio, *El Pensamiento Vivo de Sandino*, Costa Rica, 1980.

Randall, Margaret, *Sandino's Daughters*, London, 1981.

Selser, Gregorio, *Sandino*, translated by Cedric Belfrage, London, 1981

Vilas, Carlos, *The Sandinista Revolution*, New York, 1986.
Weber, Henri, *Sandinista Revolution*, London, 1981.

Other publications
The following have been particularly useful:

Barricada Internacional, international weekly of FSLN, published in English from Managua.
Central America Report, weekly publication of Inforpress Centroamerica, Guatemala City.
Envío, monthly journal of the Instituto Historico Centroamericana, published in English in Managua.
NACLA (North American Congress on Latin America) *Report on the Americas* (bi-monthly publication).
Pensamiento Propio, bi-monthly journal of the Instituto de Investigaciones Economicas y Sociales (INIES), Managua.

Also a piece by Dan Stanislawski, 'The Transformation of Nicaragua 1519–1548', in *Ibero-Americano*, vol. 54, California, 1983.